MAN'S BEST FRIEND
ON THE ROAD AGAIN WITH

A Selective Guide to the Southeast's Bed and Breakfasts, Inns, Hotels, and

🐾 🐾 🐾 🐾 Resorts that Welcome You and Your Dog 🐾 🐾 🐾 🐾

Dawn and Robert Habgood

A Dawbert Press Publication
MACMILLAN · USA

To G.B.
For Your Whimsical Spirit

Macmillan General Reference
A Prentice Hall Macmillan Company
1633 Broadway
New York, NY 10019

Howell Book House
MACMILLAN is a registered trademark of Macmillan, Inc.

First Edition

ISBN: 0-87605-708-3

Editors: Pamela Gerloff
Barbara M. Hayes
Interior Artwork: Glynn Brannon
Selected Line Drawings: Lynne Phipps

Manufactured in the United States of America
10 9 8 7 6 5 4 3 2 1

Contents

Introduction

Like millions of others in this country, we cherish our dogs and their unique place within our family. Our two golden retrievers are an integral part of our lives, and we find it difficult to leave them for extended periods of time. From the earliest days of our marriage, we loved to pack our bags and hit the road in search of new, undiscovered terrain. Each of the regions in our country is so distinct from the next, we thrive on the new pleasures and discoveries around each bend in the road. However, our unwillingness to abandon our pets soon clashed with our questing, traveling spirits.

So twelve years ago, we started including our dogs on weekend vacations. We began compiling lists of pet-friendly accommodations. Before long, we owned virtually every regional guidebook, but had unearthed only a handful of decent lodgings. Brochures could be deceptive, and the places were not always as nice as we expected. Our dogs did not care, but we did.

Finally, we decided to solve the problem ourselves and went "on the road again" in search of a variety of accommodations that would not only appeal to us, but to other people who wanted to vacation with their dog and who were seeking quality places with character, regional flavor, and charisma.

On The Road Again With Man's Best Friend is the result — a series of regional travel guides that are both selective and comprehensive. We include listings of all accommodations that accept travelers and their dogs; however, we highlight only those that merit special attention. For over a decade, we have been traveling to, and writing about, places to stay with dogs, allowing us to provide readers with our personal, first-hand impressions. If we think a place is great, we let you know, and if there are areas that could be improved, we mention them as well. We are able to do this only because we make a point of personally visiting and revisiting each entry in each of our guides.

In looking through this book, prospective guests will discover a wide range of vacation destinations that should appeal to their senses, as well as to their pocketbooks. And remember, traveling with a dog can be a delightful experience, but it is also a responsibility that, if misused, can not only completely ruin your vacation, but can deny the opportunity for others to visit that establishment in the future.

We hope you will find *On the Road Again With Man's Best Friend* to be an informative and helpful guide, and one you will include when planning any vacation with Bowser. We have found our dogs enjoy being "on the road again" just as much as we do.

How do we Select "the Best" Accommodations?

We choose our dog friendly entries by sifting through all the accommodations that welcome dogs in a given region, looking for places that exude a warmth, charm, and quality that even dog-less vacationers would find appealing. For instance, we include cottage communities that have been around for decades and, although some are rather rustic, attract a strong following of devoted patrons. Intimate B&Bs are added for their personalized attention and ambiance, while resorts are appealing for their diversity of activities. Elegant country inns and small hotels often top our list, but equally important are the family-run farms in the countryside.

Once selected, we pay an unannounced visit to the establishment, always maintaining our anonymity. This allows us, in most cases, to provide future guests with a concise overview and detailed descriptions that are not influenced by any type of special treatment. Because we accept no money from the innkeepers or owners, we can remain objective and you can feel more comfortable with our recommendations.

How to Use the Book — General Information

Each entry begins with pertinent general information about the establishment, including the address, telephone number, owner or manager's name, acceptable methods of payment, and number, type, and cost of the various guest rooms. We also describe any pet policies, and restrictions regarding children, if any. This section tells you more about each area we cover.

Types of Accommodations:

B&Bs: These are often private homes and guests should treat this experience

as though they are staying with a friend. B&Bs are usually short on amenities and on-site activities, but long on personalized attention. You can expect to find comfortable guest rooms, a common area with perhaps a television and stereo, a Continental breakfast, and a warm and friendly host who genuinely enjoys having houseguests. B&Bs generally do not serve lunch and dinner.

Inns: Inns can sometimes be confused with B&Bs. Most have the same type of intimate feeling, but with just a few more rooms. One of the biggest differences is they have either a restaurant or can serve at least breakfast and dinner. Inns are more highly regulated and must meet the various state and national health and access codes. Also, they provide more activities and creature comforts than do traditional B&Bs.

Cottages: The cottage complexes we feature vary greatly in size, amenities, and activities — but even the most rustic are very clean and well maintained. Although the cabin or cottage might offer only the bare essentials, there is always plenty to do on the premises or in the nearby area. There is almost always a main lodge with a great restaurant. In some cases, all guests eat here, and in others they have a kitchenette that gives them the option of dining in their cottage or at the main lodge. We usually choose a cottage complex because it offers a picturesque setting with plenty of open space for both owner and dog to explore.

Hotels and Resorts: Smaller hotels often label themselves inns because they feel it makes them appear more intimate. We try to warn readers of this early and explain exactly what they can expect. Hotels usually have fifty or more rooms, and are located in large towns and cities. They traditionally deliver a full range of amenities, which could include an indoor or outdoor swimming pool, concierge services, multiple restaurants, a large staff, and a health club. Resorts, on the other hand, are generally located on the outskirts of popular tourist destinations or in the countryside. They offer a wide variety of guest rooms, as well as an expansive list of amenities, activities, and on-site programs.

Motels/Motor Lodges: These vary greatly in cost and features, although guests can usually expect standard rooms, a few amenities, and perhaps a restaurant either on the premises or nearby. They do not usually warrant a description, which is why we have provided our comprehensive appendix, "The Best of the Rest," which gives readers the names, addresses, and telephone numbers of these establishments.

Rooms:

Because guestrooms vary a great deal from one establishment to the next, it is important, when making a reservation, to be very specific about your requirements. Read the descriptions carefully and decide which amenities are important, whether they are a private bathroom, a bedroom with a big closet, a firm mattress, a room on the first floor, or a separate sitting room. Do you want a room that could be out of the pages of *House Beautiful,* or modern conveniences such as televisions or Jacuzzis? Please be specific.

Rates:

The range of rates listed with each description gives you a good idea of what to expect at a particular establishment. Many of these accommodations offer special discount packages, off-season rates, weekly rates, or interesting theme weekends. Always inquire about what's offered. Almost all of the accommodations listed in our books have "shoulder" seasons too — quiet times immediately before or after the busier times of the year. In addition to saving a little money, people traveling during these months will have a better choice of rooms, be able to eat out without making reservations, and enjoy sightseeing without all the usual crowds. Guests should also be careful to check if the rates are based upon single or double occupancy and if they include local taxes, fees, and so on.

Meal Plans:

We always indicate the type of meal plan offered by a given establishment.

* Bed and Breakfast (B&B) rates includes a Continental *or* full breakfast.
* European Plan (EP) does not include any meals.
* Modified American Plan (MAP) includes both breakfast and dinner
* American Plan (AP) is all-inclusive, providing breakfast, lunch, and dinner.

Method of Payment:

While most of the smaller establishments would prefer to be paid in cash or by personal check, the larger inns, hotels, and resorts accept an array of credit cards, abbreviated as follows:

* **AE** - American Express
* **CB** - Carte Blanche
* **DC** - Diners Club
* **DSC** - Discover
* **ENR** - EnRoute
* **JCB** - Japanese Credit Bank
* **MC** - Master Card
* **VISA** - Visa

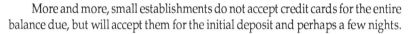

More and more, small establishments do not accept credit cards for the entire balance due, but will accept them for the initial deposit and perhaps a few nights.

Children:

We provide this category to inform prospective guests about any additional rules, regulations, or benefits concerning their children. Legally, people traveling with children cannot be discriminated against; however, we have found that there are certainly places where parents with young children would be uncomfortable. When we mention appropriate ages, it is at the request of the innkeeper or manager. More often, though, there are special discounts for young children and those under the age of 12 often stay free of charge when accompanied by a parent.

Dog Policies:

This category outlines any restrictions concerning guests' canine companions. These can include size requirements, the age of the dog, and management concerns such as leaving dogs alone in the room or walking them off the property. Some establishments offer an array of doggie treats for their canine guests, which could be homemade biscuits or extra dog beds and bowls.

Opening and Closing Dates:

Seasonal openings and closings are outlined in this section. Many of the accommodations are open all year; however, during the off-season it is fairly common for B&B owners or innkeepers to shut down and go on a short vacation. Always, call ahead to make sure the establishment is open when you are planning to visit.

Planning Your Trip

In our experience, and we are sure fellow travelers agree, planning ahead of time is the best way to avoid mistakes that make for unpleasant experiences. Here are some of our time-tested guidelines.

Traveling by Car - Planning & Precautions:

If you've never traveled with your dog before, think twice about setting out on a four-day vacation together. To ease the uninitiated dog into travel mode, start with a day trip, then an overnight or weekend jaunt, then book a longer stay somewhere. If your dog has a tendency to bounce around the car, you should buy a travel crate or a car gate — something to confine him to the rear of the vehicle so that you can drive safely.

Before you set out on your trip, take your dog for a leisurely walk. This will not only give him a chance to work off a little energy, but may also coax him into sleeping during the trip. Do not feed him or give him substantial amounts of water just before leaving. Once in the car, make sure the dog's area is either well-ventilated or amply air-conditioned. Plan frequent pit stops (every two hours or so), where you can exercise your dog on a leash.

Even if the day is not hot, a car can heat up to very high temperatures in very little time. Take the following precautions to prevent heat stroke, brain damage, or even death to your dog:

* Try to park the car in the shade and leave the window open enough to provide ample ventilation.
* Do not leave your dog for long intervals of time.
* Before you leave the car, fill his bowl with cold water to ease any effects of the heat.
* *Never leave a dog in a hot car!*

Traveling by Plane - Planning & Precautions:

There are certain legal guidelines and restrictions for air travel with a dog. The United States Department of Agriculture (USDA) and the International Air Transport Association (IATA) govern air travel for pets. The airlines themselves have regulations, and they differ, so you should always contact your airline in advance to review their procedures and requirements. Regardless of your carrier, these are important guidelines to consider:

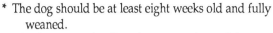

* The dog should be at least eight weeks old and fully weaned.
* The dog cannot be ill, violent, or in physical distress.
* The dog should have all the necessary health certificates and documentation.
* The travel crate must meet the airline's standards and be large enough for the dog to lie down comfortably, turn around, and stand freely in it.

Try to book a non-stop flight, and take temperature into consideration: In the summer, try to fly at night when it's cooler; in winter, fly during the day, when it's warmer.

Plan your trip well in advance and make sure you are following all the rules.

What Your Dog Needs to Enjoy the Trip:

Just as you have to pack appropriately for your vacation, your dog will need certain items to ensure he has a comfortable and enjoyable time, too. These include:

* A leash and collar with ID tags.
* A few favorite toys, chew bones, and treats.
* A container of fresh drinking water from home.
* A supply of his regular dog food.
* Food and water bowls.
* A dog "bed," whether it is a towel, mat, or pillow, or the dog's travel crate.
* Grooming aids, including extra towels for wet dogs and muddy paws.
* Any medication your veterinarian has prescribed or suggested.
* The dog's vaccination records, especially a rabies certificate or tag.

When You Arrive:

Many of the hosts and innkeepers we have met have expressed their general concerns about guests who bring their canine companions. So that your visit is an enjoyable one, we wanted to list them so you can keep them in mind.
* Dogs should be kept leashed while on the grounds.
* Dogs should not be left alone in the bedrooms unless management allows. In that case, the dog should be left in his crate or confined to the bathroom with some favorite toys.
* Always clean up after the dog, and try to walk him away from the main grounds.
* Use the dog's bedding to lessen the chance of damage to the furnishings. Never let your dog sit or lie on any of the furnishings.
* Because of health codes, dogs are generally not allowed in any area where food is made or served.

Disclaimer

Please keep in mind that the hosts, managers, and innkeepers are under no obligation to accept your dog. The management of each establishment listed in our guides has indicated to us, both verbally and in writing, that they have welcomed dogs in the past, had positive experiences, and will accept them in the future provided they are very well-behaved. Prior to publication, each of the establishments was contacted again to ensure they still welcome guests traveling with dogs. We cannot, however, guarantee against last minute changes of heart. Sometimes circumstances exist that require them to decline admitting our canine friends. They may already have a few dogs there, or be hosting a special function that would make it impractical for them to have your dog stay with you. *It is imperative you notify the establishment that you will be traveling with your dog when making your reservations.*

North Carolina

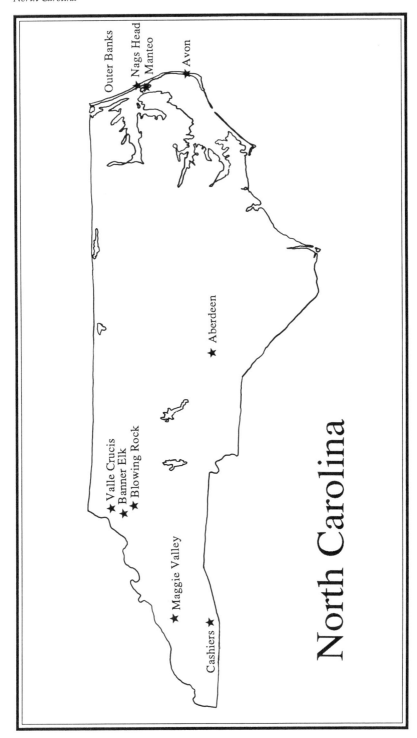

Inn at the Bryant House

214 North Poplar Street
Aberdeen, North Carolina 28315
(800) 453-4019, (910) 944-3300, Fax (910) 944-8898

Innkeepers: *Abbie and Bill Gregory*
Rooms: *8 doubles*
Rates: *$45-75 (B&B)*
Payment: *AE, DSC, MC, and VISA*
Children: *Welcome*
Dogs: *Very well-behaved dogs are welcome, provided they are controlled*
Open: *All year*

The quiet and unpretentious hamlet of Aberdeen is well known among golfers who come to play the 30 area courses. History and architecture buffs, on the other hand, might be more interested in the town's quaint historic district. Settled in the late 1880s, Aberdeen soon thereafter drew a number of regional industrial magnets who based their railroad, lumbering, and turpentine operations out of Aberdeen. During the next few decades, which were regarded as the "Blue-Page Era," business boomed and the town prospered. The gentlemen responsible for the thriving local economy built handsome homes that reflected their wealth and stature. Today, their houses are a part of Aberdeen's historic district, and one of them has been converted into a charming little inn called the Inn at the Bryant House.

When we arrived at the inn, we found Abbie just getting ready to walk her daughter's Irish Setter. She graciously postponed their walk to chat with us and give us a tour of the inn. A side door opens to reveal a charming, sunlit chamber decorated with a green, lattice-patterned wallpaper. A trunk, set off to the side, is bustling with colorful handmade quilts, and a few white wrought iron chairs are placed on the pickled hardwood floors. An adjacent room, festooned with colorful paisley wallpaper, serves as the breakfast area, where guests dine around a large circular table surrounded by white wicker chairs. The Continental meal offers a wide variety of cereals, including Abbie's delicious homemade cereal. A platter of fresh fruits and a variety of baked goodies are placed, buffet style, on the sideboard. A milk-painted hutch is brimming with dishes and glassware.

Another doorway leads to the foyer and staircase that climb to the upstairs guest rooms. Compared to the bright paisley and green trellis wallpapers, the pink striped wallpaper in the hallway is rather subtle. White wicker furniture is merely the backdrop to the colorful quilts draped over the bannister and the array of hats hanging from a rack. Before walking upstairs, though, guests may like to relax in one of the two spacious sitting rooms, located just off the foyer. A piano is the centerpiece for one, with a pair of slip-covered sofas arranged in an intimate grouping around a coffee table and central fireplace. The other sitting room is a library, where an entire wall of shelves is filled with books, collectibles, and decorative plates. One of the more notable aspects of this chamber is a glass-fronted cabinet filled with antique dolls. Once again, the decor is beautiful, with floral fabrics nicely complementing the green or white wicker furnishings.

Guests traveling with a dog are permitted in any of the guest rooms; however, we found the first floor bedroom was probably the most appropriate, as we could easily access the outside from it. This expansive corner chamber was originally part of the porch. The high ceilings and the five windows create a sense of space and light, while the blinds and blue floral draperies framing the windows make it quite private. Our white brass and iron queen-size bed was festooned with six fluffy pillows and a lovely embroidered coverlet. The hardwood floors are painted a handsome navy and set with a colorful dhurrie and several wicker furnishings. The good-sized private bathroom is equipped with a tub and a shower. The inn is set on a quiet side street, and any potential noise is absorbed by the whir of the ceiling fan or air conditioner. Upstairs, there are a variety of chambers. One cozy room, located at the top of the stairs, has a double bed set into a windowed alcove. Another bedroom is furnished with a white iron and brass bed and decorated with colorful rag rugs. The dried wreaths and flower arrangements provide delightful accents to the coral pink wall treatment. This corner room is also privy to a good deal of afternoon sun. Each of the bedrooms has pastel-colored walls, traditional furnishings, and a variety of charming collectibles. We liked the small sitting area on the second floor landing, where gray-hued floors are a neutral base for the window seat and the pair of sofas covered with floral fabric.

This inn is so appealing that there seems little reason to go anywhere else, although walking around the historic district is always pleasant and quite interesting. There is a good map that shows visitors where the homes, churches, and cemeteries are located. It covers 88-acres and has over 100 historic buildings. While Bowser will enjoy these walks, the Morrow Mountain State Park will really allow him to kick up his heels. Set on nearly 4,700 acres, visitors may hike, boat, swim, fish, and picnic throughout the park. Another doggie diversion is a visit to the Sandhills Recreation Area. The most popular activity without the dog has to be a trip to Pinehurst. The latter is home to a lovely resort, which consists of a charming shopping area, a tennis court facility (site of the United States clay court championships), and the renowned Pinehurst Golf Course, which has hosted many professional golf tour events.

Avon Cottages

Box 7 (off Highway 12)
Avon, North Carolina   27915
(919) 995-4123

Managers: The Younces
Rooms: 19 cottages
Rates: $250-950 per week (EP)
Payment: Personal checks
Children: Welcome
Dogs: Welcome with prior approval and a $15 fee
Open: All year

The Outer Banks region of North Carolina provides countless ways for vacationers to truly "get away from it all," offering a wide array of accommodations and an equally diverse range of prices. Generally speaking, people who have been coming to this region for years have settled on a particular town, for sentimental reasons. Many enjoy the old style cottages of Nag's Head, a town situated in the heart of this 125-mile string of islands. Along both sides of the road lie a variety of relatively inexpensive cottage communities that are close to both the water and a wide choice of recreational options, shops, and amusement centers. For the most part, the cottages here are densely packed, reducing the overall sense of space and privacy.

Some prefer to head further north to Duck, where there are newer cottage and condominium communities that are rimmed by denser vegetation and a more substantial feeling of privacy. Others lean in the other direction and head south toward the wilder and more natural dunes of the south coast. The latter is where we found the low-key Avon Cottages, which are situated 40 miles south of Nag's Head and surrounded by miles of National Seashore. The town of Avon is comprised of a few restaurants (like the Froggy Dog), sailboard and kite shops, and bait and tackle stores. This unassuming village is an ideal spot for anyone who wants to avoid congestion, spend the days relaxing in the privacy of a dune, and fish, fish, fish.

The Avon Cottages are a group of 20 weathered-shingled buildings set to the rear of even more understated roadside motel units. As new arrivals drive in past the motel rooms toward the huge beach dunes, they will find the small office and reception area. If being located right along the ocean is more important than staying in a deluxe resort, then this is the place for you. As with most of the Outer Banks architecture, the two- and three-story dwellings here are built on pilings, both to

5

maximize the water views and minimize the damage when the water occasionally breaches the dunes.

As one would expect, we liked the oceanfront cottages best. There are six of these buildings, ranging in size from a duplex with two bedrooms, a living room, dining room, and kitchen to an enormous three-story, four-bedroom, and four-bathroom cottage that includes a Jacuzzi. The interiors are spacious with cathedral ceilings and cedar paneled walls that exude a mountain cabin ambiance in a beach-side setting. The living room and kitchen are on the top floor, and the bedrooms are located just below them. The commanding water views, seen through sliding glass doors and walls of crank-out windows, are the focal point for the top-floor common areas. Equally pleasant, especially for the breezes and sunshine, are the wraparound decks and porches situated just off the top two floors. Back inside, wall-to-wall carpeting is used in the high traffic areas while linoleum covers the floors in the kitchen and bathrooms. The greatest emphasis is on the third-floor rooms, where kitchens are fully equipped with microwaves, large refrigerators, and other modern appliances, and the living rooms and dining areas have plenty of heavy oak and maple furniture for relaxing. While the color televisions have cable, the overall atmosphere of these accommodations exudes an old-timey feeling. The bedrooms, for instance, are utilitarian and usually just large enough to accommodate a bed, a dresser, and a chair or two. Guests will enjoy a few modern conveniences, such as central air conditioning and washers and dryers, which can be found in most of the cottages.

When choosing a cottage, we recommend trying to get as close to the ocean as possible. The brochure has a detailed map and photographs of all the cottages. Guests should keep in mind that the interior shots are of the nicest cottages. The units set one row off the beach are fine; however, the third and fourth rows are not nearly as desirable. Guests will discover that those situated on the outskirts of the property are usually well-spaced in distance from each other, while those in the center of the complex are more tightly bunched. Although there are very few shrubs and trees, the grounds are relatively well maintained. When we were visiting, there were also a number of repeat guests who seemed to be booking their favorite cottages for the following year. The busiest times of year are during fishing season; however, this is also fast becoming a sailboarding mecca as well. To accommodate the fishermen, there are outdoor cleaning tables and running water already set up.

Visitors to the region will have little difficulty finding something to do. Short trips lead to the magnificent Cape Hatteras National Seashore. Longer trips may be taken on the free ferry that takes visitors to nearby Ocracoke Island. Guests may explore this unique habitat, which is literally a world unto itself. Neat old funky houses are set along sandy streets lined with moss-laden oak trees. In addition to being the former hangout for Black Beard, the pirate, this island is a great place to take a bicycle ride and enjoy the abundance of natural wildlife. North of Avon, there is the 5,880-acre Pea Island National Wildlife Refuge, which is home to over 250 species of birds. Dogs are not permitted on the nature trails and lands bordering the west side of Route 12, but they are allowed on the beaches, where they can walk for miles. This day-long adventure will undoubtedly be one of the more memorable parts of visitors' vacation on the Outer Banks. Of course, there are also wonderful beaches that are literally just a stone's throw from the Avon Cottages, where guests will see wooden stairs leading over the dunes onto the Atlantic sands.

The Banner Elk Inn

Route 3, Box 1134
Banner Elk, North Carolina   28604
(704) 898-6223

Hostess: *Beverly Lait*
Rooms: *4 doubles, 1 suite*
Rates: *Doubles $75-100 (B&B), Suite $120-140 (B&B)*
Payment: *MC and VISA*
Children: *Most appropriate for children over five years of age*
Dogs: *Welcome, provided they are "loving animals, housebroken, and are not left alone in the room"*
Open: *All year, except for November 15 - December 15 and the end of April or May*

7

Visitors to the northwest corner of North Carolina might be coming to ski, to enjoy the natural beauty of the Mount Pisgah National Park, or to escape to a quiet, rural setting. In the sleepy town of Banner Elk, at the intersection of two rural roads, they will find a most charming Bed & Breakfast. The faded cranberry clapboard house is accented by green shutters and colorful perennial gardens lined by rock walls. We thought the house resembled a classic New England farmhouse; however, we were surprised to learn it was built in 1912 as a country church.

More recently, it was bought and renovated by Beverly, who is an affable hostess, as fascinated with her guests as they are with her. Originally from South Carolina, Beverly has led many lives, most of them overseas in South America and Europe. Today, she is not only a portrait artist, tapestry weaver, and real estate agent, but also a full-time innkeeper. She has had plenty of practice taking care of visitors, having acted as an official hostess for functions at overseas United States embassies. During her years abroad, she also collected an eclectic and lovely array of furnishings, carvings, crafts, and artifacts that she proudly displays throughout the B&B's guest and common rooms.

This is an exceptionally intimate B&B, with nooks and crannies that always seem to contain intriguing treasures. Our first look into one of these nooks and crannies revealed a large armoire, whose glass doors displayed stacks of handmade sweaters that may be purchased by guests. Just off the foyer containing the armoire is a small chamber Beverly wants to transform into an intimate breakfast nook. She plans to set a sideboard with assorted cereals, muffins, and other morning delectables that will more than satisfy the needs of Continental breakfast-goers. Those who prefer a full meal may continue to gather in the great room on the opposite side of the foyer. This is the largest room in the house, where dark stained paneling and hunter green ceilings combine to create a handsome decor. A leather sofa and side chairs, set around a white area rug, are perfectly positioned to maximize the warmth from the stone fireplace. Tati, Beverly's cat, is often resting on the television. A large dining room table in here serves as the gathering place for Beverly's hearty and memorable breakfasts. This substantial affair is served on fine china, and may include cottage cheese pancakes, baked muesli apples, or a Parmesan soufflé with cheddar cheese sauce. This expansive spread is often supplemented with freshly baked muffins and sourdough bread topped with a variety of jams and preserves. After breakfast, some guests like to prolong the relaxed mood by taking their cup of coffee and curling up with a good book in front of the fire. If the weather is warm, they usually head out to the side porch. We were especially attracted to this spot, where we could recline on the wicker furnishings and admire the lovely gardens that surround an antique fountain that Beverly rebuilt.

As we walked through the house, it was obvious that green is a color Beverly finds appealing. It is visible in the forest green and burgundy paisley-patterned wallpaper in the hallways and in many of the striped wallpapers in the bedrooms. Beverly's international collection of carvings and crafts is interspersed with more traditional antique furnishings, creating a strong sense of whimsy balanced with a slight formality. What is known as Lin's Peach Room contains an antique Victorian bed, while Jeanne's Mauve Room is highlighted by a double brass bed. Both have large new private bathrooms with octagonal windows that allow the sunlight to pour in. Jeanne and Linda's Room may be booked in combination with Bonnie's Blue Room to make a comfortable suite for four people. In here, as in the rest of the guest chambers, the beds are topped by fluffy European down comforters. The day we visited, Beverly was just putting the final coat of paint on the third floor rooms, which she refers to as the Honeymoon Suite. This is accessed by ascending a rather steep staircase and navigating through a narrow doorway. It is an interesting space, with various cozy rooms. A king-size bed occupies the bedroom situated under the eaves, while a bathroom and a separate dressing room (with a double Jacuzzi) are found off to the side. Beverly expects to furnish the dressing room with a pair of lounge chairs, a dressing table, and a few decorative knickknacks.

The Banner Elk Inn is well located for many outdoor excursions that will delight both guests and their dogs. The library contains an array of brochures, pamphlets, and area maps, including Beverly's own "Fun Map" of great things to do, both in town and in the general vicinity. The B&B is located on a quiet road that is good for walks. In the summer time, guests can even find their way up to the blueberry farm. Just off the Blue Ridge Parkway, are Simms Pond and Price Lake, where many guests and their dogs can swim or take an invigorating hike. The town of Banner Elk is located in the 500,000-acre Mount Pisgah National Forest, where leashed dogs are welcome. Hiking, swimming, picnic, and boating activities will tire even the most energetic souls, and we can't think of a better place to rejuvenate than at The Banner Elk Inn.

Cameron's Country Cabins
at the Circle "C" Ranch

Route 1, Box 644
Blowing Rock, North Carolina   28605
(704) 295-4836, Fax (704) 295-4761

Hostess: Pamela and Gordon Cameron
Rooms: 8 cabins
Rates: $125-150 per day (B&B), $790-950 per week (B&B)
Payment: MC and VISA
Children: Welcome
Dogs: Well-behaved dogs are welcome with prior approval
Open: All year

When we think of North Carolina, we immediately focus on the Outer Banks and the lush, forested areas around the Great Smoky Mountains. Traveling up the Blue Ridge Parkway out of Asheville, visitors will see villages like Little Switzerland, Linville, and Valle Crucis. Just beyond these enclaves is one of our favorite choices, Blowing Rock. Not only are there virtually limitless outdoor activities, but the countryside is absolutely spectacular. We especially liked the look and the feeling of Cameron's Country Cabins, as they are not only attractive, but also offer incredible views of the Globe Valley and Grandfather Mountain.

After we finished exploring the intimate hamlet of Blowing Rock, we drove down a winding rural road that meandered through stands of tall trees, traversed high ridge lines, and passed by lovely old mountain retreats. Five miles later, we came upon the charming cabins. The inspiration and centerpiece for the group is the 100-year-old original log cabin that is constructed out of hand-hewn, wormy chestnut logs. The bentwood furniture and rocking chairs rest comfortably on the intimate front porch, with the rocking chairs whimsically painted black and white to resemble cows. Baskets of flowers add color to the porches, but what we liked most were the red tin roofs that produce a melodious sound during rain showers. Once inside the antique cabins, the old-fashioned charm enveloped us. A classic woodstove, set on a large stone hearth, fills one corner. The mounted animal heads, set against rough-hewn walls, gave us the impression of visiting a hunting lodge. These are interspersed with old-fashioned farm implements and other assorted collectibles. The comfortable furnishings in the great room beckoned us to relax and stay awhile, but we were drawn to the windows to check out the views of Grandfather Mountain. Guests may choose from sleeping accommodations in either the small, queen-bedded chamber or upstairs in a low-ceilinged sleeping loft. While the original cabin is very clean and fairly well appointed, the overall ambiance is authentically antique. A short distance away, we located a group of cabins and the reception area.

We found Pam and her husband Gordon chatting with some old friends who had been coming to the cabin resort for many years. We left them to talk a bit as we explored further. Just beyond the reception alcove, where the front desk is tucked, we walked into a large, beamed-ceiling common room. The antique simplicity of the first cabin is not evident here, where overstuffed couches and armchairs sit upon Oriental carpets, and a large- screen television is set up to entertain the guests. While the atmosphere is extremely appealing, it cannot begin to compete with the 75-mile views, which can be enjoyed both through the windows and from the expansive deck.

Along the driveway, other cabins are nestled behind pine trees, and also offer fantastic views of the Globe Valley and the Pisgah National Forest. Most of these sleep six people; however, their floor plans and list of amenities vary. The Little House has lovely views not only from its wraparound deck, but also from the windows in the cathedral-ceilinged great room. A lovely assortment of antiques are placed around the massive stone fireplace in here, along with a modern concession, a television. The king-size bed in the master chamber completes the picture. The Wicker Cabin, created from cedar logs, is slightly different in feeling. Iron bedsteads and white wicker furniture are interspersed with country antiques to create a more informal atmosphere in the two bedrooms. Once again, there is a large great room, which is enhanced in character by a woodstove. The Old Homestead, on the other hand, contains a carved cedar, king-size bed in the master bedroom, and a private Jacuzzi for relaxing just before bed. The great room has comfortable couches and chairs, along with a freestanding fireplace, which is not only decorative, but also serves to warm the upstairs loft. The Yonahlosse (which, translated, means "the trail of the bear") is decorated around a Southwestern theme. It, too, was built with soaring cathedral ceilings and a massive stone fireplace in the living area. Braided rugs cover the pine floors, and an abundance of windows provides some of the most memorable views of the valley and mountains below. The king-size, four-poster bed made of carved logs is appealing, as is the two-person Jacuzzi bathtub. The small, but modern, kitchenette allowed us to create our own meals. The array of amenities and pleasing decor both surprised us and appealed to us, as did the idea of feeling so removed from civilization.

Aside from the truly remarkable views, guests will appreciate the 25-acres of grounds they can explore with Bowser. Along the way, they are certain to come across the oversized Jacuzzi in the gazebo. While

Bowser may not be overly impressed with the birds flitting around the assorted feeders, he might pick up the scent of the deer, cougars, and black bears that have been known to wander through portions of these parts. The cabins are close to Grandfather Mountain, which guests may enjoy climbing one day with their canine companion. Another option is the neighboring Flat Top. With a tired out Bowser, guests may be able to check out the Blowing Rock stables for horseback riding or perhaps visit the Tweetsie Railroad. The latter is a small Western theme park, whose main draw is an antique, narrow gauge railroad. After exploring the village at the base of the mountain, guests may feel inclined to jump on the chairlift and enjoy the scenic views up to the top. Here, in a recreated mining town, visitors can pet some animals or pan for gold. It is a really fun and unique way to spend a portion of the day.

Peacock Ridge Cabins

Route 2, Box 78
374 Charlies Way (off of Possum Hollow Road)
Blowing Rock, North Carolina 28605
(704) 295-3783

Hosts: Jim and Annette Sauder
Rooms: 3 cottages
Rates: $95-135 per day (EP), $550-750 per week (EP)
Payment: MC and VISA
Children: Welcome (cribs, high chairs, and babysitters are available)
Dogs: Welcome with a $10 fee
Open: All year

Blowing Rock is a small town situated along the scenic Blue Ridge Parkway on the outer fringes of the Pisgah National Forest. This region is popular in the summer months because the mild temperatures and picturesque surroundings make it ideal for horseback riding, fishing, and golfing. In the winter months, many people like to ski at any number of the nearby downhill resorts. Those who are curious about how Blowing Rock got its name can better understand it by visiting the actual Blowing Rock. This outcropping of granite, lying above St. John's River Gorge, is most unusual. When the updrafts are just right, any light object thrown off the rock will float back upward.

Certainly the blowing rock attracts its fair share of visitors, but travelers return year after year because of the climate and the area's intrinsic beauty. One of the newest additions to the area are the Peacock

Ridge Cabins. This is not the sort of place people find by accident. While we always recommend calling ahead for reservations, in this case it is almost a necessity. Sheer luck would be required to locate these cabins without directions. Situated only a couple of miles from town, they may be fairly close to civilization, but guests would never know it.

The Peacock Ridge Cabins are reached by way of a steep driveway that wends past a trout pond and eventually leads to the crest of a hill revealing nice views of the surrounding area. Here, we ran across Annette, who led us part way back down the hill to the cabins. At Peacock Ridge, there are three rough-hewn log cabins, built of wormy chestnut and cedar. Although the cabins are perched fairly close together on the hillside, their interior spaces and expansive wrap-around porches have been designed with an emphasis on privacy. In the first cabin we were impressed by the good sized-common room, where hardwood floors and Oriental rugs set the initial tone. Multiple pairs of windows, framed by pretty floral tab curtains, allow the afternoon sun to lighten this beamed-ceilinged chamber. We initially thought the stone-faced fireplace would be the primary draw to this room, but we soon discovered that the inviting sofa bed, arm chairs, and rocking chairs provided the welcoming touches most guests are looking for in a good-size family room. Most will also probably enjoy using the remote controlled television resting on a shelf in the corner. The adjoining dining area and fully-equipped kitchen were open to the living room, allowing guests to easily converse with the chef. The two bedrooms, one with twin beds and another with a queen bedstead, were as spacious as they were appealing.

From this cabin we could walk down to the second, in which the floor plan, style of furnishings, and country decor were almost identical to those in the first. The third cabin, on the other hand, was obviously the newest addition to the group. As we rounded the hillside, we found Jim and a few helpers not only putting the finishing touches on the front staircase, but also redoing some landscaping that had recently washed away. We clambered around them, up the stairs and into a cavernous cathedral-ceilinged common area. The full kitchen was off to the left and the spacious living area off to the right. Traditional braided rugs were placed on the hardwood floors around the rocking chairs, futon sofa bed, and contemporary wood framed chairs. While this light and airy chamber is rimmed by windows, it was the French doors opening onto a deck that were most appealing to us. From the expansive deck, we could either entertain the thought of a little sunbathing or just enjoy the great views of the surrounding woods. On cooler evenings, guests will also enjoy gathering near the floor-to-ceiling fieldstone fireplace situated in the corner of the room. To the rear of the cabin there is a spacious master bedroom containing a king-size bed that rests upon navy carpeting. The room is rather Spartan in terms of furnishings;

however, the floral draperies and green sponge wall treatment add to the minimalistic decor. Just off the master bedroom is a spacious modern bathroom. Upstairs, a loft space contains a pair of twin beds covered with coral-colored spreads. While this configuration would be ideal for families with older children, the low railings would definitely make the loft area a little too dangerous for smaller children.

The Peacock Ridge Cabins are an ideal place to bring dogs, as they will thoroughly enjoy exploring the 20-acres of wooded grounds. Some of the preferred walks include a visit to the trout pond, creek, or following one of the assorted trails that wend through the property. South of Blowing Rock, off the Blue Ridge Parkway, there is the Julian Price Memorial Park, which is situated on over 4,000-acres. Trails abound, and summertime hikers marvel at the clusters of beautiful wild flowers and flowering bushes that bring these forests to life. Many also visit the scenic Linville Falls, where cascading water and picturesque gorges combine to create a spectacular effect. Trails lead to scenic overlooks, where visitors will be impressed with the lovely views. Closer to home, the charming town center of Blowing Rock is as much fun for people to investigate as it is for them to take their canine cohort for a leisurely stroll.

High Hampton Inn & Country Club

P.O. Box 338
Route 107
Cashiers, North Carolina   28717-0338
(800) 334-2551, (704) 743-2411, Fax (704) 743-5991

Managers: Will and Becky McKee
Rooms: 130 doubles, 10 suites, 25 vacation homes
Rates: $72-95 per person (AP)

Payment: *AE, MC, and VISA*
Children: *Welcome (cribs, cots, babysitters, high chairs, and children's programs are available)*
Dogs: *Welcome, provided they stay in the inn's kennel*
Open: *All year*

Anyone wanting a traditional antebellum resort, surrounded by forests, lakes, and mountains, should definitely consider the High Hampton Inn. Located in the heart of the Blue Ridge Mountains and close to the intersecting borders of Georgia, North Carolina, and South Carolina, the inn was formerly the home of Wade Hampton. He built this impressive hunting lodge in the early 1800s, using the labor of slaves he brought up from the lowlands. The houses and land have stayed within the domain of two families, the Hamptons and the McKees, for nearly 200 years. Hampton's son, a Confederate General and the eventual Governor of South Carolina, owned the estate for some time. General Hampton's niece and her husband, Dr. William Halstead, then bought the estate and owned it until 1922. Dr. William Halstead is most notable for his pioneering efforts with anesthesia and for founding the first school of surgery at Johns Hopkins. His family created the extensive landscaping that includes the magnificent Halstead Dahlia garden we see today. After Dr. Halstead's death in 1922, E.L. McKee purchased the 1400-acre estate and converted it into a resort. Three generations of McKees have taken great pains not to alter the overall atmosphere or character of the High Hampton Inn. Anyone who stayed here 70 years ago could return today and find comfort in the fact that very little has changed.

As new arrivals pass through the large stone pillars flanking the main entrance, they will notice split rail fences backed by stands of hemlocks and rhododendrons. Further down the drive, the famous golf course appears, after which the tennis courts come into view. The expansive inn is the most impressive sight of all; resting on a knoll, it offers bucolic views of the colorful gardens, as well as of the more distant Hampton Lake and surrounding mountains. An inn of this size deserves a wraparound front porch, and this one is no exception. The porch on the High Hampton Inn is usually filled with guests relaxing in their rocking chairs and visiting with one another. The massive lobby, just inside, is dominated by a huge stone chimney with fireplaces set on four sides. The beamed ceilings, knotty pine walls, and comfortable furnishings set the low-key tone for the entire inn. Throughout the space, there are dozens of sitting areas. Some of the more desirable are those that have been created around the fireplaces or next to the walls that are lined with windows. Before meals, people tend to gather here in this common area, as the dining room is located just off of this space.

This elongated room maintains the same simple elegance found throughout the rest of the inn. The atmosphere is always relaxed and convivial. During the day guests may dress casually, but in the evening the guests are asked to don more formal attire. Men are requested to wear a jacket and tie, while women should put on a dress or skirt. A long buffet table is always laden with delectables. Some of the perennial favorites are the cream of peanut soup, cranberry Waldorf salad, served with the High Hampton fried chicken, prime rib, or freshly caught trout. The sunny silver pie, a luscious lemon icebox pie creation, and the plum duff, a prune pudding cake, are just two of the many desserts that have enjoyed continued popularity over the years. This simple yet excellent home-cooked fare has survived the test of time.

Guests at High Hampton have several lodging options, most of which center around the inn's rustic decor and simple ambiance. Inn bedrooms lie on the second and third floors, while the 19 cottages and array of private homes are scattered over the additional acreage. Long-time guests definitely have their favorite spots. Some prefer the main inn's bedrooms, where pine paneled walls are the backdrop to the equally unpretentious pine furnishings. Beds are covered with white cotton spreads. The most noticeable touch of color is found in the vases of fresh flowers placed in the rooms. Telephones and televisions are not a part of this experience. These thin walls might reveal the hum of a quiet conversation next door, but guests will more likely remember the cool breezes and sounds of rushing water that drift into the rooms through the windows.

The assorted cottages, too, are aged and full of character, offering fireplaces to take the chill off cool mountain nights. One of our favorites is the Honeymoon Cottage, which is set in the old gristmill on the edge of the lake. Most of these are a short distance from the inn. Not only do they offer privacy, but they also allow guests to more fully appreciate their natural surroundings. The private vacation homes are the most modern portion of the resort. They are equipped with a full complement of up-scale amenities, along with a choice of 2, 3, or 4-bedroom configurations. Cathedral ceilings provide a sense of space, and plate glass windows let in plenty of light and forest views. While these accommodations are definitely deluxe, we preferred the simplicity of the old inn. Here, there are no frills or luxurious amenities, just a sense of blending in with the natural environs, which are such an integral part of this inn. This resort is so unique that we even modified our standard requirement that guests be able to bring their dogs with them into the bedrooms. Those traveling with their canine cohorts must lodge their dogs in the inn's kennel, which is located just 100 yards from the lodge, between the putting green and tennis courts. Guests may spend time with their dogs anytime they wish during the day, and then return them to the kennel at night.

People-oriented diversions are abundant at High Hampton. There is an 18-hole golf course on the premises, complete with a golf professional, and a variety of programs geared for all levels of play. One red-clay and five fast-dry tennis courts are also available. These are as well utilized for private play, as they are for round robins, clinics, and private lessons. In addition, there are a multitude of lawn sports, including English croquet, badminton, bocci, volleyball, tetherball, shuffleboard, archery, and a putting green. Naturalists will enjoy the pristine setting and the goodly number of hiking trails that wend through the property. (There are also a few trails for mountain biking.) Over 150 different bird species have been observed on the grounds. The inn's 35-acre Hampton Lake is also the site of many activities, including swimming and fishing. The inn's flotilla includes sail boats, row boats, canoes, and pedal boats. Children can look forward to organized programs that include everything from nature walks, arts and crafts, and hay rides to Mexican Fiestas and theme cookouts, such as the Teddy Bear's Picnic. A recreation room is fully stocked with indoor activities, such as a pool table and ping pong. Adult tastes are not overlooked. Afternoon tea and bridge are a nice way to end the day, and, in the evening, cocktails and dancing may be enjoyed in the Rock Mountain Tavern. There are also a variety of adult workshops available, covering such themes as basket making, quilting, watercolor painting, and wild flower arranging.

Creek Wood Village

P.O. Box 640
Soco Road
Maggie Valley, North Carolina 28751
(704) 926-3321

Hostess: *Sonja Michels*
Rooms: *7 log cabins*
Rates: *$90-130 per night (EP), $475-695 per week (EP)*
Payment: *MC and VISA*
Children: *Welcome (cribs are available)*
Dogs: *Welcome with prior approval and a $5 nightly fee*
Open: *All year*

Maggie Valley, population 200, is a popular destination for people wanting a simple, rustic family-oriented vacation. Many come to the valley and use it as a home base to explore the Great Smoky Mountains National Park and the Blue Ridge Parkway. According to local lore, the valley was named by the Postmaster General. One would think he could have chosen just any name, but instead he chose to name the region after one of the local residents' daughters, which, you guessed it, happened to be...Maggie. Throughout the town, new arrivals will find a variety of cabin complexes, which fill up quickly in the summer months. One of the more notable of these, which is set just off the main road, at the end of a long gravel driveway, is the Creek Wood Village. As guests approach the reception area they will pass a line of cabins that are placed alongside a series of ponds and look out toward the southern rim of the valley.

Each cabin has a front porch, complete with rocking chairs, where guests can spend relaxing evenings taking in the valley views and enjoying the refreshing breezes. The interior spaces are almost as appealing, with their knotty pine walls and cathedral ceilings. The floor plans vary somewhat, but guests may expect to find a good-sized living room and full kitchen. The homey decor is inviting, usually consisting of two chairs and a sofa set around the woodstove to create a simple living room arrangement. A master bedroom is generally located just off the living room. The larger cabins have enough additional space to accommodate a small dining room table and chairs. In these units, the upstairs bedrooms are often just expansive lofts with double beds placed against the back walls and twin beds edged into the eaves of the roof. Earth tones predominate throughout these spaces, ranging from the hunter green carpets and cream-colored lace curtains to the almond-colored bathrooms and coffee-colored decks. We found that the naturally stained pine walls, cathedral ceilings, and multiple windows made each cabin appear even lighter and more spacious. For romantics or newlyweds there is also a 100-year-old honeymoon cottage, which is usually reserved months in advance.

While the cabins are a great place to begin and end one's day, in between, most guests are anxious to investigate the array of sights and attractions available in the area. Some like to test their angling skills in one of the village's trout ponds or along a rushing creek. Ghost Town in the Sky is another popular diversion, with separate mining, western, and mountaineering towns re-created all along a nearby mountaintop. An inclined railway or shuttle bus brings visitors up to the park, where they will see mock gun fights, saloon shows, and an array of characters dressed in western regalia. There are also dozens of Native American shops filled with a wide choice of goods. These are located between Maggie Valley and Cherokee. Although some might not consider this an area ideal for skiing, there are, however, some excellent slopes at the Cataloochee Ski Area.

Country Cabins

21 Bradley Street
Maggie Valley, North Carolina   28751
(704) 926-0612

Hosts: Dana or Cheryl Easterling
Rooms: 7 cabins
Rates: $60-110 per day (EP), $325-550 per week (EP)
Payment: Personal checks, but will accept credit card deposit if necessary
Children: Welcome (cribs are available)
Dogs: Housebroken dogs are welcome with prior approval and a $25 fee
Open: All year

The Maggie Valley area is a popular destination for a variety of reasons. Some people retreat to this picturesque mountain region to escape the summer's heat and humidity, which permeates much of the south. Others are attracted to the array of sightseeing opportunities and cultural attractions available throughout the region. Maggie Valley's mountain setting also supplies just the right combination of golfing, white water rafting, canoeing, fishing, and hiking opportunities. While visitors may have many different reasons for coming to the valley, most would agree that they thoroughly enjoy the relaxed feeling of the Country Cabins.

We visited in the springtime, a quiet but beautiful time of year in Maggie Valley. From the main road bisecting the valley, we spied the narrow lane that leads up to the intimate cabin complex. As we turned into the hedge-lined drive, we spied a handful of children playing on the lawn off to the side of the Easterling's home. Some were batting a whiffle ball around, others were bouncing on the trampoline, and still others were climbing on the wooden jungle gym and busying themselves in the playhouse. Against this backdrop of children playing, we noticed the sounds of a rushing stream, coupled with the aroma of spring flowers.

A path leads to the main house, which fronts a small group of cabins that are surrounded by large shade trees and rhododendrons. Dana, with toddler in tow, came out to greet us. We headed toward the cabins, up a hillside path that meandered around mature plantings. As we ascended the front stairs to the two-story Wildcat cabin, we learned it was one of two 150-year-old cabins on the premises. The good-sized front porch is set with rocking chairs, a picnic table, and a gas grill. Most prefer to prepare their meals on the grill, especially when it's a nice evening outside. Once inside, we found a homey decor in the living room, a nice complement to the pine-paneled walls and beamed ceilings. From the look of the comfortable sofas pulled up around the fieldstone fireplace, they have been well used over the years. A television is set off in a corner, just in case guests forgot or can't find a good book. The hardwood floors are often spread with braided rugs. With all of this history, we were surprised and pleased to find a kitchen that is not only spacious, but also relatively modern. A stairway leads up to one large loft space, which can accommodate up to six people on the pair of twin and double bedsteads. Another bedroom, just beyond this chamber, contains a double bed with an adjoining full bathroom. This cabin configuration is probably most ideal for a large family or a group of good friends who do not mind walking through each others' bedrooms to get to the bathroom or down the stairs. The second antique cabin is tiny, a 15 x 15 foot studio, containing only a double bed and a bathroom. While the overall decor in the cabins is similar from one building to the next, the two 150-year cabins have darker interiors than the more contemporary ones near the main house.

Built about six years ago, the newer group of cabins seem decidedly brighter than the older ones, due to their honey-colored pine walls and their refreshing country decor. The floor plans are basically the same from one cabin to the next. Guests will find that the good-sized great rooms extend to include a kitchen and dining area. The kitchen, set against one wall, consists of a sink, stove, microwave, and a little counter space. The kitchen is modern and quite functional, but guests shouldn't expect to create too many elaborate meals here. Just next to the kitchen is the pine dining room table, which is covered with a colorful tablecloth and surrounded by ladder-back chairs. Best of all, diners can eat their meals while also enjoying a crackling fire in the stone fireplace. Knickknacks add even more character to these cabins, with mantels dressed up by dried flower arrangements and side tables topped by coffee table books or duck decoys. Comfortable couches and armchairs complete the picture. One double-bedded guest room is located just off this great room, with added sleeping space provided in the loft. During both day and evening hours, guests usually drift out to the wraparound porch or deck. Best of all, Bowser can easily access the outdoors, where there are plenty of attractions to occupy his time.

Most guests like taking a trip to the Great Smoky Mountains National Park. Little do they know, they are already within the confines of the park and need go only a little distance to find a trailhead, an intriguing picnic site, or a stream for fishing. If this is a family sojourn, guests may want to take the children and the dog over to Sliding Rock, where everyone can ride the current as it flows over the rocks. For human visitors, there are the Stomping Grounds, where they can listen to mountain music and watch a little clog dancing. There are also a variety of craft shops, restaurants, and amusement areas within walking distance of the cabins. A scenic drive into the next valley will lead guests down into the Cherokee Indian Reservation, where there are a variety of interesting sights and attractions. Visit during the winter months and try out the downhill skiing at the Cataloochee Ski Area.

Maggie Mountain Villas & Chalet

8 Ivy Lane
Country Club Cove
Maggie Valley, North Carolina   28751
(800) 308-1808, (704) 452-4285

Hosts: Tom and Sue Koziol
Rooms: 2 villas, 1 chalet
Rates: Villas $105-165 per day (EP), $595 per week (EP),
       Chalet $195-255 per day (EP), $995 per week (EP)
Payment: Personal checks
Children: Welcome
Dogs: Well-behaved pets are welcome with prior approval, however please,
       "no alligators"
Open: All year

Maggie Valley is a small town tucked along the western edge of North Carolina, set directly between the spectacular Great Smoky Mountains National Park and the equally picturesque Pisgah National Forest. Most visitors to the area have been coming for years, but newcomers may be surprised to discover this peaceful, wooded valley surrounded by such immense natural beauty. Mother Nature supplies an array of diversions for visitors; however, humanity has also added an assortment of shops and restaurants lining the rural route that bisects the valley. At the entrance to Maggie Valley, before emerging into the more commercial thoroughfare, visitors will find the lush green fairways of the golf course. Upon arriving at the entrance to the country club, guests may proceed up past the main club house to a series of private roads that lead to the Maggie Mountain Villas & Chalet.

Tom Koziol and his wife Sue own the villas and chalet. The couple is originally from New York, where Tom worked for 17 years at IBM. During a visit with an uncle in nearby Franklin, the Koziols decided to explore the surrounding area and they came across Maggie Valley. Instantly connecting with the relaxed pace and beauty of the region, a short time later they purchased a home. It won't take long for guests to understand why Tom and Sue were so smitten.

After a long ascent up the steep hillside, new arrivals come at last to the driveway that leads to the villas. These two units are contained in one building, which is set into the hillside. Both units in this duplex—with one villa situated on the first floor and the other on the second—share similar floor plans, amenities, and decors. Pine paneled walls set the tone in these spaces, coordinating with the comfortable country decor. In this home-like setting, guests feel at ease relaxing on the camel-colored carpet in front of the fireplace, and playing a board game or watching television. Those who prefer to dwell above floor level will be just as happy in one of the soft armchairs or on the sofa. Rattan tables and additional side chairs complete the scene. The spacious living room opens into an intimate dining nook and fully-equipped kitchen, allowing for easy conversation between the two areas. The white walls make this already expansive chamber all the more light and airy. During the summer months the covered deck is truly the place to be, as it affords some of the best valley views, visible between the canopy of trees. Rocking chairs and porch swings are frequently the gathering spots of choice, allowing guests to take advantage of the refreshing breezes that predominate at 3,300 feet. In the evening, guests may retire to one of two bedrooms located toward the rear of the villa. A hallway leads past a large bathroom to a room with a queen bed, and another with a pair of twin beds. The country collectibles are nice accents to the comfortable furnishings.

Extended families or couples traveling together may want to consider the expansive chalet. It is situated on another hillside, only a short distance from the villas. Tom and Sue have just spent a good deal of time, energy, and money refurbishing this home. A tightly twisting driveway brings guests up the hill another 100 feet to a wood framed dwelling. Perched on the hillside, safely tucked behind a massive, newly constructed retaining wall, is the chalet. From the outside it is difficult to imagine what the interior looks like; however, a step through the door leads into a cavernous cathedral-ceilinged living room. We especially liked the massive stone fireplace, whose chimney can be seen rising through the ceiling. More spectacular still are the views of the valley seen through the wall of windows. The good-sized dining area to the rear of the room can easily hold all the house guests and a few more. A kitchen is well stocked for creating meals, although most prefer to do their cooking on the barbecue. After a strenuous day of hiking and a long, leisurely evening meal, the outdoor hot tub is the perfect way to truly rejuvenate.

There is a wide array of sleeping arrangements in this house. On the main floor, just off the living room, are two bedrooms, one with a queen bed and another with two twin beds. The full bathroom is shared between these two spaces. We thought the large loft space was used quite creatively. In it, a sofa bed is positioned directly across from a pair of twin beds and a queen bed is placed behind a privacy curtain. Guests who choose the chalet will enjoy not only the ample space, but also the unobstructed valley views.

It would be sacrilegious to come to the area and not visit the Great Smoky Mountains National Park. It extends just over a half million acres of land, and is considered the oldest rise of land in the world. These mountains may be old, but they are still fairly high, in some places reaching altitudes of over 6,000 feet. Visitors should bring a leash so Bowser can also enjoy the beauty of the park's lakes, rivers, and mountain peaks. (Unfortunately, Bowser is not permitted to hike on the trails.) Adding to the visual beauty is the blue-tinged haze that generally hangs over the area. (Hence the name, Smoky Mountains). Access to the park is most easily gained at the Oconaluftee Visitor Center. Other fun outings around Maggie Mountain are white water rafting, gem mining, and a visit to the Cherokee Indian Reservation. Visitors may want to stay in Maggie Valley to check out the Soco Gardens Zoo and the Ghost Town in the Sky (theme park), as well as the clog dancing and miniature golf. People may also wish to hit the links at the championship golf course, which has its own dining room. Perhaps one of the most popular diversions is to just meander about the quiet roads surrounding the villas and chalet, giving both guests and their canine companions a chance to really appreciate the surrounding valley.

Pirate's Cove

P.O. Box 1879
Highway 64 & 264 (just off the Nags Head/Manteo Causeway)
Manteo, North Carolina   27954
(800) 537-7245, (919) 473-6800, Fax (919) 473-6412

Manager: Elena Wilkinson
Rooms: 56 Condominiums, 18 houses
Rates: Condominiums $725 - 1,015 per week (EP),
*   Houses $1,300-2,250 per week (EP)*
Payment: MC and VISA
Children: Welcome (high chairs and cribs are sometimes available in the units)
Dogs: Welcome in three condominiums, with a $53 flea extermination fee.
*   One pet per unit.*
Open: All year

North Carolina's Outer Banks is a string of islands and extended peninsulas that line over 125 miles of its coastline. Visitors who have never visited this region will be pleasantly surprised by the excellent fishing and boating opportunities, as well as the magnificent beaches. Bird watchers flock here hoping to enjoy the abundant wildlife and catch a glimpse of a new species to add to their journals. The ocean and sound waters not only set the natural borders for the area, but are also the source for most of its recreational pursuits. Roanoke Island sits in the center of it all, situated between the Croatan and Roanoke Sounds and just minutes from Nag's Head. Pirate's Cove is a private complex of luxury condominiums and homes, where residents and renters have easy access to the waterways that practically encircle the property.

Just a short drive from Manteo's charming town center lies the entrance to Pirate's Cove. During our visit, this expansive condominium and cottage community was in full gear readying itself for the upcoming summer season. A guard station limits access to residents and renters only, and once past the gates, these people will see a zigzagging line of condominiums that make up Buccaneer Village. This seemingly convoluted configuration not only creates a sense of privacy, but also allows the units to have unobstructed views. One of the first condominiums we visited was located in Building One, which is conveniently located next to a variety of recreational outlets. A swimming pool and a pair of tennis courts are situated right next door, and a volleyball court, basketball court, and wooden jungle gym are located just across the drive. We checked out a third floor, 1 1/2 bedroom unit. It was extremely well designed, with cathedral ceilings and an abundance of windows that maximized the feeling of space and light. Outdoor living is achieved through covered patios that are accessible from both the master bedroom and the living room. The condominiums flow well, with the central living area consisting of a spacious family room, fully-appointed kitchen, and a dining nook. Although each unit is individually decorated by the owners, each has standard amenities. For instance, the fireplaced living rooms contain televisions, VCRs, and stereos. The master bedrooms have either queen- or king-size beds and the second bedroom usually has a bunk bed. In addition, the master and second bedrooms are separated by a full bathroom.

Another condominium that we liked was in the recently completed Building Seven, also in Buccaneer Village. These units are far more spacious, and slightly more luxurious, than those in Building One. We entered one ground floor condominium and immediately came across two bedrooms furnished with double beds. The living space is further inside the unit, where guests will find the combined kitchen and dining nook. Bar stools line one side of an island counter top and there is a separate area for the dining room table. The family room and dining nook feel far more spacious than they actually are, because of the cathedral ceilings and the absence of walls separating the cooking, eating, and gathering areas. The spacious master bedroom is off by itself, and, once again, has access to a covered back patio. The third unit that accepts pets is in Building Nine. This is also a ground floor condominium, with a configuration similar to those in Building Seven, except it has far better views of Roanoke Sound and the Outer Banks. As of this writing, the units in this building were just being finished and furnished by their respective owners.

While the condominiums generally have a standard layout, the interior decor varies, according to each owner's personal taste. Not only were the condominiums we saw very traditionally furnished, but they offered a complete host of amenities that would make travelers more than comfortable during their stay. Guests may expect central air conditioning and heating, washers and dryers, outdoor showers, televisions with VCRs, and stereos. Second televisions, surround sound stereos, and other goodies, including crab pots, are sometimes added by the owners.

In addition to living in the lap of luxury, Bowser will also be delighted by the abundance of walks around the grounds. We advise guests to follow the docks and boardwalks to their conclusion. Curious dogs might check out the buckets of crabs that people collect off these docks, or just enjoy quiet meanderings through the complex. There are still plenty of open lots that are waiting to be developed into private homes, but until then, they make for excellent walking areas. A drive into Manteo, or over the bridge towards Nag's Head, reveals another host of diversions. The beaches along the Outer Banks are still open to dogs, but there is talk of limiting their activity to the quieter times of day. Pea Island is just south of Pirate's Cove and makes for a great day trip. There are no houses in the preserve and leashed dogs still have unlimited access to the beach.

Laughing Gull Cottages

P.O. Box 1119 (Milepost 17 1/2)
Nags Head, North Carolina   27959
(919) 441-7423, (919) 441-5751, (804) 596-1182

Manager: Billy Vance
Rooms: 8 cottages
Rates: $320-1,500 weekly (EP)
Payment: MC and VISA
Children: Welcome
Dogs: Welcome in all of the cottages except for Unit 8. There is a $30 fee and dogs must adhere to pet policies. Pets cannot be left unattended, they must be leashed on premises, waste must be scooped up, and pet must have a current health certificate, along with a tick and flea collar and identification.
Open: All year

We can still clearly remember the many family vacations we took as children. Although these adventures varied, they were always highly anticipated trips. Whether we visited the seashore or the mountains, they remain strongly ingrained in our memories. If we were to go back today to the vacation spots of our youth, we might be disappointed with the changes that have occurred over the years, but most likely we would fall back easily into our old routines. Anyone who has spent summers in Nags Head would understand what we mean, for as much as the area has developed, visitors can still find its simple side. Returning visitors can slip easily into this other world, because they have either owned or rented the same cottage for years. This is certainly the case with the Laughing Gull Cottages, where some guests have been coming for 20 years. Given a repeat record like that, we wanted to know more about the resort's facilities and cottages.

During our stay on the Outer Banks, we learned that looks can sometimes be deceiving; often the most innocuous-looking places turn out to have the most character. The Laughing Gull Cottages are no exception. The eight cottages are built on stilts and line either side of a sand-covered lane. At the end of the lane we could see the primary reason for the cottages' popularity—the expansive beach. As we walked around, we saw a couple coming off the beach with their Golden Retriever. We looked over to another cottage's observation deck and saw a German shepherd, a terrier, and a beagle hanging out with their human friends. This was reminiscent of a scene out of Our Gang, but instead of being surrounded by children, we were surrounded by dogs. A little later, we ran across yet another doggie vacationer, a Siberian Husky. It was becoming fairly obvious to us that the Laughing Gull Cottages might more appropriately be called the "Laughing Dog Cottages," as all the canines seemed to be having a fine time.

After encountering so many dogs, we were hoping the cottages would live up to their reputation, so that we could recommend them to our readers. Fortunately, they did. This place is not fancy, by any means; it is just classic old Nags Head. The rectangular buildings are three stories high and covered with weathered, gray cedar shakes. Guests enter on the first floor, where most of the bedrooms are located. A staircase leads upstairs to the main living space, where the ocean views begin to unfold. This upside-down arrangement might seem unusual if this were not the Outer Banks, where large dunes tend to block ocean views on the first floor. Each cottage has a slightly different configuration, but most contain three bedrooms and at least two bathrooms, making them quite expansive. Furnishings are attractive, but rather simple, with few knickknacks cluttering the rooms. Nothing is overdone, making this a perfect spot for a relaxing beach-style vacation. In each cottage, there is generally an oversized living room/ dining room combination, which easily accommodates large groups of people. This opens onto a screened-in porch that faces the ocean. An outside staircase leads up even higher to an observation platform. While the decor may be simple, there are still plenty of modern amenities. Living areas contain televisions with VCRs, along with stereos and radios. Like the rest of the cottage, the kitchens are exceptionally clean and fully equipped. Other helpful amenities include the outdoor showers, barbecue grills, central air conditioning, and even electronic bug zappers. When booking a cottage, guests should keep in mind that the ones closest to the ocean are more expensive—and they are worth every penny.

Vacationers who are wondering how they will spend their time at the Laughing Gull Cottages can take a short walk over the dunes. During the off-season dogs are allowed on the beach at any time of day. The town has plans to limit beach access for dogs in the summer months, to just the morning and evening hours. Those looking for other walking options may wish to try the road that runs along the back of the cottages. Nags Head is also well situated for day trips further south. One of the more popular visits is to Cape Hatteras, where visitors will find miles and miles of unspoiled beaches and the famous Hatteras Lighthouse, circa 1870. Dogs are welcome all along the beaches down here and will have a fine time romping and swimming. These beaches are unforgettable, and well worth the drive.

The staff obviously has a fondness for animals. If the dogs themselves hadn't given their secret away, then the little framed quote inside the front door of one of the cottages surely did: "Pets are welcome here. We never had a pet who smoked in bed and set fire to the blankets. We never had a pet who stole our towels, played the television too loud, or had a noisy fight with his traveling companion. We have never had a pet who got drunk and broke up the furniture. So if your pet can vouch for you, you are welcome, too."

Toad Hall Cottage

324 West Soundside Road
Nags Head, North Carolina 27959
(919) 441-1297

Hostess: Megan Vaughan
Rooms: One 4-bedroom cottage
Rates: $400-750 per week (EP)
Payment: Personal checks
Children: Welcome (a crib is available)
Dogs: Well-behaved dogs are welcome for a $40 fee, and must adhere to the
    guidelines of the rental agreement.
Open: All year

The old-fashioned cottages in Nags Head have long been summer homes for countless families. As the sea has encroached, some have been moved back off the dunes; however, a far more crucial change has come through the encroachment of human beings, who have continued to develop the area. The attraction is understandable, as this area offers wonderful beaches, pristine expanses of national seashore, and an abundance of water-oriented activities, all of which draw people to this bustling summer resort. It is becoming increasingly difficult to find the original Nags Head, which is now sometimes overwhelmed by strip malls, amusement areas, and restaurants. Fortunately, we finally tracked down one of the most classic examples of old Nags Head at the Toad Hall Cottage. Moreover, just as we were about to go to press, we also learned that the Vaughns had recently acquired another cottage, located just around the corner from Toad Hall. This second "dog-friendly" cottage is called Awesome Austin (after the former owners) and is also situated on the sound side of Nags Head. Unfortunately, we were not able to visit Awesome Austin, but we were assured by others that it shares many of the same qualities and attributes that Toad Hall offers.

During our visit to Nags Head, we headed down a quiet back road along Roanoke Sound, where we came upon a brown-shingled cottage set upon stilts. We didn't know it at the time, but the balloon frame construction of this building represents a fine example of a traditional, old-fashioned Nags Head cottage. It was originally built for the Walker family in the 1930s by the then-renowned Mr. Twine. Some argue that the house was formerly situated in the shallows of the Roanoke Sound, while others believe it has always occupied its current site. This controversy is unimportant for visitors today; it is the charm and rich character of the cottage that make it so wonderful.

We ascended the staircase, which climbed from the sandy drive to the expansive wraparound covered porch, where a customary Nags Head hammock was swinging in the breeze and white wooden chairs seemed to be waiting for someone to come and sit awhile. A side door leads into the living room, where richly hued pine-paneled walls, hardwood floors, and exposed beams create a sense of repose. We loved the neat, old-fashioned armchairs and soft sofas, which nicely complemented the white rattan furnishings fitted with festive royal blue chintz cushions. There is an understated sophistication to this place, which somehow manages to maintain a traditional and homey feeling. The television, VCR, and stereo are thoughtful conveniences, but most prefer gathering around the original brick fireplace. The living room flows out to the rear of the house, where an antique dining room table is set in a windowed corner nook, surrounded by eight chairs. The adjoining kitchen seems larger, because of the beamed cathedral ceiling. Although the kitchen retains plenty of Old Nags Head charm, it is also fully equipped with many modern conveniences. A week's worth of food can easily be stored in the large refrigerator, and preparing each of the meals is made simple with the food processor, blender, toaster, and microwave that have been thoughtfully provided.

Toad Hall may look deceptively small from the road, but it can easily sleep ten people. There are two bedrooms off the living room, which look onto the front porch. One contains a queen-size bedstead, while another has a pair of twin beds. As with the other bedrooms and common rooms throughout the cottage, the polished hardwood floors are covered with braided area rugs and the windows are framed by sheer curtains. These chambers use the spacious downstairs bathroom, which appears larger both because of the juniper-paneled cathedral ceiling and because an exterior door opens to a fully screened-in garden deck. A flight of stairs leads to the second-floor bedrooms, which are privy to the best views in the house. The eaves up here create all sorts of interesting nooks and crannies, which enhance the overall charm of this cottage. The oversized master bedroom is actually a self-contained family suite, as it has a queen-size bed, bunk beds, and a sofa bed love seat. There is also a walk-in closet, which is large enough to double as a nursery. In addition to an antique mahogany dresser and a chest of drawers for storing clothes, the room contains a telephone and color television. The spacious bathroom is terrific, but we especially liked the four-foot shower that is outfitted with a bench. The other upstairs bedroom is a little smaller than the master bedroom, but it is furnished with a queen-size bed, large oak armoire, a dressing table, and a bureau. There are plenty of windows in this chamber, allowing guests views of the sound. There is also a private entrance, which opens to reveal an expansive "flight deck."

Aside from lovely interior spaces, there are several outdoor amenities that make this one of our favorite finds on the Outer Banks. A Weber grill is set up on the downstairs brick patio, where guests will also find a large fish-cleaning area. After a day on the beach, most will want to rinse off in the double outside shower. A partition can be either opened or left closed to form two separate shower spaces. The washer and dryer make it easy to keep up with the vacation laundry situation. Guests will also appreciate the good-sized storage area for beach toys and other paraphernalia.

Bowser will be equally happy whether inside or outside Toad Hall Cottage. Guests may take him on a leisurely stroll along the quiet lane, over to the Jockey's Ridge State Park, where there are 400 acres of sandy dunes and beachfront to explore. This is an excellent swimming and windsurfing spot that is tucked away from the crowds and from the Atlantic surf. The Outer Banks is also quite a haven for dog owners. While all of the beaches are accessible to those with dogs, we recommend some of the less crowded areas to the south of Nags Head. For "birders," a drive south to Pea Island will lead to an area rich in wildlife. Bowser is allowed on the Atlantic side of the refuge, but not on the sound side. Driving north to Corolla, an entirely different feeling pervades—that of a planned resort community. Guests should drive carefully, as there a number of wild horses that still wander throughout this northern section of the Outer Banks.

Not only is Toad Hall the most authentic cottage we found in Nags Head, but it also offers the most privacy. It is beautifully maintained, filled with inherent charm, and certainly a place we would be able to enjoy with our family, friends, and dogs.

Outer Banks House Rentals

Real Estate Companies

B&B on the Beach
P.O. Box 564, 1023 Ocean Trail
Corolla, North Carolina 27927
(800) 962-0201, (919) 453-3033
Rental Range: $1,050 - 4,100 per week
Rental Period: Three consecutive days (off-season), weekly (in-season)
Reservations: Pre-reservations made one year in advance by previous
renters, all others are one year less a week in advance.
Dog Policy: "Pets are limited to two domestic, housebroken pets with a
weight limit of 75 lbs each, unless otherwise noted. There is a
$45 extermination fee. Let us know when making your
reservation if your furry friends are coming along."

Sun Realty
P.O. Box 163
Kill Devil Hills, North Carolina 27948
(800) 334-4745, (919) 441-8011
Rental Range: $525 - $3,650 per week
Rental Period: 2-3 consecutive days (off-season), weekly (in-season)
Reservations: Accepted December 1 of year preceding rental, ie. December
1, 1995 for 1996
Dog Policy: "Cottages allowing a pet are limited to not more than two
housebroken dogs. A $65 fee, plus sales tax, is charged for flea
extermination. No cats allowed."

Atlantic Realty
4729 North Croatan Highway
Kitty Hawk, North Carolina 27949
(800) 334-8401, (919) 261-2154
Rental Range: $525 - 2,250 per week
Rental Period: Three consecutive days (off-season), weekly (in-season)
Reservations: Accepted January 2 of the year beginning the season, i.e.
January 2, 1996 for 1996 season.
Dog Policy: "Pets are allowed in any rental unit stating 'Pet
Allowed.'There will be a $65 charge for extermination of pet
units. Pet owners are financially liable."

North Carolina's Outer Banks were first colonized in 1585, when the English settled on Roanoke Island. Over the next hundred years or so the fishermen, farmers, and Native Americans who lived here led a relatively undisturbed life. The only major changes continued to be provided by Mother Nature, who sent wild storms crashing onshore to reshape the inlets, coves, and dunes. Man-made change finally crept onto the Outer Banks beginning in 1903, when Wilbur and Orville Wright successfully flew their motorized airplane from Kill Devil Hills. The notoriety of the flight and its origins soon attracted visitors, who quickly recognized the area for something else entirely. The sleepy towns along the coast were not only an idyllic escape from the summer's inland humidity, but also for the miles of unspoiled beaches and dunes. Fishermen were blessed with abundant sportfishing areas, and birders reveled in the rich variety of birds that would regularly migrate through the area.

Today, the coastline continues to be reshaped, and the wildlife and fishing remain abundant, but the flavor of these once sleepy towns has markedly changed as private home construction and commercial development increases. The Outer Banks has several distinct areas whose activities center on the major towns along the island chain. Most people who come for a week generally rent houses or cottages through real estate agencies. Just as each town has a distinct personality, so do the multitude of agencies. We chose the three that most impressed us. Having rental access to dog-friendly units was obviously very important to us, but so were the quality of the listings and the area covered. These three companies offered not only a good number of accommodations that welcomed dogs, but also a diverse array of houses and prices.

First, though, how does one pick the town to stay in? Nag's Head is one of the more popular, accessible, and affordable, because it lies near the main causeway connecting the Outer Banks to the mainland. An extra two lanes of road were added to the causeway in 1995, which should alleviate the headaches people experience on weekends when they are either coming on or going off the Outer Banks. In Nag's Head, as well as Kill Devil Hills and Kitty Hawk, visitors will find weathered, shingle cottages and houses resting on stilts set one next to the other along the Atlantic ocean. Vegetation is rather sparse, with the exception of beach grass. On the Pamlico Sound, there are more modern complexes. These include low-rise condominiums and houses that are part of private communities. There are plenty of commercial diversions, ranging from outlet malls and restaurants to sailboarding, kite and novelty stores, and miniature golf complexes. Visitors may drive south through Pea Island Wildlife Sanctuary to leave the array of amusement centers and strip malls behind.

Here, the landscape becomes decidedly more bucolic, with miles of protected conservation lands lining the Cape Hatteras National Seashore. There are small towns such as Salvo, Avon, Buxton, Hatteras, and Ocracoke. Visitors will discover that the southernmost destinations are the most isolated, and reminiscent of the Outer Banks of old. To the north of the Nag's Head/Kitty Hawk area are the tiny towns of Duck and Corolla. As one local described it to us, each group of towns from Nag's Head on northward corresponded to a decade of development. Nags Head, Kill Devil Hills, and Kitty Hawk were developed in the 1970s, Duck and Sanderling in the 1980s, and Corolla in the 1990s. Thus, as a general rule of thumb, the rental houses and condominiums become more refined, up-scale, and well-appointed as travelers drive north. As an aside, not only are accommodations in Duck, Sanderling, and Corolla spaced a greater distance apart from one another, but they also have denser vegetation and more elaborate landscaping. Corolla is one of our favorite areas. With the right sticker and a four-wheel drive vehicle, visitors can drive onto the beach and head north beyond the houses to the far northern reaches of the island. Corolla is also home to 18 wild horses that are allowed to roam freely throughout the area.

There are plenty of low key motels along the Outer Banks, interspersed with some interesting B&Bs and a few inns. These are generally popular for extended weekends, but most find that longer vacations require the use of a house, which in turn may be rented through any number of real estate companies. Before prospective guests begin the selection process, they should first understand that there is a huge variety of properties available. Some cottages are within whispering distance of their neighbors, while others are set off by themselves and surrounded by shrubs. Many are part of exclusive communities, and several neighborhoods are located near commercial areas, within easy walking distance of restaurants and shops. Beach-front houses vary greatly in price, depending on where they are located. A house in Corolla may be rented for $3,000 per week, while a house in Nag's Head is available for half that price. One might offer every creature comfort; the other may have few amenities and a more casual overall atmosphere. Prospective renters should think about what they want, what price range is best for them, and then send away for the thick, magazine-style brochures and enjoy the reading.

B&B on the Beach:
    We were most impressed with the types of accommodations offered and the dog-friendliness of the **B&B on the Beach** in Corolla. The front cover of its 1995 catalog is terrific, with a black and white 1920s-style photograph showing the staff posing in front of the office. The office looks like an old hunt club, and the staff is clothed in full hunting regalia. Scattered about the staff members are their dogs and decoys. The dogs get as big a mention as the staff; they are listed in the photo credits as Goose, the black dog; Traveler, the fat dog; and Lily, the baby dog. Inside the impressive four-color brochure, which shows both interior and exterior shots, prospective renters can easily identify the dog-friendly accommodations. The brochure uses a line drawing of Lily (the baby dog), as the whimsical pet symbol. Most of these units are circa 1990s and even the older ones are exceptionally well maintained and attractive. It is tough to go wrong with this outfit, whether choosing a waterfront rental, a house off the water, or one situated along the sound.
    Each unit is individually decorated and furnished and we couldn't find a mediocre one in the bunch. Whatever the amenities, they were usually provided. A variety of housing options are available, including a house set off in the dunes by itself or one with a private swimming pool or tennis court. Vacationers may want to try Corolla Light, a resort village offering a clubhouse, swimming pool, biking and hiking trails, and a sports center. All accommodations have modern and fully-equipped kitchens, central air and heat, televisions and VCRs, barbecue grills, beach chairs, and outdoor showers. Additionally, **B&B on the Beach** supplies a long list of services. A concierge is available during the high season and will go out of his/her way to assist guests, whether it be securing theater tickets, babysitters, tee times, or horseback riding lessons. Conch Club homes are designated by a conch shell. These are

generally the most exclusive listings, because the Conch Club homeowners subscribe to an extended service, which renters may also use. Beds are made prior to arrival and linens are supplied. Starter baskets of shampoos, conditioners, razors, paper towels and coffee are more reminiscent of a hotel than a house. Guests renting houses that are not part of the Conch Club service may opt for linen rentals or bring their own. **B&B on the Beach** is as full-service and professional as can be found, just about anywhere. This agency will rent only to families — no undergraduates or people unrelated to each other.

Sun Realty:

The second agency, **Sun Realty**, had the largest number of rentals. These were slightly more expensive, on average, than those offered by **Atlantic Realty**, but were less costly than the **B&B on the Beach** rentals. Their black and white photographs are small and harder to distinguish, but their terrier symbol for dog-friendly houses is easy to spot. Moreover, the number of rentals that welcomed dogs was probably two to three times the number offered through the other two agencies. An added benefit is **Sun Realty's** detailed maps of the area, which use numbers to indicate the location of each rental property. Renters know exactly where their house or cottage will be, taking some of the guesswork out of making a decision. Available properties include listings from Corolla to Avon (offering listings located further south than those available through either of the other two agencies). Soundfront and oceanfront were best. Oceanside, set one house off the beach, came in a close second. Oceanfront does not necessarily mean ocean views, however, so renters must be sure to read the fine print. We checked out many of the dog-friendly houses and were impressed with a number of them. For instance, one coffee-colored, Cape-style, shingle house was considered to be oceanside, and although renters had no view of the ocean, they could walk 100 yards up a sandy lane and be on the beach. The house had been recently renovated and updated, with new windows, amenities, and a fresh decor. Another appealing pair of cottages lay at the end of a private lane in South Nag's Head. Two dark gray, weathered board cottages sat next to one another on a dune, with unsurpassed ocean views. The pair could be rented by extended families, or they could be reserved as separate rentals. Further south, on the outside of Avon, we found a spectacular property on the sound. It is a contemporary gray, shingled structure with a private dock the juts into the sound. It is set at the end of a lane, in a stand of trees and bushes that conceal it from other houses. From the driveway, there are few windows, increasing the sense of privacy. From the sound, though, there are plenty of windows and exceptional views. Anyone renting through **Sun Realty** should know that the agency rents only to family groups, and not to groups of unrelated friends.

Atlantic Realty:

The third agency is **Atlantic Realty**, which has a comprehensive assortment of listings and includes rentals from Corolla down to Bodie, just south of Nag's Head. This agency, too, features interior and exterior color photographs of each listing, as well as maps showing the exact location of its houses and cottages. Because the agency's listings cover the entire Outer Banks, there is greater diversity available, but of highly variable quality. Thus, it should not be too surprising to find an older three- or four-bedroom house available for $650 a week, while a newly constructed four-bedroom might command up to $2,250 a week. Clearly, the latter offers a full array of amenities, access to the ocean, and everything from a swimming pool to a dog run. Renters should read through the standard location descriptions in the front of the brochure. We felt that most of the houses located "between the highways" were affordable, but mediocre. There are a number of pet-friendly houses, designated by the indicator, "Pets Allowed," set in bold letters. We checked out a number of these places and found that price was a very good bench mark for quality and level of amenities. Inexpensive rentals could be found near the beach, but renters there had to contend with noisier roads or tinier living spaces.

Regardless of the real estate agency travelers may choose, we recommend booking as early as possible, within the agency guidelines. This region is very welcoming to dogs. They are generally allowed on the Atlantic Beaches, which are the ultimate early morning and late evening walking spots. Many also enjoy bringing Bowser along for a leisurely jog along a quiet side road, or perhaps taking him on a bicycling adventure around the picturesque paths that line the Outer Banks. Whatever vacationers and their canine cohorts decide to do, both will find a wonderful assortment of houses and cottages available through these rental agencies.

Valle Crucis Log Cabins

P.O. Box 554
Valle Crucis, North Carolina   28691
(704) 963-7774, Fax (704) 963-6209

Manager: *Sherry Miller*
Rooms: *9 cabins*
Rates: *$125-175 per day (EP), $550-750 per week (EP)*
Payment: *Personal checks*
Children: *Welcome*
Dogs: *Welcome with prior approval and a $35 fee*
Open: *All year*

Following the Blue Ridge Parkway out of Asheville, travelers very quickly find their way into North Carolina's High Country. We were enchanted by the many little hamlets tucked into the woods along the scenic back-country roads. One of these is Valle Crucis, which, translated, means valley of the cross, referring to the confluence of the three creeks that run through here. Anyone who seeks a simpler way of life will thoroughly enjoy Valle Crucis, as one of its larger commercial ventures is the general store, which dates back to 1883. Inside, a piece of history is revealed in the old advertisements lining the walls, the ancient woodstove, and even the antique scales that are still used to weigh and measure goods. The Valle Crucis Log Cabins don't necessarily share the same antiquity, but they do exude the same charming Appalachian ambiance that is found in the general store.

We have seen plenty of log cabins in our time, and have noticed that many are very much like soldiers, all lined up and facing a focal point such as a lake or a golf course. In contrast, at Valle Crucis, the cabins are linked only by their name, *Evergreen,* and by the company that rents them out. In every other way they are quite individual. Guests are also treated as individuals. There are no organized programs, get-acquainted cocktail parties, or the like. The guests here seem to prefer it that way. The newly constructed, Appalachian-style cabins are set into the hillsides surrounding Valle Crucis. Clusters of white pines, hemlocks, and rhododendrons create a sense of privacy around the cabins. It takes a little skill and patience to navigate the winding rocky gravel roads leading to the cabins, but rest assured that any inconvenience is worth the end result. Each of the hand-hewn cabins is fronted by a wraparound porch set with a half dozen rocking chairs. The exteriors may look authentic, but inside are thoroughly modern amenities and charming guest quarters.

The light pine walls and multiple pairs of windows combine to naturally brighten the cabins, especially in the cathedral-ceilinged family room found in each of the cabins. The family room is furnished with an emphasis on maintaining the light and comfortable mood. There are overstuffed sofas and armchairs, but anything else that might seem utilitarian is missing here. Instead, there are hand-painted tables, sweater chests, country antiques, and assorted pine furnishings used as tables and accent pieces. An array of country collectibles quite literally fills the walls. Dried flower wreaths, pewter cookware, baskets, and duck decoys are just the start. There are also snowshoes, oxen yokes, and framed prints that either occupy other wall spaces or hang from the beams. Although there are color televisions, most guests find they are more apt to enjoy a crackling fire in the authentic, dry stack stone fireplaces. We appreciated the fully-equipped, modern kitchens where microwave ovens and dishwashers add to the ease of vacation living. Those who prefer an outdoor flavor to their foods will be happy to find that each cabin has a gas grill. The dining areas contain Windsor chairs set around rectangular tables. Corner hutches, decorative plates, and assorted other collectibles are also usually found in these chambers.

Many of the cabins are set on the side of a hill. This arrangement allowed the designers to situate a majority of the bedrooms on the lower levels, leaving the upper floors for the common areas, where the views are best. (This is not to say that the bedrooms are without views, as they are privy to them as well.) Another feature of the bedrooms that derives from the cabins' design is that they tend to stay cooler in the summer months and warmer in the wintertime, because they are located down on ground level. The interior configurations of the cabins vary. Some offer two bedrooms, two private half baths, and a shared full bath. The standard arrangement consists of a queen-size bed in one room and a pair of twins in another. We thought the most interesting bedrooms were in the loft, set behind the chimney. The king-size bed there is terrific by itself, but with the stereo and television it becomes a well-appointed suite. Each of the bedroom decors varies as well, but guests may expect brass lamps on pine side tables, area rugs on the wood floors, and a warm and inviting country motif to predominate. Saving the best for last, many of the cabins have hot tubs, which are certain to be well utilized. Some of the more basic, but very important amenities, such as washers and dryers, telephones, and linens are also supplied. We were impressed by these cabins, and would agree with the brochure, which describes them as "private mountain retreats."

Bowser will undoubtedly enjoy getting out and exploring the surrounding region. Many guests like to take a drive along the magnificent Blue Ridge Parkway, but travelers should plan on going slowly and not try to cover too much territory in one day. Closer to home, visitors will find the Linville Falls and gorges, where winding trails give hikers a dramatic view of the falls. This is a great picnic spot and many like to spend the better part of a day here. Others might prefer some leisurely trout fishing, or, if the season is right, visitors may investigate the annual Grandfather Mountain Highland Games. The warm months here are highlighted with the blooming of the rhododendrons, mountain laurel, and roses. In addition to hiking in the Moses Cone and Price National Parks, many come for the white water rafting, swimming, and boating options available within a few minutes' drive of the cabins. The colder months bring such diversions as sleigh rides and ice skating, as well as downhill and cross-country skiing, which are available at nearby Beech Mountain. During the day, Bowser will undoubtedly opt for just about any of the outdoor pursuits; in the evening he will surely enjoy an informal walk up the quiet private roads that wend through the hills.

South Carolina

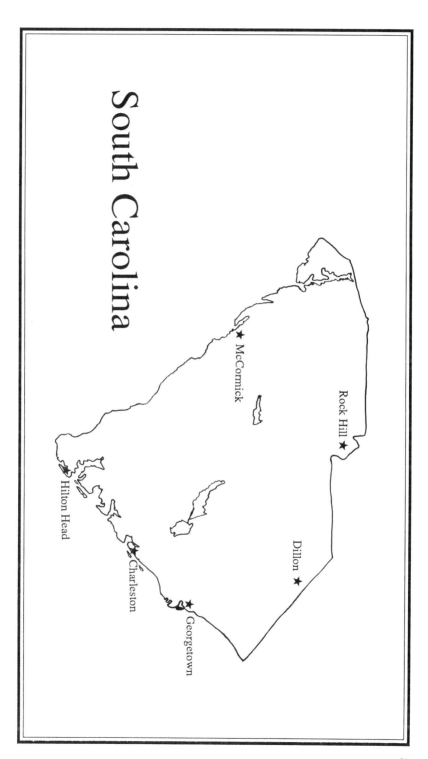

South Carolina

McCormick ★

Rock Hill ★

Hilton Head

Charleston ★

Dillon ★

Georgetown ★

Capers-Motte House

69 Church Street
Charleston, South Carolina 29401
(803) 722-2263

Hosts: Jessica and Keith Marshall
Rooms: 7 doubles
Rates: $95 (B&B)
Payment: MC and VISA
Children: Welcome
Dogs: Welcome with advance notice and prior approval
Open: All year

Many visitors to Charleston are enamored with the historic heritage of this charming city that has managed to hold onto its small town feeling and intrinsic beauty. The quaint market places, antique homes, beautiful old churches, and scenic waterfront certainly piqued our interest. While some people are partial to learning about the past, others are more intrigued with actually experiencing it. One of the best ways to do the latter is to reserve a room in one of Charleston's historic Bed & Breakfasts. We know of a great, low-key B&B located in the heart of the historic district—The Capers-Motte House. Besides being within walking distance of the picturesque Battery Park, this 20-room mansion is reputed to be the largest pre-Revolutionary War house in Charleston. Moreover, Church Street, where it is located, is commonly referred to as "the most interesting street in America." Given the combination, how can guests go wrong?

The house was built in 1735 by a merchant named Richard Capers. A short time later, it passed into the hands of Jacob Motte. The most interesting story culled from his tenure here involves his daughter-in-law who tried to convince the Revolutionary soldiers to burn down the house while it was occupied by the British. Fortunately, she failed in her mission, and the subsequent owners, the Smiths, kept the house in their family for the next 170 years. In 1971, Jessica and Keith Marshall, the present owners, purchased the old mansion and began the arduous task of restoring it to its former condition.

In one of their initial probes through the house, the Marshalls ran across articles of antique clothing stored in the attic, which they donated to a Charleston museum. They then hired a crew of local artisans and craftsmen to tear down and recreate portions of the house that were not historically correct. The first items on the list were the porches. Working on these, it was found that a few of the house's interior walls had also been altered. While restoring them, the Marshalls learned that the house had been constructed mostly out of massive timbers taken from old sea going vessels. These rough-hewn beams and boards, being cured by the salt water, were decaying more slowly than untreated lumber. The Marshalls now knew that if all else failed, at least the house was extremely well supported. After spending nearly $150,000, the Marshalls had recreated a masterpiece, having restored old moldings and detailed woodworking to places where it had been removed over the years. They also decided to paint and furnish the house in much the same manner as it would have been hundreds of years ago.

As guests walk down the appealing, tree-lined Church Street, what they will find is a three-story, faded brick red facade accented by black shutters. As we entered the elegant foyer, we were immediately drawn to the dining room, where a formal three-pedestal table is surrounded by Chippendale chairs and set on an Oriental rug. In the morning, fine English china is used for the full, hearty breakfast that is served in here. On the other side of the foyer is the spacious living room, where the cypress paneling has been enriched with a light stain and windows are enhanced by the Indian shutters. Georgian-style antiques, set around a fireplace, are combined with lovely portraits and crystal chandeliers. To the rear of the foyer—which holds a splendid tall case clock and a gracefully curving staircase—we finally found the kitchen, where an assistant was helping with the post-breakfast chores. The house's original kitchen, known simply as the cook house, is located out near the garden and pool area. This cottage has been renovated to accommodate two guest rooms. Unlike the rooms in the main house, these are furnished with period reproductions, rather than antiques. Bowser probably cannot tell the difference and he may be a little happier out here, as the ease of access to the outdoors is appealing.

Bed chambers in the main house are completely authentic, with high ceilings, traditional color schemes, and a collection of lovely antiques. Four-poster rice beds grace some rooms, while pairs of finial-topped twin beds are found in others. Most guests, though, thoroughly enjoy the second floor drawing room, where they may sip a refreshing libation. In addition to the elegant furnishings in here, the stained, paneled cypress walls are authentic, as are the impressive examples of the Adam fireplace mantel. Even without understanding the incredible history and detailed restoration of the house, guests are certain to appreciate the expansive common areas and charming bedrooms. The Marshalls have truly helped us gain a better appreciation for life as it must have been back in the 1700s.

In addition to exploring the historic district in Charleston, visitors may want to walk down to the handful of marketplaces nearby. Here, they can easily check out the vast array of boutiques, antique stores, and larger shops that comprise much of the downtown area. Others might enjoy taking Bowser on one of the many informal, self-guided walking tours of Charleston, where there are plenty of architectural and historic sites, as well as green areas to explore. This is a walking city, and one where dogs feel as comfortable as their human companions. The plantations just outside of the Charleston are also worth a visit. Visitors may view their impressive gardens and learn more about the lifestyle on the plantations back in the 1700s and 1800s. Charleston is also a terrific base for trips to Folly Beach County Park and James Island County Park, located on islands just south of Charleston.

Hawthorn Suites Hotel

181 Church Street
Charleston, South Carolina   29401
(800) 766-2644, (803) 577-2644, Fax (803) 577-2697

General Manager: Adrian Wewers
Rooms: 181 suites
Rates: $85-155 (B&B)
Payment: AE, DC, DSC, MC, and VISA
Children: Welcome
Dogs: Smaller dogs are welcome with prior approval and a $30 fee
Open: All year

After touring all along the Carolina coastline, we were pleasantly surprised to come upon the enchanting city of Charleston. The historic downtown area is as enjoyable for casual walks as it is for its plethora of intriguing boutiques, antique stores, galleries, and fine restaurants. Most will also delight at the impressive well-preserved homes, public buildings, and churches that can be found throughout this portion of the city. In the midst of it all is the historic City Market, which dates back to 1841. The assortment of souvenirs, local wares, and crafts found throughout the marketplace makes it worth a special trip. Of course, guests staying at the Hawthorn Suites Hotel don't need to go out of their way to find City Market, as it is located only a block away. This expansive, five-story granite building was designed to complement the City Market's historic architecture, yet within these walls guests will find an elegance and an assortment of amenities more befitting a modern, four-star inn or hotel.

The gray granite facade is accented by a small, beautifully detailed front entrance consisting of a pair of windowed doors flanked by small Roman Corinthian columns. Inside the lovely reception area, still more columns are illuminated by enormous brass chandeliers. Georgian-style reproductions are placed in intimate sitting areas; interspersed among these are lovely flower arrangements and potted plants. Creamy wall treatments are the backdrop for the assorted botanical, nautical, and Audubon prints. On our way to the bedrooms we were able to look into the dining room, where yellow floral wallpaper combines with a green, lattice-patterned carpet to create a garden-like setting. As we passed through the dining room, we emerged onto a long, brick and granite courtyard, highlighted by a large fountain. A dozen or so white umbrellas shading glass-topped tables are placed about the courtyard. Wrought iron benches, interspersed with huge clay pots containing palms, and others overflowing with flowers, are set around the perimeter. Although many like to take their buffet breakfast out here, we found that guests naturally gravitate to this lovely spot any time of day.

While there are an assortment of inns in the Charleston area, these usually can't provide the array of amenities found within the Hawthorn Suites' guest chambers. Visitors will find three different suite styles from which to choose. The most common configuration features a well proportioned living room, which includes a small dining area. It is set with good quality, Georgian-style reproductions that might include a butler's tray table surrounded by an overstuffed sofa and a pair of Queen Anne-style wing chairs. The television is often placed inside a formal cherry armoire. The colors in the striped and floral fabrics are a mixture of deep cranberry, royal blue, and hunter green. Guests who step further into this standard chamber will find on one side of the hall a well designed, modern bathroom with all the amenities. Across from this is a wet bar/kitchenette, situated in a recessed alcove. This gives guests the opportunity to prepare a few simple meals using the microwave, stove, refrigerator, and coffee maker. The master bedroom is located to the rear of the suite, where either a pair of double beds or a king-size bed will be found. The striking finial headboards back bedsteads covered in quilted floral spreads and dust ruffles, which are coordinated with the fabrics framing the windows. Another room design places the living room on one level and the master bedroom upstairs in a loft space. Accents in here and throughout the suites include brass lamps, Oriental bowls filled with plants, and historic prints lining the cream-colored walls. Finally, there are over a dozen rooms whose double French doors open directly onto a courtyard equipped with a Jacuzzi. We were impressed with the contrast between light and formality in these spaces, but equally appealing is the hotel's proximity to downtown Charleston's historic district.

Most enjoy taking their canine cohort for a leisurely stroll through Charleston. Visitors may investigate the intimate parks, or walk along the sea wall out by The Battery. There are so many things to do in and around Charleston that exploring this area could easily involve a week of one's vacation. For those who are planning longer stays, we also suggest driving south to visit such scenic destinations as Beaufort, Hilton Head, and Savannah. After exploring these lovely areas, some might also enjoy heading north to Pawley's Island and Myrtle Beach. The latter boasts of an incredible number of area golf courses—90!

The Meeting Street Inn

173 Meeting Street
Charleston, South Carolina   29401
(800) 842-8022, (803) 723-1882, Fax (803) 577-0851

Manager: Alan Johnson
Rooms: 56 doubles
Rates: $75-160 (EP)
Payment: AE, DSC, MC, and VISA
Children: Welcome (cribs and rollaways are available)
Dogs: Welcome
Open: All year

Charleston is one of the more popular destinations in the south and is certainly one of our favorite cities. This is a place that is best explored on foot, allowing visitors to gain an appreciation for the city's historic homes, churches, and commercial buildings, which have been beautifully preserved and restored. Visitors can meander along the picturesque waterfront and around Battery Point, take in the wonderful Festival of Houses and Gardens springtime tour, or just explore the numerous shopping areas. Set amidst all this history and beauty is the Meeting Street Inn. The inn was built in 1841 and today stands in the heart of the historic district, just a few blocks from Battery Point.

The inn's three-story coral pink facade presents the same type of "single house" front that many of the other buildings in this part of the city have. Local lore has it that homeowners were originally taxed on the basis of their street frontage. Consequently, most homes were designed so that only a small portion was exposed to the street. Thus, the better part of these buildings runs from the front to the back of the property, and usually encircles a spacious courtyard or garden. In keeping with the other historic buildings in the neighborhood, the Meeting Street Inn has decorative stonework around the windows. It also has a series of porches, on each level, that run the entire length of the structure.

The spacious reception area sets the decorative tone for most of the other rooms in the inn. Here, guests will find an array of formal antiques, interspersed with leather couches and wing chairs that form intimate sitting areas. An antique clock graces one wall, while a ship's model rests on a beautiful antique secretary. This room serves not only as the reception area, but also as the gathering place for the hearty Continental breakfast presented to the inn guests each morning. This repast may be enjoyed right here in this room or out on one of the brick courtyards, where birds flit in and out of the lush plantings, sometimes stopping to bathe and drink from one of the decorative fountains. It was springtime during our visit and the flower gardens were in full boom, and quite stunning.

The guest rooms are located along the side and to the rear of the building, on one of three levels. While Meeting Street tends to be quite busy during the day, after dinner it quiets down, as tourists and shoppers head home. Anyone who is especially concerned about potential street noise should request a room near the rear courtyard—where there also happens to be an outdoor Jacuzzi. New arrivals will find their guest quarters by walking through one of the courtyards or along the porches, both of which are accented with black wrought iron benches and chairs. As we entered the rooms, our eyes were drawn to the high ceilings. The walls, papered in delicate old-fashioned floral prints, are sometimes enhanced by decorative wainscotting. Most rooms are furnished with a pair of queen-size beds, but there are five that have king-size bedsteads. These finial or four-poster rice beds are placed on Oriental rugs, which protect the original hardwood floors. A writing desk is generally set off to one side of the room and a television is discreetly tucked into an armoire. The walls have decorative accents, such as Queen Anne mirrors, dried flowers and wreaths, and an assortment of paintings of local scenes or Audubon prints. Even though the bedrooms have an antique feeling about them, the bathrooms, fortunately, do not. They are good-sized, modern, and outfitted with an array of toiletries.

Although there is not a restaurant on the premises, there are many excellent dining options available just a short distance from the inn. Travelers may look for local favorites such as She crab soup and the wide variety of Low Country dishes. As guests walk through town, they may be interested in learning more about Fort Sumter's role in the Civil War. Or they might pay a visit to the aircraft carrier, the U.S.S. Yorktown. Even non-shoppers would be remiss if they failed to investigate the various nearby markets, including the restored City

Market, the Rainbow Market, State Street Market, and Market Square, as well as the myriad galleries, boutiques, and antique stores that are nearby. Some may like to take Bowser for a drive north of the city, where they will discover an assortment of magnificent plantations, whose grounds are resplendent with color in the spring. Charlestowne Landing, which was founded by the English in 1670, is a 660-acre park that allows leashed dogs to explore its grounds. Another popular outing is found just outside Summerville in the Old Dorchester State Park, an historic site set on 325 acres. The community of Dorchester, founded in 1696, was eventually abandoned, and then finally destroyed by the British. Bowser will appreciate the fact that within the city limits, there are not only plenty of parks worth investigating, but also leisurely walks and waterfront areas to romp along.

Rutledge Victorian Inn

114 Rutledge Avenue
Charleston, South Carolina   29401
(803) 722-7551

Hosts: Lynn, Mike, and B.J. Smith
Rooms: 10 doubles
Rates: $80-120 (B&B)
Payment: MC and VISA
Children: Welcome (cribs, cots, and babysitters are available)
*Dogs: Small dogs are welcome with prior approval, provided they sleep in
        the bathrooms*
Open: From February through December

Charleston epitomizes everything one envisions about gracious southern living—charming old cobblestone streets, historic churches and homes, and an abundance of formal gardens found both in the city and on the sprawling plantations. Despite catastrophic fires, enemy attacks, and devastating hurricanes, Charleston has managed to survive. Part of its resiliency lies in the people, who have fought hard to ensure that the city's heritage and its over 2,000 historic buildings remain intact. The twentieth century may have moved in around the perimeter of this quaint coastal city, but it has altered very little of Charleston's core.

Staying in the historic district is a must for visitors who want to experience the city's past. Vacationers seeking a relaxed, unpretentious, and low-key environment should look into the Rutledge Victorian Inn. Set close to the Old Museum Park, the 1880s inn is notable for its decorative Italianate style of architecture, a style unusual for Charleston. Walking toward the white wrought iron fence, we could see colorful flags waving in the breeze alongside the 100-foot, wraparound front porch. A few guests were relaxing on the rocking chairs, while a pair of seemingly sated cats basked in the warm morning sun.

We knew from our research that the Smiths had spent a great deal of time restoring the inn. Once inside the foyer, we were able to get some idea of the extent of this project. One of the more obvious undertakings was the intricately carved cherry and mahogany staircase. Layers of paint had to be hand stripped, sanded, and cleaned—an arduous task that took many painstaking days to complete. This expansive lavender-hued chamber is decorated with an eclectic assortment of Victorian furnishings that are far from museum pieces; but they allow people to feel comfortable in this informal Bohemian setting. The adjacent dining room, with a large table surrounded by straight back chairs, is the site for an expanded Continental breakfast that is a true serve-yourself affair. Guests may help themselves to the juice and coffee, and to an assortment of muffins, nutbreads, pastries, bagels, and croissants. Cold cereals and fresh fruit accompany the baked treats. Guests may return at the end of a day's explorations to sample one of the assorted cookies from the large glass jar.

As with the common areas, the guest quarters also have twelve-foot ceilings enhanced by delicate plaster moldings, walls trimmed with wainscoting, and original fireplaces. Not only are these bedrooms individually decorated and furnished, but they are also quite substantial in scale. Aside from some king- and queen-size Victorian and finial bedsteads, many of these chambers have enough space left over for additional beds or sitting areas. One room, just off the foyer, has multiple hues of blue and peach brightening the walls and furnishings. One double bed is tucked into a windowed alcove, and another is placed across from the tiled fireplace. The wall of seven-foot windows is accented by balloon shades and floral jabots. The strong colors in here might be somewhat overwhelming were it not for the white cotton spreads covering both beds. Another guest room's corner location appealed to us. There, sunlight pours in through the windows for most of the day. There is an old-fashioned feeling to this space, created by the floral Victorian-era wallpaper that is complemented by the royal blue tie-back draperies. At the foot of the king-size bed a country quilt is neatly folded. Another popular room, situated toward the rear of the house, contains a four-poster canopy bed. A small crystal chandelier illuminates the intimate sitting area found just in front of the fireplace. The modern amenities have not been overlooked, as the bathrooms are private, the guest rooms air conditioned, and each of the rooms contains a television.

The heart of the Historic District is about a 15-minute walk from the inn. Guests might walk out to The Battery, or stroll down to circa 1841 City Market, which is a fun place to investigate with a canine friend. Shoppers will find the Rainbow Market, State Street Market, and Market Square all to be worth exploring. History buffs will surely be interested in visiting the Fort Sumter National Monument, the Patriots Point Naval and Maritime Museum, and the Charles Towne Landing Park. One of the more popular seasonal exhibitions is the Historic Charleston Foundation's Festival of Houses, where many of the city's noteworthy private homes and gardens are open to the public. Some may want to jump in the car with Bowser, and drive out to one of the old plantations, located just a short drive from Charleston.

Magnolia Inn Bed & Breakfast

601 East Main Street
Dillon, South Carolina 29536
(803) 774-0679

Hosts: Jim and Pam Lannoo
Rooms: 4 doubles
Rates: $55-65 (B&B)
Payment: AE, MC, and VISA
Children: Welcome by prior arrangement (a high chair is available)
Dogs: Welcome with prior approval
Open: All year

"Snowbirds" who make the annual trek south, will probably remember passing a town called Dillon, but will undoubtedly be hard pressed to remember exactly where it is. This diminutive spot on the map is located just a few miles south of North Carolina's border and a short distance from I-95. It will take visitors only a few minutes to navigate the back roads leading to town, but once in town, they will be pleasantly surprised by Dillon's charming neighborhoods. We were pleased to find the Magnolia Inn Bed & Breakfast set in the middle of it all. A pair of old, magnificent magnolia trees flanks the brick pathway leading to the columned, wraparound porch. The porch is set with brick red rattan chairs and sofas, and lined with planters brimming with flowers. We were awfully tempted to sit and converse with the other guests; however, we wanted to have a look at the interior, so we stepped through the formal entrance and into a central foyer.

The home has rich period detailing, reflected in the glossy white, paneled wainscoting, hand-carved moldings, and original hardwood floors. We were drawn to the Corinthian columns, located near the base of the stairs. The architectural interest is enhanced by the muted, period striped wallpaper and collection of American antiques. We then walked through a pair of pocket doors and into Miss Georgia's Victorian Parlor. A potpourri of Victorian furnishings and knickknacks are accented by a collection of dolls displayed on tables, in children-sized chairs, and on the fireplace mantel. We then meandered across the hall to the Andrew David Bethea Library, which maintains a much homier atmosphere. A pair of rust-and-camel-colored sofas, set in opposite corners of the room, are well placed to take advantage of both the fireplace and the television set. The darkly stained, elaborately carved wood surrounding the fireplace makes the fireplace, too, appear to be antique. A standing globe, assorted duck decoys, and a tugboat model give the room an additional inviting atmosphere that would make children of all ages feel right at home.

Just down the hall is another cheery space, the Magnolia dining room. Linen and fresh flowers cover the oval table, encircled by fan back Windsor chairs. Once again, though, it was the elaborately carved mantel around the fireplace, topped with an antique shelf clock, that drew our attention. Each morning, Pam serves a full southern-style breakfast in here—which has earned her accolades from both guests and reviewers, near and far. A handsome sideboard placed in a small alcove completes the room's decorative appeal.

Just as each public room has a personality, so do the guest rooms. One of the more feminine is the Camellia Room, where plenty of lace fabrics and pale peach colors create just the right backdrop for the delicate white iron bed with matching heart-shaped head and foot boards. While this may sound a bit contrived, the effect is surprisingly subtle. A ceiling fan circulates the air on still days, while air conditioning cools hot summer nights. We thought the step-up bathroom was also an interesting aside. Across the hall from the Camellia Room, is the Dogwood Room, which contains a Victorian Oak Mansion bed, positioned so that guests can see the flowering dogwood trees through the windowed alcove. The antique furnishings include a cherry high boy and a small, marble-topped bedside table. The traditional floral wallpaper is accented by blue wall-to-wall carpeting. The Jessamine Room, named after the state flower, is one of our favorites. This already light and airy corner room is heightened by white wicker furnishings coupled with a profusion of pale pink and blue floral accents. The antique heart-of-pine bed, with delicately carved decorative trim, is placed at an angle in the room. Matchstick paneling and wainscoting create even more interest along the lower half of the wall. The fireplace in here can provide additional warmth on cool winter nights, and help set the tone for a romantic evening. Equally festive is the Azalea Room, where the subtle yellow wall treatments surround an old-fashioned southern rice bed, framed with a hand-tied fish net canopy.

As we mentioned, there are two formal sitting areas on the first floor; however, for those who want a little privacy, we recommend the second-floor parlor, Wisteria. It reminds us of an intimate garden room, although instead of live plants, we were surrounded by ivy patterned wallpaper and white wicker furnishings. Guests may choose from the assorted *Southern Living* magazines that are placed atop the side table, and further immerse themselves in the relaxed atmosphere.

There are many reasons for visiting the Magnolia Inn B&B. Some people might want to use it as an overnight stop on their way north or south. Others might consider staying awhile, as there are an assortment of things to do with Bowser in the area. We thought anyplace with a name like Little Pee Dee State Park might merit further investigation.

Once there, we appreciated the 835-acres of picnicking, hiking, and canoeing opportunities. A little further afield is the Cheraw State Park, which has more than 7,000 acres of similar offerings. Other areas include the Sandhills State Forest and the Carolina Sandhills National Wildlife Refuge. Many visitors to this region arrive in the late summer and early fall, when the cotton is being ginned and the tobacco auctioned off. We liked the Magnolia Inn B&B because it offers guests a dose of low-key, unpretentious southern hospitality.

Mansfield Plantation

Route 8, Box 590
Highway 701 North
Georgetown, South Carolina   29440
(800) 355-3223, (803) 546-6961

Hostess: Marybeth Vanpelt
Rooms: 8 doubles
Rates: $75-95 (B&B)
Payment: MC and VISA
Children: Welcome
Dogs: Well behaved dogs are welcome with prior approval
Open: All year

Georgetown is an historic coastal community, dating back to the 1700s, which still contains a large number of well preserved, pre-Revolutionary homes and buildings. Today, it is known as a deepwater port, but in the mid-1800s it was tied more strongly to the region's rice production. Rice plantations were commonplace, and their owners grew wealthy harvesting the abundant crops from these fertile lands. Mansfield Plantation, set along the banks of the Black River, was just one of these many plantations. The land was first granted to John Green in 1718, but it was not until 1846, when Francis S. Parker took over, that the acreage was put to use for growing rice. During his lifetime, Parker purchased two other plantations, which ultimately resulted in a quadrupling of the collective annual yields. First-time visitors to this region who are interested in learning more about the area's historic plantations should plan an overnight stay at the Mansfield Plantation.

Visitors will navigate a long, rutted dirt drive that cuts through dense woods and arrives eventually at two large, brick pillars—which mark the true entrance to the 760-acre plantation. As we gazed out upon the scene before us, it was easy to feel transported back in time. Stands of large black oaks draped with Spanish moss line the drive, next to the original slave quarters, which are set behind split rail fences. We stopped for a bit to look at these dwellings. As it turns out, they are the five original antebellum slave cabins, plus a slave chapel, and two replicas that were built in the 1930s, when Colonel Robert Montgomery owned the property. The original winnowing house, used to separate the chaff from the rice seed, can also be visited. We finally pulled ourselves away, and drove further down the drive toward the charming "Big House," dating back to 1812. This building is comparatively smaller than those commonly found on most plantations, primarily because Mr. Parker spent little time here, preferring his other houses to this one. Although the Mansfield Plantation lacks a formal estate house, visitors are treated to an authentic plantation setting.

The morning we visited, Marybeth was busy sending off a group of visitors who had just enjoyed a guided tour of the plantation, and was taking a brief break before another small group of people arrived. We walked together up to the "Big House," and along the way came across several brick-lined fish ponds that were interspersed along the walkways. The pesky black flies were beginning to swarm, but Marybeth assured us that motion generally attracted them, and if we stood fairly still they would not light upon us. As we slowly walked over to the North Guest House, situated to the left of the main house, we learned about an upcoming International Festival of Wines, an annual fundraiser held at the plantation, where proceeds are used to restore the slave village. Twenty or more wineries were being represented at this year's tasting, and besides sampling the wines, guests would be treated to gourmet foods and live jazz. All participants were encouraged to dress in "Great Gatsby" attire, to help recreate the ambiance of the plantation's heyday.

As we entered the charming, two-story brick North Guest House, we discovered spacious bedrooms, enhanced by high ceilings and intricate decorative moldings, painstakingly hand carved by local craftsmen. Pastel walls and hardwood floors provide the framework for the fine reproduction and antique furnishings set upon Oriental carpets. The waterside chamber contains a king-size bed and river views. A pair of twin beds are set amid chintz fabrics and accents in a back bedroom. We liked the angles of the upstairs ceilings, created by the eaves. Through the windows, beyond the branches of a moss-laden black oak, we were treated to pretty river views. Our next stop was in the smaller South Guest House. The overall atmosphere in here is a little less sophisticated, with a pair of twin beds in one chamber and a larger than normal double bedstead in the other. Lastly, there is the Old School House, which also offers lovely accommodations with traditional furnishings and a similar decor.

Most guests look forward to the daily pilgrimage to the "Big House," where they are treated to a full breakfast. Guests may want to spend a little time in the formal library before moving into the dining room to enjoy this delicious meal. This spacious, elongated chamber is impressive in its own right; however, the exquisite collection of formal English antiques is what makes it truly outstanding. Guests gather around the multi-pedestal mahogany table for this hearty repast. The menu changes with the day, but most look forward to the freshly baked muffins and breads created by the pastry chef, who now works on the plantation full-time. This breakfast spread is supplemented by spinach quiche or French toast, with gourmet coffee and fresh juices as welcome accompaniments. Afterwards, guests may enjoy walking the acreage with Bowser, inspecting the old slave village, or just taking a closer look at some of the other out buildings.

Bowser will undoubtedly love exploring the expansive grounds, and may want to check out the dock, where guests can frequently be found fishing for bass and brim. The plantation feels like a nature preserve with fox, deer and wild pigs roaming the woods and beaver, otter, and yes, alligators, occupying the wetlands and rivers. Of course, this abundant wildlife also makes the plantation popular among the hunt set. The recently established Mansfield Duck Hunting Club offers annual packages that include ten hunts, overnight accommodations, and a full country-style brunch. We thought this was a fabulous place, but Marybeth reminded us that it isn't for everyone, especially those seeking an oceanside setting—found 20 minutes away on Pawleys Island. The people who stay at the plantation usually want to immerse themselves in the history of this place and enjoy the natural setting. We would have to agree that after traveling down that sandy drive, we, too, felt as though we had stepped back in time.

Player's Club Resort

P.O. Box 7468
35 DeAllyon Avenue
Hilton Head Island, South Carolina 29938
(800) 777-1700, (803) 785-8000, Fax (803) 785-9185

General Manager: Jim Metrakos
Rooms: 98 doubles
Rates: $89-99 (EP)
Payment: AE, MC, and VISA
Children: Welcome (cribs, cots, and high chairs are available)
Dogs: Welcome with a $10 fee
Open: All year

Hilton Head Island, situated off the coast of South Carolina, is the largest coastal island between New Jersey and Florida. The Spanish, English, and French colonists tried to settle here in the late 1520s, but were continually attacked by Native Americans, who made it difficult for them to gain a foothold. In the 1660s, Captain William Hilton, for whom the island is named, arrived by boat and wrote glowing reports about the incredibly lush landscape and headlands. Over a period of several hundred years, the Native American population gave way to the English, who built plantations that yielded abundant crops of indigo, rice, and cotton. After the Civil War, the plantations lost their cheap labor and were broken up, allowing the island to return to a more natural state. A good number of the freed slaves (or Gullahs, as they are known locally) began to migrate to these shores, where they lived a simple existence. Hilton Head Island remained relatively isolated until 1956, when a bridge was finally constructed linking it to the mainland. Before too long, and with a great deal of planning, year-round communities began to spring up, giving visitors the ability to bask in the mild climate and enjoy an array of recreational options. Today, rising up around the old plantations are their 20th-century counterparts. Tourists in the 1990s will see, not fields of rice and cotton, but instead, an abundance of tennis, golf, and boating opportunities in this ever expanding resort area.

Whether visitors are coming to the island for the PGA Tour's Heritage Golf Classic at Harbour Town, or to enjoy the abundance of recreational options available on the island, they would seem to be able to pick from a wide variety of accommodations. Unfortunately, people traveling with a dog have an extremely limited number of choices, even in the motel category. However, we did find one spot that would appeal to a wide range of vacationers and their canine companions. The

Player's Club has it all, including a fine tennis complex, modern spa facilities, and access to most of the 22 golf courses on the island. Situated near Hilton Head's southern shore, the resort maintains a low-key atmosphere, making it an ideal place for singles, couples, or the entire family.

The property is surrounded by tall stands of palm trees and interspersed with quiet lagoons teeming with ducks. Long, unobtrusive, two-story buildings house the many guest rooms. We can safely say that while these are nice accommodations, they are also fairly standard, both in decor and in amenities offered. Most are furnished with one king or a pair of queen-size beds surrounded by light oak and pine Scandinavian-style furnishings. Brass lamps provide good reading light, while pastel floral fabrics and potted plants add a decorative dimension. We thought the framed caricatures of tennis players fit in well with the "player's club" atmosphere. Often, these are set alongside other prints reflecting bucolic headland settings or waterfront vistas. A wet bar, containing a separate sink and refrigerator, is set off in an alcove. The good-sized, modern bathrooms are tiled and have Corian counters and sinks.

Even though the accommodations are rather mainstream, the array of diversions are not. Guests of the Player's Club may play tennis at the VanDeer Meer Tennis Center, where they may also choose their surface: hard court, clay, or an all-weather indoor court. (The latter is the only one of its kind in Hilton Head.) In addition to an array of clinics and instructional sessions, there are also tennis camps in which guests may enroll. After a great workout, it is always enjoyable to drift over to the spa. In addition to an outdoor swimming pool, there is a 50-foot indoor lap pool, saunas/whirlpools, racquetball courts, and plenty of high-tech Nautilus equipment. After an eventful day, some grab a drink at the Hap Player's indoor lounge; others enjoy bringing their drink to the outside patio. We liked the look of the hotel's restaurant, The Greenhouse, where brass chandeliers and wood-paneled walls are mere accents to the expansive, two-story atrium. The Continental fare ranges from gourmet pizza and thick steaks to fish caught locally and innovative pasta dishes. Undoubtedly, there are better restaurants in Hilton Head, but very few offer this type of atmosphere.

Bowser will surely enjoy meandering about the seven acres of grounds, or perhaps taking a walk down to Forest Beach. Those visiting in the off-season may take their canine companions out on the beach, but in the summer months, dogs are generally forbidden during the day. Some of the more popular activities *sans* dog that give visitors a chance to enjoy their natural surroundings, include visits to the Sea Pines Forest Preserve, the Pinckney Island National Wildlife Refuge, and the Audubon Newhall Preserve. While the streets around Hilton Head are terrific for cruising with a dog, there are also some excellent day trips from the island. A short drive to the north leads guests to Beaufort. The town was established in 1711, making it the second oldest community in South Carolina. Visitors and their dogs can walk the quiet streets, check out the antebellum and pre-Revolutionary homes, and then continue on to Hunting Island State Park. It is easy to spend an entire day at the park, with over 5,000 acres to explore and even a lighthouse to visit.

Hickory Knob State Resort Park

Route 1 (near Route 378), Box 199-B
McCormick, South Carolina   29835
(800) 491-1764, (803) 391-2450, Fax (803) 391-5390

Park Superintendent: Ted Williams
Rooms: 74 doubles, 3 suites, 18 cottages, 1 house
Rates: Doubles $36-40 (EP), Suites $72-80 (EP), Cottages $50-300 (EP),
*   Guest House $80-480 (EP)*
Payment: MC and VISA
Children: Welcome (cribs, cots, and high chairs are available)
Dogs: Welcome in the kennel facilities on the premises, but not in the
*   accommodations.*
Open: All year

Hickory Knob State Resort Park is a slight departure from our standard recommendation. First and foremost, dogs are welcome in the park and at the resort, and may enjoy all corners of it with their human friends. However, the management does require that during the evening hours dogs be placed in the on-site kennel, and that they not enter the guest accommodations. At first, we were a little hesitant to include Hickory Knob; however, once we learned of all the activities and diversions available during the day, for both guests and their canine friends, we thought we could make an exception to our normal standards.

After driving under the canopy of wisteria near the front entrance, we felt immediately transported from civilization to a rather remote wilderness oasis. Even though the park is just a 45-minute drive from Augusta, Georgia, it seemed as though we were hundreds of miles from any major city. Miles of tree-lined roads wend through the park, revealing vistas of Strom Thurmond Lake, golf course fairways, and wooded valleys, until visitors finally emerge at the low-key resort complex. Keep driving past the tennis and volleyball courts, and eventually the main lodge appears. This single-story series of adjoined buildings houses a good-sized restaurant, an expansive common room/ game area, and a small sport shop. Check-in is a painless affair, and afterwards guests can stop briefly in their rooms before heading out to explore the grounds.

Guests may choose between the motel rooms, lakeside rooms, or the cabins. All have either natural shingles or earth-tone wood siding to better blend in with the natural surroundings. The standard motel accommodations are located behind the lodge, by the swimming pool area. The decor is basic and just what one would expect, with a pair of double beds set on low maintenance wall-to-wall carpeting. Wildlife prints spice up the plastered or wood-paneled walls, and a television provides a little entertainment. While there is nothing fancy about these rooms, they are very clean and are also centrally located with regard to the rest of the complex. Families requiring more space and/or cooking facilities may wish to reserve the one available suite in these buildings. The master bedroom contains a pair of twin beds, while the sitting area is coupled with a kitchenette.

Guests may also request one of the lakeside rooms, which are located across the drive and away from the lodge, just beyond the nature center and wooden jungle gym—at the end of the peninsula overlooking the lake. We preferred these to the motel units, as they are slightly more upscale and provide guests with far more scenic surroundings and vistas. There are two suites available in the lakeside rooms, should guests require a little more space or the use of a kitchenette. The two 400 buildings are adjoined by a large deck, where guests tend to congregate and enjoy the lovely views of the sparkling waters below. These units are rather contemporary; however, they are in the process of being remodeled, which will undoubtedly make them even more appealing.

Separate cottages and cabins are also available to overnight guests. One interesting option is the charming and historic Guillebeau House, dating back to the 1700s. From the exterior, this is perhaps the most appealing place, with a tiny porch, dark shingles, and an old stone fireplace. Inside are two bedrooms, one containing a double bed and another a pair of twin beds. The furnishings in here may be antique, but the kitchen is modern, as are the telephone and television. Anyone willing to give up a lake view in favor of more space and charm should consider the cabins located on the south side of the complex. We walked in and found a dining nook off to one side and a full kitchen to the other; but what truly clinched it for us was the living room. It is generally found to the rear of these expansive chambers, where a wall of windows provides bucolic views of the woods and distant water. A sofa and series of comfortable armchairs are well positioned to take best advantage of the outdoor scene and television. The master bedroom contains a pair of double beds placed over hunter green carpeting that nicely contrasts with the oak trim. Best of all, the kennel facilities are located within a minute's walk from these units, making it easy to get Bowser in the morning or put him to bed at night. The kennels are located in the woods, and are self-service affairs, where guests are totally responsible for their dogs' well being. Some like to think of it as tent camping for dogs.

Bowser should sleep well, as there are plenty of things to tire him out during the day. Many take their dogs for walks along the nature trails or a trip along the four-mile, bird dog field trail. Golf and tennis are options, but we thought the water looked awfully inviting. Guests may bring their own boat or canoe and easily launch it from one of the two good-sized dock areas on the lake. In addition to sailing and water skiing, fishing is probably the most popular water-oriented activity at the resort. Those who are so inclined may utilize the archery or the skeet shooting facilities, located just across from the club house. After a full day of activity, many people are eager to sample one of the hearty meals at the lodge. We liked the festive, yet relaxed atmosphere in the restaurant, which specializes in hearty southern cooking. Offerings such as fried catfish, southern-fried chicken, sautéed pork chops, and grits are well worth sampling. Whether it be breakfast, lunch or dinner, guests may opt for the buffet or order off the menu.

We usually try to recommend interesting areas to visit with Bowser that are within a short walk or drive of the accommodation. In this case, the accommodations are in the midst of 1,000 wooded acres, where the possibilities for activities are virtually endless. Travelers will want to take advantage of this place, where an adventure lies, literally, just outside the front door.

The Book & Spindle
Bed & Breakfast

626 Oakland Avenue
Rock Hill, South Carolina   29730
(803) 328-1913

Hosts: Pam and Warren Bowen
Rooms: 4 doubles
Rates: $55-70 (B&B)
Payment: MC and VISA
Children: Welcome
Dogs: "House broken and quiet dogs are welcome"
Open: All year

The town of Rock Hill was originally named for the white rock used in the construction of several of the railroad systems that traversed the state. This quiet rural county has seen several prosperous periods, one associated with the booming cotton industry and another with the development of the hydroelectric dam on the Catawba River. In 1895, Winthrop College came to Rock Hill, giving the town a firm economic base. Whether new arrivals are first-time visitors or parents of incoming freshmen, they will certainly find themselves in the town's historic district. In the center of it is the charming Book & Spindle Bed & Breakfast.

Originally built in 1930, this handsome Georgian-style brick home was designed by the same firm that designed the historic buildings on the Winthrop College campus. The Bowens purchased the house approximately ten years ago. When they finally decided to open it as a B&B, they felt the name Book & Spindle was especially appropriate in this college town. "Book" for the influence of the college, and "spindle" because it reflects the town's textile past. When we arrived, Warren was just finishing a little touch-up paint project on his columned front porch. The weather was beginning to look slightly ominous, giving Warren the perfect excuse to finish early—a prospect that seemed to make him gleeful.

We walked with him into the house, where we found Pam, who graciously led us into the charming front parlor. The lovely effect of the salmon walls served to nicely complement the period furnishings and floral draperies framing the unusually long windows. From here, we ventured through a large, double arch into the long and narrow living room painted dove gray. This inviting chamber is furnished with a pair of wing chairs flanking a camel back sofa and coffee table that rest in front of the fireplace. The lustrous hardwood floors gleamed in the midday sun that was emanating through the windows. We came back in the evening to find the light from the cut glass chandelier, along with the candles in the wall sconces and decorative table lamps, casting a soft glow across the room. The personality of the owners comes through in every corner. This was true whether we were looking at a pair of Oriental vases placed on the mantel, family photographs nestled together on the antique end tables, or the ruddy glow of the sherry in a crystal decanter surrounded by matching stemware. We visited briefly with Pam in the sitting room and she asked if we wanted to see some of the bedrooms. Of course, we did.

We followed an Oriental rug runner to the upstairs chambers, where our first stop was the Charleston Suite. True to its name, this suite is reminiscent of a bedroom in a gracious Charleston home. The four-poster rice bed is draped with a lovely floral canopy that coordinates with the draperies around the windows. English antiques in the main portion of this room are offset against more casual wicker furnishings in the private sunroom. The Camden Suite, on the other hand, is more formal still, with hunter green walls that enhance the hunt and equestrian prints hung against them. The fireplace is a welcome feature, but during most of the year, guests are usually more appreciative of the canopied, private outdoor patio. As one might expect, there is also a guest room named after Winthrop College. This light and airy room reflects the days when the college was renowned as a leading school for women. Lace curtains frame a multitude of windows, while a woven floral carpet tops the lustrous hardwood floors. Lovely coverlets grace a pair of twin beds, further expressing the feminine side of this space. Finally, we came to the Glencairn Room, which, except for the Oriental rug, boasts a strong Scottish decorative theme. A Scottish plaid blanket rests at the foot of the four-poster bed, and antique wooden golf clubs line one of the walls. We enjoyed the distinct personalities of each bedroom, and also appreciated the modern conveniences, such as private bathrooms and remote control televisions. Anyone who wants a little more room and independence should reserve one of the two suites that also contain well-appointed kitchens.

After a hearty Continental meal breakfast, Bowser will undoubtedly enjoy the opportunity to explore the grounds of the expansive campus. Afterwards, visitors may want to walk through the historic district for a little taste of southern architecture and history. Nearby, the 12,455-acre Lake Wylie offers some excellent water-oriented diversions that any canine will surely want to try. There are also hundreds of acres in which to romp, in the Andrew Jackson, Chester, and Landford Canal park areas. Whether guests want to spend the night in Rock Hill while en route to another vacation spot or are here just to visit a student, the elegant common areas and gracious southern-style guest rooms make the Book & the Spindle a must for B&B enthusiasts.

Georgia

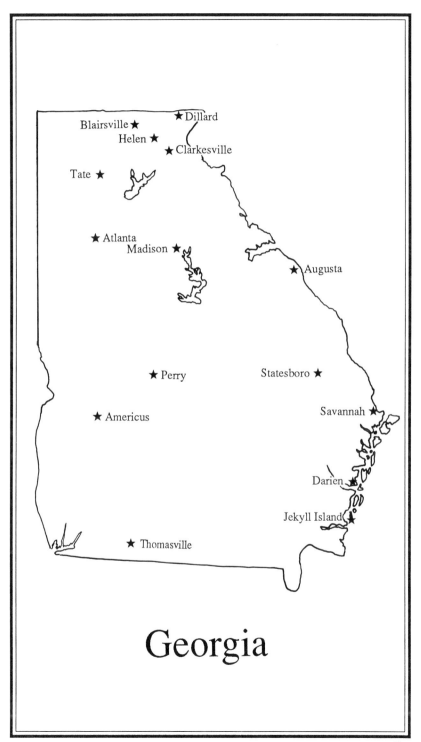

Blairsville ★
★ Dillard
Helen ★
★ Clarkesville
Tate ★

★ Atlanta
Madison ★

★ Augusta

★ Perry
Statesboro ★

★ Americus
Savannah ★

Darien ★
Jekyll Island ★

★ Thomasville

Georgia

The Cottage Inn

Highway 49 North
Americus, Georgia   31709
(912) 924-9316 or 924-8995

Hosts: Jim and Billie Gatewood
Rooms: 4 suites
Rates: Suites $55-60 (B&B)
Payment: MC and VISA
Children: Welcome
Dogs: Well-behaved dogs are welcome with prior approval
Open: All year

There are times when, to rejuvenate, we need nothing more than a couple days in a quiet place away from home. Travelers who need to get away from it all should consider staying a few nights at The Cottage Inn, whose elegant country setting is certain to help them relax and unwind. Set on the outskirts of Americus, a small Georgian country village, The Cottage Inn is a lovely, antebellum raised cottage. It was built in 1852, not in Americus, but in Gulthert, Georgia. Just before the cottage was to be torn down, Jim and Billie found it, bought it, and had it moved to their five-acre pecan orchard alongside their house.

As new arrivals turn off the rural route and into the drive, they will find this charming cottage set well back on the property, amid mature plantings and large shade trees encircled by perennials. A front path covered with pine needles and lined with boxwood hedges leads guests to the expansive front porch. Accented by decorative lacy trim and colorful hanging plants, the atmosphere seems to invite passers-by to pull up a rocking chair and relax awhile. As with most southern homes, this one was built with a wide center hall that runs the length of the cottage. Along the hallway are an array of impressive antiques, adorned with graceful vases set on Oriental rugs. In the spacious guest suites, located on either side of the central hall, are similar collections of antiques, which rest below 18-foot high ceilings.

We walked into the sitting room of one suite, where Oriental rugs, along with *objets d'art*, set the tone for this most inviting space. We could have spent our time on one of the comfortable couches or armchairs centered around the fireplace, but instead, we wandered around the room looking at all the exquisite collectibles. A windowed alcove contains a table topped by a lovely antique bird cage, and the walls display a collection of exquisite paintings. On sunny days, an abundance of light pours in through the 12-foot high windows. Just beyond this chamber, guests will find the bedroom, where a pair of finial twin beds flank a side table set with an Oriental vase lamp. In here, as with the rest of the bedrooms, guests will find beautiful old handmade quilts. The suite on the other side of the hallway is virtually a copy of the first. The only difference is that an enchanting four-poster bed occupies the bedroom.

Step back out into the central hall, meander out the back door, and guests will find two other storybook cottages. To reach one of these, we proceeded down an even narrower path covered with pine needles. This cottage, too, was slated to be demolished, but the Gatewoods came to the rescue and moved it to its present site. Inside, a four-poster bed is the focal point for the good-sized chamber. However, in the foreground is an intimate sitting area containing an overstuffed sofa and an antique pine table with lovely picture books on top. Brass sconces and decorative plates line the walls. Throughout the space guests will see an equally distinguished array of collectibles. We thought the entire effect created a most inviting private retreat. To the rear of this cottage is a separate kitchen, which is accessed through a private entrance on the back side of the building. This facility is available to any of The Cottage Inn's guests.

A third cottage, decidedly the smallest and simplest of the group, is located just a stone's throw from the other two. Oriental rugs cover the hardwood floors, while an assortment of period furnishings and antiques are placed throughout the sitting room and bed chamber. Whichever of the cottage suites guests ultimately select, they can expect modern amenities, such as renovated bathrooms, air conditioning, and cable television. Extra sleeping space is generally available on those overstuffed sofas we mentioned, as most fold out into queen-size beds.

While the cottages are exceptionally appealing, it is the bucolic setting around them that is truly alluring. Most guests feel comfortable lingering over their Continental breakfast, while quietly rocking on their porch and perhaps watching one of the local peacocks parade by the cottage. This quiet setting is conducive to complete relaxation; however, those in search of a little activity will also find it within steps of their cottages. A swimming pool and a clay tennis court are situated on the hosts' property, and guests may use these with prior permission. Newcomers to these parts may wish to explore the historic part of town and investigate the many beautiful antebellum homes around Americus. We also suggest visiting the Civil War town of Andersonville, the Little White House in Warm Springs, and both the Callaway Gardens and the Camellia Gardens. The Andersonville National Historic site is close to Americus, where visitors can learn more about the Civil War's most famous prison. Further south is the Georgia Veterans Memorial, which rests on over 1,300 acres. Visitors may fish, swim, and explore the area with their dog. While Bowser can accompany his human companions on most of these outings, both man and beast will probably be eager to return to the relaxed atmosphere of The Cottage Inn, where there is plenty of open space for romping and large shade trees to sleep under.

Doubletree Hotel

Seven Concourse Parkway
Atlanta, Georgia 30328
(800) 528-0444, (404) 395-3900, Fax (404) 395-3918

General Manager: Creston Wood
Rooms: 365 doubles, 5 suites
Rates: Doubles $69-175 (EP), Suites $175-300 (EP)
Payment: AE, CB, DC, DSC, DC, ENR, MC, and VISA
Children: Welcome (cribs, cots, high chairs, and babysitters are available)
Dogs: Dogs 30 pounds and under are welcome with a $75 refundable deposit
Open: All year

When staying in a large city, it isn't always easy to find great accommodations at a reasonable price. Throw in a dog and the prospective choices narrow even further. We like the idea of having plenty of green space around us when traveling with a dog, as well as easy access to it. We thought the Doubletree Hotel was a great choice, as it is just a short drive north of Atlanta and set in a 64-acre wooded corporate park. In the midst of the complex, there is a good-sized lake encircled by expansive lawns and tree-lined walking paths.

Stepping inside the hotel, guests will see that the reception area replicates the lush exterior, with its cavernous two-story atrium that runs along the rear of the building. The decor and furnishings contained in this contemporary, 20-story facade are both sophisticated and comfortable. The abundant potted plants and flower arrangements are enhanced by the green and rose color schemes. This same ambiance extends into the guest rooms, but here, a combination of soft earth tones and pastels create subtle stripes and floral patterns in the fabrics that cover the traditional furnishings. Dark cherry woods are used in the Chippendale chairs and armoires containing the televisions. Brass accents provide a nice complement to these decors.

An array of sleeping configurations should please most travelers. The standard rooms contain either a king-size bed or a pair of doubles, while the junior suites have a king-size bed with a separate sitting area and lake views. Guests may reserve a room on the Concierge Level for a complimentary Continental breakfast and evening hors d'oeuvres, coupled with a more personal level of service. Or perhaps this is a special occasion and the two-bedroom suite would be more to the traveler's liking. These expansive accommodations, with names like the Senator, Governor, and Ambassador, have a master bedroom set just off a central living room. All of the accommodations share a wide array of standard hotel amenities, but what many remember most are the fresh chocolate chip cookies awaiting guests each evening.

There are plenty of ways to get some exercise, both at the hotel and in the surrounding area. A three-story, 85,000 square foot Concourse Athletic Center, located just down the way, provides everything from indoor/outdoor swimming pools and squash and tennis courts to a padded indoor jogging track, sun tanning center, and a comprehensive weight room. Guests may want to take Bowser along the extensive paths that weave through the surrounding acreage. Canine companions may also want to explore sections of the Chattahoochee River National Recreation Area, where there is an extensive system of trails. Further north lies the Amicalola Falls State Park, which is home to the state's highest waterfall and is surrounded by 1,000 acres of open space. Another interesting day trip is to Lake Sidney Lanier and the Buford Dam. Here, people and their dogs can swim, hike, and picnic along the lake shore or rent a boat and investigate the entire lake.

After a busy day, many are eager to return to the hotel for dinner, as Acacia is an award-winning restaurant whose seasonally changing menu reflects a variety of innovative dishes. The entrées include a petit filet with a merlot sauce, grilled salmon with a choice of dill sauce, or a wild mushroom lobster sauce. The lamb loin, encrusted with pistachio nuts and served with a port wine glaze, is a longtime favorite of the regulars. The deluxe mixed grill should satisfy anyone who is looking for a varied meal, as it contains a choice of double lamb chops or beef tenderloin, along with jumbo shrimp stuffed with crab. A minted port wine, wild mushroom, and herb cream sauce is drizzled over the top. Doubletree's chocolate chip cookies are put to good use in a chocolate chip cookie cheesecake. Guests may also think about trying the white chocolate Napoleon with fresh raspberries and a raspberry sauce or the peach flan with an almond cream. Those visiting over the weekend may also sample the Sunday brunch, which has won numerous accolades from . Bowser will undoubtedly enjoy a leftover or two from this feast.

Whatever one's reason for visiting this area, guests will surely agree that the hotel's lush surroundings, substantial guest rooms, and close proximity to Atlanta's more notable diversions make the Doubletree a natural for those who want to be close, but not too close, to the center of town.

Beverly Hills Inn

65 Sheridan Drive, N.E.
Atlanta, Georgia 30305
(800) 331-8520, (404) 233-8520 (Tel & Fax)

Manager: Mitt Amin
Rooms: 18 suites
Rates: $75-125 (B&B)
Payment: AE, CB, DC, DSC, MC, and VISA
Children: Welcome
Dogs: Welcome with advance notice
Open: All year

Visitors who want to experience Atlanta, but who don't need to stay downtown, will be happy to know about the Beverly Hills Inn. Built in the late 1920s out of block, brick, and stucco, the building today distinguishes itself from others in the surrounding neighborhood by its avocado-green facade, highlighted with white iron balconies and corners that are edged in overlapping white blocks. This three-story house formerly accommodated apartments, before its more recent incarnation as an intimate inn. We arrived one sunny spring morning to find the flower gardens in full bloom. As we entered the inn, Mitt was in the midst of a long conversation with Evelyn Keys, a native Atlantan who is perhaps best known for her role as Scarlett O'Hara's sister in Gone with the Wind. After reminiscing for a little while, Ms. Keys was on her way, but promised to return soon.

Mitt is a charming man, with a vibrant personality that is enhanced by his English accent. Running the Beverly Hills Inn is his latest venture in hotel management. As he gave us a tour, we discovered that an old-world European atmosphere, intermixed with southern charm, permeates the common areas. A cozy first-floor parlor is accessed by way of a pair of leaded glass French doors, where guests relax amid the period antiques. Cream-colored walls and draperies soften the decor, while potted plants and freshly cut flowers add a certain homey ambiance.

Each of the bedrooms has an individual style, with one constant: all are furnished with lovely, English antiques and reproductions. Guests enter these chambers through a leaded-glass French door, stepping across hardwood floors covered with area rugs and carpets. Four-poster, canopy, or finial beds are found alongside intimate sitting areas. White wicker brightens the mood in some spaces, while dark floral prints and traditional pieces lend an air of formality to others. The art is especially noteworthy, with Japanese screens, original oil paintings, and hunt or botanical prints hanging on the walls. A complimentary bottle of wine and a dish of Hershey kisses are set out for newly arriving guests. Since these were once apartments, there is the added convenience of fully-equipped kitchenettes. Guests will also appreciate the telephones and televisions that are found in each of the bedrooms. We thought the white wrought-iron balconies off some of the rooms were especially appealing. Unlike many European-style hostelries, here at the Beverly Hills Inn, guests may expect their own private bathrooms.

Each morning, breakfast eaters are invited to partake of a hearty, Continental meal served in the cheery first-floor garden room. The colorful murals will certainly help most people wake up, if the coffee doesn't do the job first. Guests interested in enjoying the meal in their rooms will be happy to know that the staff will deliver. Our favorite spot for breakfast, however, is on the sunken patio beneath the umbrellas. Here, guests can peek out onto the surrounding neighborhood as it, too, begins its day. While the brick courtyard and garden are enticing spots for reading the morning paper, Bowser will probably be more interested in exploring the park and playground located at the end of the street. The neighborhood, too, is a pleasant place for a leisurely stroll. The inn is situated just 15 minutes from Atlanta's mid-town area, in the heart of the Buckhead neighborhood. This portion of the city is renowned not only for its wonderful old homes, but also for its excellent shopping. The perfectly manicured estates and expansive traditional homes, as well as the Governor's Mansion and Atlanta Historical Society, are found just a short distance from the inn. Shoppers will thoroughly enjoy nearby Lenox Square and Phipps Plaza, where hundreds of small, upscale shops are interspersed among retailers such as Lord & Taylor, Saks Fifth Avenue, Neiman Marcus, and Macys. Just barely out of town is the Chattahoochee National Forest, with numerous parks dotting a 48-mile stretch of the Chattahoochee River. There are also hiking trails that start right outside of the city and wend through forested areas and along the river. Trail maps are available through the park service.

The Beverly Hills Inn is unique. The proprietors know it, and we appreciate it. There is an emphasis on personal attention, but not a lot of extra fluff. The owners feel, as do we, that "only some will understand—but then—we don't have room for everybody."

Ansley Inn

253 Fifteenth Street
Atlanta Georgia   30309
(800) 446-5416, (404) 872-9000, Fax (404) 892-2318

Manager: Tim Thomas
Rooms: 12 doubles, 2-bedroom cottage
Rates: Doubles $115-250 (B&B), Cottage $175 (B&B)
Payment: AE, DC, DSC, ENR, MC, and VISA
Children: Appropriate for older children
Dogs: Small dogs are welcome
Open: All year

Host to the 1996 Olympics, Atlanta has long been a bustling city with a wide variety of accommodations. The Olympic games may come and go, but places like the Ansley Inn should last indefinitely. The charming, albeit somewhat eclectic, inn is situated in the historic Ansley Park neighborhood in the heart of Midtown. Surrounded by five parks, this peaceful area has quiet winding roads that wend past lovely old homes and impressive mansions.

The handsome, yellow brick, English Tudor-style Ansley Inn is accented by green shutters. The semi-circular drive leads visitors to the inn that is fronted by a hillside of ivy, rhododendrons, azaleas, and dogwoods. This enchanting inn once served as the residence for wealthy philanthropist, George Muse. More recently, it was used as an exclusive boarding house for young ladies. Unfortunately, after WW II, the house and its property headed into a decline. In the late 1980s, the mansion was finally purchased by its current owners who, after two years of restoration, re-established an aura of grandeur.

In the old days, people used to enter the mansion through the formal front entrance, but today it is far more convenient to walk in through the enclosed porch around the side. Once inside, a concierge greets new arrivals and gives them a short tour of the inn's first floor. In the adjacent living room, boxed-beam ceilings and crystal chandeliers set the tone for the array of Chippendale and Queen Anne antiques set around a marble fireplace. A pair of red leather sofas face one another across a brass coffee table, and Chinese jars and impressionist art are just two of the many tasteful accents. Each afternoon, hors d'oeuvres and refreshing libations await guests. The adjoining barrel-ceiling dining room is even more striking, as the walls are painted a rich salmon hue presenting a strong contrast to the darkly stained wood moldings. A three-pedestal mahogany table awaits morning revelers, who usually eat their Continental breakfast here. A wide selection of fresh fruits, croissants, and other baked goodies are placed on the sideboard, while morning newspapers are resting upon the window seat.

A good night's sleep is almost inevitable, with the individual decor lending a personal and homey feeling to each of the bedrooms. There is something for everyone, from rooms decorated in pastels or bold colors, to those with florals or stripes. Avery, a charming lavender-colored chamber, has a queen-size brass bed that is lit by brass lamps. A yellow wicker chair is placed alongside a drop leaf table topped with an assortment of knickknacks. This guest room is located to the rear of the inn and has its own private entrance, which many dog owners find especially convenient. Avery's bathroom is modern, and it, along with all the others at the inn, has a Jacuzzi bathtub. Lafayette, on the other hand, has hunter green walls and 12-foot ceilings. A four-poster bed, and several English antiques are placed on the coral-colored carpet, but it is the fireplace that makes this room truly special. Peachtree, boasts a window seat and Oriental accents, while the gabled ceilings in Westminster make this the most spacious and probably the nicest room at the inn. Cozy doubles and extra large rooms with sitting areas are tucked away in all the nooks of the Ansley Inn, and the amenities are apparent at every turn. We expected the ceiling fans, individual climate controls, televisions, and private telephones; however, the Jacuzzis and wet bars were enticing extras. All of these modern touches are beautifully tempered by the wide variety of Chippendale and Queen Anne mahogany antiques and reproductions. Those who are traveling as family or with friends may prefer the two-bedroom cottage, which also has a fireplace and the added convenience of a kitchen.

Bowser will certainly love investigating the abundant green areas in this neighborhood and in the surrounding parks. Head out between six and eight p.m. to walk Bowser, and look forward to encountering an assortment of new friends with the local canine contingency. In addition to meandering along the charming back streets, many people also choose to stroll or run along the scenic portions of Peachtree Street (be sure to ask the concierge which Peachtree, we understand there are about 40 different ones in town). A short drive out of Atlanta brings visitors and their dogs to Stone Mountain Park set on 3,000 acres. There are hiking trails that wind around this 300 million year old granite dome, and even a short trail that climbs up to the top.

Hotel Nikko

3300 Peachtree Road
Atlanta, Georgia   30305
(800) NIKKO-US, (404) 365-8100, Fax (404) 233-5686

General Manager: Masaaki Kawanabe
Rooms: 416 doubles, 22 suites
Rates: Doubles $115 - 240 (EP), Suites $300-1,200 (EP)
Payment: AE, CB, DC, DSC, JCB, MC, and VISA
Children: Welcome (cribs, cots, and high chairs are available)
Dogs: Welcome with permission from the management
Open: All year

In recent years Atlanta has been revitalized, due in part to the region's improved business climate and to the 1996 Summer Olympics. Travelers who are interested in visiting this thriving metropolis will find an abundance of downtown hotels and historic inns, as well as accommodations located in the prestigious Buckhead neighborhood. Those seeking accommodations outside of downtown, who enjoy luxurious chambers and a good deal of pampering, will find that the Hotel Nikko will more than fill their needs. Opened in 1990, this relative newcomer is well situated in the heart of Buckhead. The hotel's 25-story Georgian-style facade is fronted by a columned portico and enhanced by lush plantings. In a hotel of this size we expected to walk into a cavernous lobby. What we experienced was quite different—and not only set the decorative tone for the entire hotel, but also evoked a complete sense of serenity.

The designers accomplished this feat by creating an intimate interior rotunda, just inside the front doors. As we walked across inlaid marble floors, our eyes were drawn away from the creamy colored, curved walls to an immense Japanese flower arrangement set on a black marble pedestal in the middle of the room. Brass sconces and lights, hidden within the recesses of a single dome, cast a soft glow over this space. The room's simplicity was stunning. As we passed through this chamber, we emerged, finally, into the magnificent reception area that we had been expecting originally. It is a cavernous, columned lobby, backed by a series of floor-to-ceiling Palladian windows that reveal views of beautifully landscaped Japanese gardens. In the garden is a 35-foot waterfall. This expansive space is imbued with a sense of tradition, with its crystal chandeliers and brass accents, royal blue draperies backed by paneled walls, and handsome reproduction furniture; yet there is a progressive undertone to it, as well.

We had to look carefully to find the reception area, as it is unobtrusively tucked off by itself. The staff is very professional, working with expedience, yet always exuding a helpful and gracious manner. As we made our way off to see the guest rooms, we passed an assortment of impressive flower arrangements, interspersed among the hotel's fine collection of art—at last count, numbering more than a hundred pieces. These pieces range from elegant Japanese screens and paintings to museum-quality vases and sculptures. The art collection truly enhanced each of the common areas we passed through. In the guest rooms, we found a sophisticated look, pervaded by a certain calm.

Whether guests choose a standard double, a spacious room on the Nikko Executive floors (which also have private lounges), or one of the expansive suites, there is always a strong sense of tradition. For the most part, the dark woods of the Georgian-style furnishings complement the guest rooms' warm color schemes. In each of these spaces, subdued stripes and floral-patterned fabrics have been carefully selected to frame the windows, cover the beds, and adorn the armchairs and sofas. Brass lamps sit atop large writing desks, which are generally placed kitty-corner to the intimate sitting areas. Windows provide plenty of indirect light. Each room contains three telephones and a private bar. Guests will also luxuriate in the large marble bathrooms containing both signature terry cloth bathrobes and an array of toiletries. While there is a sense of European tradition about these rooms, the designers have not overlooked their Asian roots. There is one Tatami suite, which is decorated and furnished in traditional Japanese style.

This is one of the first Japanese hotels in the Atlanta area. Guests will find a gracious simplicity reflected throughout the Hotel Nikko, especially in the fabulous hotel gardens. There is also a state-of-the-art health club, as well as an outdoor swimming pool, which is surrounded by white umbrella tables. After guests' aesthetic and athletic needs have been met, they may treat their palates to the fine foods served in the hotel's two restaurants. The restaurant, Cassis, features an excellent Continental cuisine, which we thought was quite innovative; however it was the restaurant, Kamogawa that intrigued us. For over 300 years, Kamogawa has operated as a restaurant in Japan. In order to create the right environment for their restaurant in America, its interior was constructed in Kyoto, Japan and shipped to Atlanta, where it was assembled inside the Hotel Nikko. Guests may enjoy equally authentic Japanese dishes in either the traditional Tatami rooms or amid a more Western setting.

We think Buckhead is a terrific place for walking dogs. Visitors may take Bowser for a leisurely stroll through Buckhead's lovely residential neighborhoods, where dogs and humans can admire the estates. An abundance of shopping alternatives are available in either Phipp's Plaza or Lenox Square. Both dogs and their humans will be pleased to know that there are almost as many scenic walks around Buckhead as there are picturesque parks.

The Suite Hotel
Underground Atlanta

54 Peachtree Street (at Upper Alabama)
Atlanta, Georgia   30303
(800) 477-5549, (404) 223-5555, Fax (404) 223-0467

Manager: Renae Kassam
Rooms: 156 suites
Rates: $135-210 (B&B)
Payment: AE, DSC, DC, ENR, MC, and VISA
Children: Welcome (cribs and cots are available)
Dogs: Dogs under 30 lbs. are welcome
Open: All year

Atlanta has been growing at a rapid pace for quite awhile and once they were announced as the official city for the 1996 summer Olympics, the rate of new construction seemingly tripled. But along with all of the glitz and excitement, there are still the older historic sights in Atlanta. Anyone who wants to stay near one of these historic attractions should think about reserving accommodations at the luxurious Suite Hotel. This intimate European-style hostelry, a relative newcomer to the city's hotel scene, is situated next to expansive Underground Atlanta. Years ago, when Atlanta was known as The Terminus, there were just buildings, a few roads, and railroad tracks, which converged into the area we now know as Underground Atlanta. But it was tough for the trains and other modes of transportation to peacefully coexist; so the bridges and roads were raised and they began to operate over the train tracks. The buildings' first floors receded beneath the new catacomb of causeways—so much so that people began to think of them as lying "underground." The area remained relatively undisturbed for many years, until its rebirth during the mid-1980s. Now the 12-acre site draws countless tourists and locals to the more than 130 restaurants, shops, boutiques, and kiosks that fill the three-story complex. In the evening, visitors may expect a lively mixture of street and club entertainment, along with dining in some of Atlanta's more notable eateries. During the day, though, shoppers mix with others who have come to learn more about the area's historic appeal.

Just across the courtyard from Underground Atlanta, visitors will spy an attractive limestone and brick building rising 16 floors above the cityscape. The entrance is marked only by a pair of brass doors flanked by a doorman on one side, and a small brass plaque reading *The Suite Hotel* on the other. Once inside the cozy foyer, guests are enveloped by classical music, soft lighting, and muted colors. In addition to the recessed front desk, guests will thoroughly enjoy the reception area's mahogany paneling, crystal chandeliers, formal English antiques, and overstuffed sofas and armchairs. Elaborate flower arrangements are set on glass-topped tables and wooden pedestals. Check-in is effortless and afterwards a nearby elevator whisks guests up to their spacious bedroom suites.

Each of these traditionally furnished chambers is decorated in pale green and rose color schemes, accented by coordinated floral draperies and quilted bed coverlets. These rooms were designed for long-term guests, with the spacious living rooms and bedrooms separated from one another by pairs of louvered doors. Once again, luxury and comfort mingle well, with European-style furnishings set around brass and glass tables. Amenities are well conceived, with two televisions, three telephones, and combination wet/honor bars. The exquisite marble bathrooms are outfitted with a fine array of toiletries, with the most luxurious containing Jacuzzis. Our favorite guest suites are on the upper floors overlooking Underground Atlanta, which is festively illuminated at night.

Each morning a Continental breakfast is offered to hotel guests, in their rooms. The hotel does not have a restaurant, but a light dinner menu is available through room service. The cozy bar is the one public area in the hotel, and its sophisticated striped wallpaper and mahogany tables make it all the more appealing. Those interested in ordering a light fare will find that the bar offers a few appetizer-like items. We especially enjoyed sitting in front of the windows and taking in the pleasing views of the surrounding area. It is easy to stroll with Bowser along Peachtree Street. This is a good chance for people to look at some of the historic buildings, investigate the shopping alternatives, or just stretch their legs. Further uptown, there is the popular Piedmont Park, which is not only Atlanta's largest park, but also a great place to give canine cohorts a little exercise. Many of the park's streets are closed to cars, and walkers and their dogs are free to explore for miles on foot. For those who are interested, there are botanical gardens here as well, which are well worth investigating.

The Grand Hotel

75 Fourteenth Street
Atlanta, Georgia 30309
(800) 952-0702, (404) 881-9898, Fax (404) 873-4692

Manager: Gerald Gleason
Rooms: 172 doubles, 18 suites
Rates: Doubles $150-275 (EP), Suites $400-1,500 (EP)
Payment: AE, DC, DSC, ENR, MC, and VISA
Children: Welcome (cribs, cots, and high chairs are available)
Dogs: Welcome with prior approval and a $100 deposit
Open: All year

Georgia's capitol city, Atlanta, has rejuvenated not only its business climate, but also its sports profile by becoming the site for the 1996 Summer Olympics and Super Bowl XXVIII. It's no wonder that the relatively quiet old city of the south has had such a resurgence, given both its sports fame and the fact that over 400 of America's Fortune 500 companies maintain an office in Atlanta. In the heart of the mid-town area visitors will discover the lavish Grand Hotel, which was completed in 1992. Business people, sports enthusiasts, and yes, even doggie travelers will be impressed with this place. A cavernous atrium lobby is resplendent with an abundance of marble, whether it is set across the inlaid floors, carved into panels, or adorning the columns that rise three floors, past balconies trimmed with brass. Potted palms and ferns are accented by fresh flower arrangements, completing the look of this exquisite hotel. Upstairs in the bedrooms, guests will find individual settings equal to that of the public areas.

Each of the elegantly appointed guest chambers has a distinctly sophisticated European flavor. Sumptuous earth tones, highlighted by chocolate brown and taupe colors, set the refined mood. Upholstered headboards, thickly quilted bedspreads with dust ruffles, and chintz fabrics coordinate to create the luxurious effect. The traditional furnishings are copies from the Georgian period, and are grouped together with more contemporary, overstuffed sofas to create intimate sitting areas. Desks are set with parchment-shade brass lamps. But the bedrooms are not the only exquisitely decorated spaces. The spacious, marble clad bathrooms are also fitted with everything from European fixtures and an extra telephone to fluffy cotton robes and an array of imported toiletries. Travelers requiring additional space should think about reserving any of the four-bedroom suites featuring spacious living rooms that contain not only televisions and stereos, but wet bars, as well. In here, writing desks have the added features of facsimile machines and computer ports. The most impressive of the hotel's suites is the Royal Suite, located on the 19th floor. Its commanding views of the city are almost, but not quite, surpassed by its design. Both royals and commoners would approve of the dining room, full kitchen, master bedroom, and bathroom with a spa. Any of the rooms, whether built for royalty or not, are conducive to total relaxation. Step outside the bedroom though, and guests will find that the equally well appointed public areas are just as soothing.

Afternoon tea is served daily in the Overtures Lounge, where patrons may try exotic teas and nibble on delicate edibles, while a pianist provides background music. Others may prefer to wait a bit, and enjoy cocktails in the more club-like Segovia Bar. Dining options range from the relaxed atmosphere of the Café Opera to the exquisite decor and gourmet meals presented at Florencia. The Café features an à la carte menu, while the restaurant offers seven-course, gourmet meals. Florencia's guests feel as though they are dining in a formal, Mediterranean living room, as wing chairs set around a small group of tables are illuminated by brass chandeliers and candles set atop the mantel of the crackling fireplace. This Continental menu might begin with the foie gras and smoked duck fricassee in a rice crèpe, the grilled shrimp and squid ink spatzle, or the sautéed lamb sweetbreads in a puff pastry with a shallot truffle sauce. The entrée selection ranges from

Muscovoy duck breast and confit with quail egg to the roasted yellow fin tuna with a ginger black pepper and red chard sauce. Other standouts are the New Zealand red deer, the Victorian squab and wild rice crépinette, and the perennial favorite, Maine lobster.

Either after a delicious meal or before, guests may enjoy a variety of activities. On the first floor, just past the fully-equipped weight room, is an exquisitely designed swimming pavilion, with an adjacent sun terrace. The latter doubles as a great spot to star gaze. Others may prefer to take a leisurely stroll by the High Museum of Art and the Woodruff Arts Center or perhaps around the residential neighborhood over by Piedmont Park. In addition to the abundance of sightseeing and shopping alternatives available throughout the city and in the Buckhead neighborhood, within a short drive of the hotel there are a number of scenic city parks for walking with Bowser.

Swissotel Atlanta

3391 Peachtree Road NE
Atlanta, Georgia 30326
(800) 253-1397, (404) 365-0065, Fax (404) 365-8787

General Manager: *Joseph R. Kane*
Rooms: *262 doubles, 16 suites, 50 corner rooms, 30 club rooms*
Rates: *Doubles $115-195 (EP), Suites $285-950 (EP),*
Corner and Club Rooms $170-235 (EP)
Payment: *AE, DC, DSC, ENR, MC, and VISA*
Children: *Welcome (cribs, cots, high chairs, and babysitters are available)*
Dogs: *Small dogs are welcome, with prior approval and a $50 one-time fee*
Open: *All year*

Buckhead is one of the more exclusive and affluent neighborhoods in Atlanta. Travelers who want to stay right in the midst of it should investigate the Swissotel. When the Swissotel opened in 1991, it became the first European hotel to grace the Atlanta area. Situated in the heart of Buckhead, adjacent to the prestigious Lenox Square and Phipps Plaza, the 21-story building is fashioned in the trendy Bauhaus style of architecture, combining pristine white porcelain tiles with blue granite accents and an all-glass facade. The effect is striking.

The hotel's interior is cavernous. Guests will begin to understand this as they ascend the grand staircase leading up to the wood and marble laden lobby. New arrivals emerge into an ultra modern world of electrifying colors, dazzling flower arrangements, and avant-garde Biedermeier-style furnishings. The reception desk alone would overwhelm most hotel lobbies, but this long, lustrous 'wood counter is dwarfed by 45-foot high ceilings and huge, wood-paneled walls. In addition to the hotel's striking color schemes, there is also an impressive, albeit eclectic, collection of contemporary and post-modern works of art, placed about the common areas. These sculptures, watercolors, wood cuts, and lithographs represent works from both local and internationally recognized artists.

After dispensing with check-in, guests are escorted to their bedrooms. Each of the spacious chambers is decorated and furnished in much the same manner as the reception area. The purple, red, and blue Beidermeier-style furnishings nicely contrast with off-white walls and Edwardian gray carpeting. The expansive suites are the most impressive, not only because they have a fireplace and television with a VCR, but also because of their private terraces and Jacuzzi tubs. The more popular chambers are the corner rooms, which provide wonderful views of the Buckhead area and a look beyond to downtown Atlanta. A favorite configuration for families are the "17" rooms. Two chambers, one with a pair of double beds and another with a king-size bed, combine to form a mini-suite. Standard features in each of the guest rooms are the mini-bars, electronic safes, clock radios, and irons and ironing boards. The Swissotel is often a favorite stopover destination for business travelers. Consequently, each room has been designed with office-oriented features. Two telephone lines, call waiting, voicemail, fax and computer capabilities ensure that business can be conducted at guests' convenience. We were equally impressed with the spacious marble bathrooms, containing oversized bathtubs and separate showers, makeup and shaving mirrors, bathrobes, hair dryers, and an array of "environmentally friendly" toiletries.

The hotel's Executive Level rooms offer additional amenities and services. However, even the guests staying in a standard double guest room will learn first-hand why the hotel has such a great reputation for its fine staff and European quality service. Best of all, the Swissotel has a new policy of rewarding frequent visitors with little momentos and gifts. We know that few people (or their dogs) will ever see the inside of the 2,400 square foot Presidential Suite, but what the heck, we can live a little vicariously, can't we? Those who are fortunate enough to stay overnight in it will probably find the romantic in them drawn out by the fireplaces that grace both the formal living room and the exquisitely appointed master bedroom. Of course, there is also the music room, and even a kitchen for whipping up a few snacks. In addition, the outdoor terrace has a private Jacuzzi.

We found Buckhead to be the perfect place for exploring with a dog. Its residential qualities make it an ideal area for casual walks. Another popular outing includes a trip to Unicoi State Park, near Helen. There are a variety of hiking trails here, along with a huge lake and beach. A mere thirty minutes northwest of Atlanta visitors will also find the historic Kennesaw Mountain National Battlefield Park. This 2,800-acre tract of land has been set aside to commemorate the area where the famous Civil War battle took place. Visitors can follow the road to the top of the mountain, where there are marked trails to explore and old battlements to investigate.

After a busy day enjoying the sights and attractions in and around Atlanta, most will have worked up quite an appetite for a delicious meal at either the casual Café Gamay or the exquisite and world famous Palm Restaurant, which was first established in New York city in 1926. The walls of the restaurant are filled with whimsical portraits and caricatures of local notables and national celebrities. This charming eatery offers ample portions of simply prepared foods. Appetizer favorites include the clams casino, shrimp cocktail, or a jumbo lump crab meat cocktail. The house specialties feature the jumbo (3 pounds or more) Nova Scotia lobster or the aged New York strip steak for two. The double cut lamb and pork chops, prime rib, and filet mignon are tantalizing, but so are the variety of veal dishes. The choices of veal include Milanese, Piccata, Marsala, Martini, and Parmigiana. Any extra portions will surely be appreciated by well-behaved dogs.

For those who are seeking a little rejuvenation after their meal, there is an indoor swimming pool, a sun deck (good for star gazing, too), his/her saunas, and steam baths—all available for guests' use on the sixth floor. Ladies may wish to take advantage of the extensive treatments that are also offered by Claiborne's Spa. Guests will discover plenty of ways to feel pampered at the Swissotel; the trick is to decide just where to start.

Telfair Inn
A Victorian Village

326 Greene Street
Augusta, Georgia   30901
(800) 241-2407, (706) 724-3315, Fax (706) 823-6623

Owner: Herb Upton
Rooms: 30 doubles, 29 suites, 1 cottage
Rates: Doubles $67-107 (B&B), Suites $97-150 (B&B),
*   Cottage $150 (B&B)*
Payment: AE, CB, DC, DSC, MC, and VISA
Children: Welcome (cribs, cots, and high chairs are available)
Dogs: Small and medium-size dogs are welcome, fee dependent
*   upon length of stay*
Open: All year

Augusta was founded in 1737 and soon thereafter became regionally recognized for its prolific tobacco and cotton production. Golfers tend to overlook this aspect, perhaps because this is the home of the most prestigious golf tournament in the country: The Masters. Each spring, golf enthusiasts flock to this historic area to catch a glimpse of the world's most famous golf professionals as they drive, chip, and putt their way along the Augusta National Golf Course. But golf aside, most visitors, at some point, will investigate downtown Augusta and the lovely Olde Town Historic District.

This 51-block neighborhood has a wide variety of homes ranging from impressive Federals and beautiful Victorians to twentieth-century bungalows and three-room shotgun cottages. Many of Olde Town's most elegant and elaborate homes burned during a devastating fire in

1916. The area languished for many years until, in the 1980s, an extensive and intensive revitalization effort resurrected many of the historic houses. Set in the midst of it all is the expansive and distinctive Telfair Inn. The inn is named after Edward Telfair, who was both a Revolutionary War patriot and a two-time governor of Georgia. The inn began with just three restored homes in 1981. As Olde Town was restored, the number of inn buildings increased. Finally, in 1989, the inn's expansion ceased, with the acquisition of the Concierge House. This latest addition is patterned after the Ritz Carlton's club level and represents the finest of the inn's 17 buildings.

The lovely, tree-lined Greene Street leads new arrivals to the green awnings fronting the reception building. Along the way, guests can have a look at the other Victorian houses belonging to the inn, which fill the entire block between Greene and Telfair streets. Most of these are marked by good-sized front porches, interesting gables, eaves, and trim. Some of the facades would begin to look alike, except that each is painted a different color, from pale pink or yellow to sky blue or taupe. Just as each Victorian house is unique, so, too, is its decor. Regardless of the location, the rooms are authentically and attractively decorated, and furnished with antiques or very nice reproductions.

Although the houses are Victorian in style, the ornately carved furnishings of that same period are not in evidence. Instead, the appointments reflect the simpler lines of the Georgian period. The walls are painted in strong, rich colors and the windows are framed by jabots or balloon shades. One memorable room with pale pink walls and a hunter green carpet is illuminated by brass table lamps and chandeliers. A quilted chintz spread lies on the bed, backed by a Chippendale headboard and footed by a Queen Anne bench. Deep burgundy walls set the tone for another guest room, with a four-poster canopy bed and several Chippendale and Sheraton-style mahogany reproductions placed around a fireplace. A pair of pocket doors leads into a sitting room. Another bedroom, which also contains a four-poster bed, has a camel back sofa and wing chair forming a small sitting area in front of the fireplace. The adjacent kitchen is a welcome convenience. While each bedroom is different from the others, most are accented with floral fabrics and coordinated dust ruffles on the beds. The decorators have tried to highlight the period features as well, such as high ceilings, detailed moldings, and exposed brick fireplaces. Corner rooms tend to be the sunniest, as the large windows allow ample amounts of sunlight to filter inside. When making reservations, prospective guests should be specific about which of the many room configurations will best meet their needs. Most of the chambers, whether they are the expansive suites or smaller doubles, have fireplaces and whirlpool bathtubs. Little extras, such as bidets, kitchenettes, or private porches are also found throughout the complex.

The Telfair Inn offers lovely rooms, but does not have a restaurant. It does have a casual pub called the Fox's Lair; however, just across the street is a fabulous French restaurant that may as well be part of the inn. It is called La Maison, and they will prepare a breakfast tray to be enjoyed in bed, or guests may walk over to the restaurant to sample the wonderful array of fine cuisine. Eggs roulade—a puff pastry filled with eggs, spinach, and sausage topped with a light cheese —is one choice. Banana pancakes, served with a special caramel syrup, and the French toast stuffed with strawberries and cream cheese are other pleasant options. There are many types of restaurants in Augusta, but do save an evening for La Maison. One of the more popular appetizer selections includes the baked portabello mushroom stuffed with spinach, leeks, artichoke hearts, and cheese. Another is the baked oysters prepared three different ways (Imperial, Rockefeller, and Casino). Soups are delicate and rich. Some prefer the lobster bisque topped with cognac, while others lean towards the Charlestonian She Crab soup laced with sherry. (Our two favorites.) Entrées include the Dover sole sautéed with grapes, almonds, and citrus butter, and the jumbo shrimp and scallops, sautéed with a roasted garlic and white wine cream sauce, served over fresh pasta. We also liked the game sampler, which included pheasant sausage, quail, and venison. Wienerschnitzel and Yeagerschnitzel with forest mushrooms are two other intriguing offerings.

After dinner, Bowser will certainly enjoy a walk. The neighborhood around the inn has wide sidewalks and is terrific for leisurely strolls. Within a short distance there are also the Julian Smith, Allen, and Westover Memorial parks. Other nearby attractions worth visiting are the the Savannah River, Port Royal, and the Riverwalk. A 20-mile drive northwest of Augusta will bring travelers to the J. Strom Thurmond Lake, which is comprised of 70,000 acres of land. Others will enjoy crossing the border into South Carolina's Sumter National Forest, which encompasses over 335,000 acres. Hiking, boating, fishing, and swimming opportunities abound in both of these parks. Extensive trail maps provide a diverse array of walks that Bowser will surely find appealing.

Seven Creeks' Cabins

Horseshoe Cove Road
Blairsville, Georgia 30512
(706) 745-4753

Hosts: *Marvin and Bobbie Hernden*
Rooms: *6 cottages, 1-3 bedrooms*
Rates: *$55 per day (EP), $300 per week (EP)*
Payment: *AE, MC, and VISA for deposit, but prefer balance*
by cash or check
Children: *Welcome; those under 6 years are free of charge. Children over 6*
are $5 per day or $25 per week. (Cribs and high chairs are
available.)
Dogs: *Welcome, provided guests adhere to the list of pet policies. General*
guidelines require that dogs be housebroken, free of fleas, quiet, and
under voice or leash control at all times. They should not be left
alone in the room, and they may be walked only in areas that other
people are not apt to frequent.
Open: *All year*

Blairsville is a small, northern Georgia town, just a few miles from Brasstown Bald, the highest mountain in the state. Besides being one of the South's most photographed regions, its rugged mountains contain a section of the Appalachian Trail, three good-sized lakes, and an assortment of recreational diversions. As first-time visitors drive down the rocky dirt road leading to the low-key resort, they will pass corn and hay fields before arriving at a small Christmas tree farm. This was just about the time we thought we were hopelessly lost, as there were no signs pointing us in the right direction. However, just around the corner, we found the Seven Creeks' cabins.

We first encountered a small lake, complete with a half dozen resident ducks, situated at the base of a hill. Later we learned that this same lake is stocked with bream, bass, and catfish. Guests may either borrow a rod or bring their own to fish from shore or the floating dock. No license is required on this private lake. The area is also an informal recreation center, where volleyball, badminton, tetherball, and horseshoes are available, along with a picnic table for casual meals. Seeing all this, we began to understand why guests enjoyed this secluded oasis so much.

The first cabins visitors are likely to come across are Brassview and Twin Oaks, which lie on a lane halfway up the hillside, overlooking the Christmas tree farm. The dark brown, weathered Brassview cabin sleeps four people, two in the queen-size bedroom and two in a sofabed. This contemporary cabin has an L-shaped living room, which is painted a light blue and furnished with soft, comfortable armchairs and a contemporary sofa arranged around a fireplace. A ceiling fan cools the room, should the day become hot; or guests may prefer to open the doors to the deck and let the valley breezes blow through the cabin. The views of Brasstown Bald are quite spectacular from here, but most visitors will also enjoy watching the resident pony, goats, and sheep grazing in the meadow. Twin Oaks, the next cabin up the lane, sleeps six people in its queen- and twin-bedded rooms. The naturally stained, wood paneled walls in the living room give this cabin a slightly more rustic appeal.

The Lake cabin, true to its name, is located just a stone's throw from the lake. It is the oldest and probably the most rustic of the bunch, although the well maintained, light gray exterior and the lattice trimmed porch do not convey the true age of this abode. The cabin sleeps six people, with a double bed in one of the bedrooms, a pair of twin beds in the other, and another set of twin beds in the sleeping loft. Attractive furnishings fill the rooms, while area rugs cover the linoleum floors. The deep green exterior of the Garden cabin, tucked up the hillside from the Lake cabin, makes it blend in nicely with the surrounding woods. Once again, knotty pine walls set the decorative tone for this cabin, which is furnished in much the same manner as the others. Near the top of the hillside is the Ledford cabin (nicknamed Treefort), which is approximately 100 feet from the Hernden's house. This cabin is smaller than most, sleeping just four people, two in a queen-size bedroom, and two on a sofabed. The only cabin that does not accept dogs is Longview, because it has just been fully carpeted.

All of these cabins, without exception, are clean, well appointed, and informal. This allows guests to completely relax amid pleasant surroundings. These are also housekeeping cabins, where guests supply their own towels and linens and are expected to leave them as clean as when they arrived. The kitchen facilities, while not state of the art, are modern and fully stocked with just about every feature one would expect in a country cabin. Most summer guests find that they use the barbecue and picnic table extensively during their stay. Some of the other standard amenities include a television, a washer and dryer, and a few extra linens, just in case guests forget something. We thought the old fashioned "party line" telephones were a wonderful remembrance of the past. Another endearing touch are the red and blue notebooks the Herndens have placed in each of the cabins. The red notebook gives guests an idea of the local restaurants, grocery stores, and notable things to do in the area, while the blue notebook is a diary containing guests' comments on their stay. It makes for some interesting reading.

Guests and their dogs always enjoy exploring the 70 acres of pasture lands and woods around the cabins. Along the way, they will certainly encounter Tater, the resident dog who usually likes to accompany guests along the hiking trails. Naturalists will thoroughly enjoy their surroundings amid this lovely mountainous setting. A visit to the nearby Alpine village of Helen is another enjoyable option. Travelers interested in other day trips may wish to visit Vogel, a 250-acre recreation area (ten miles outside of Blairsville), which offers hiking trails and picnic sites. Lake Winfield Scott and Lake Blue Ridge are also in the vicinity; both permit visitors who leash their canine companions.

Habersham Hollow
Bed and Breakfast

Route 6
Box 6208
Clarkesville, Georgia   30523
(706) 754-5147

Hosts: C.J. and Maryann Gibbons
Rooms: 2 doubles, 2 cabins
Rates: Doubles and Cabins $85 (EP)
Payment: MC and VISA
Children: Welcome
Dogs: Welcome in the cabins for a nightly fee of $5
Open: All year

Habersham Hollow Bed & Breakfast is located in northeastern Georgia, a mountainous region with plenty of areas for Bowser to explore. New arrivals will find a pair of charming cabins situated along a gravel lined driveway surrounded by dense woods. Just beyond these is the main house, which doubles as the Gibbons' home and B&B. When we arrived, Maryann was most gracious but also seemed a bit frazzled. It did not take us long to learn that she and C.J. were still recovering from their shock when, after an extended trip, they returned to find water pipes burst and 18 inches of water on the first floor. The carpets, floors, and many of the furnishings were ruined, the second floor ceiling had collapsed, and the entire heating system was destroyed. At the time of our visit, the Gibbonses were in the final stages of repairs and improvements. The walls were being prepped for painting and the floors readied for new carpeting. French doors would soon fill the gap between the expansive living room and the enclosed porch, where breakfast is often served to the B&B guests. (Cabin guests have kitchens and can prepare their own breakfast). The Gibbonses were looking forward to moving their belongings out of the kitchen and dining room and back into the rest of the house. Maryann gave us a tour of the home where, even amidst all the restoration, we could still get a feeling for this charming B&B. The large guest bedrooms are furnished with king-size four poster beds, rocking and ladder back chairs, and draped side tables. An assortment of country collectibles, dried flowers, and wreaths provide colorful accents.

Guests traveling with a dog are welcome in either of the two cabins located back down the driveway. A ramp walkway, leading to the wraparound porch, provides access to these attractive gray buildings, whose windows are framed by blue shutters and brightened by flower boxes. Once inside, guests will discover that both cabins have similar configurations, furnishings, and styles of decor; however, the loft in one cabin is slightly smaller than the other and is not useable. Each of the cabins is essentially a studio, where the large L-shaped first floor provides enough space for two to four people. The knotty pine walls are adorned with colorful quilts, along with decorative wreaths and country knickknacks. In both cabins the queen-size beds are positioned to take advantage of the woodland views, which can be seen through the sliding glass doors leading out to the porch. One of the units contains a sleeping area up in the loft. While the loft does not offer the same views as the rest of the cabin, it is ideal for children or another couple. The kitchenette is well stocked, and there are also a charcoal grill and picnic table for outside dining. On cool nights, many enjoy stoking the woodstove, which provides more than enough heat for these cozy cabins. During the warmer months, guests always seem to be drawn to the cabin's back porch, where the canopy of trees and lush plants provide a most tranquil setting.

Visitors to this region are usually interested in investigating nearby Helen, a Bavarian village complete with boutiques, outlet stores, and restaurants, all sporting Alpine-style red roofs and window boxes. Flags flap in the breeze and colorful murals are painted on the stucco walls, making the entire hamlet a festive and popular destination. Human visitors seem to appreciate the town more than does Bowser, who would probably prefer a visit to one of the local parks or forests. Some nearby nature areas include Unicoi State Park, which is bisected by the Appalachian Trail, and the scenic Tallulah Falls, which are just a 15 minute drive from the B&B. Those who enjoy water-oriented diversions will find that canoeing, rafting, and tubing are all available nearby.

Open Gates Bed and Breakfast

Vernon Square
Darien, Georgia   31305
(912) 437-6985

Hostess: *Carolyn Hodges*
Rooms: *4 doubles*
Rates: *$45-55 (B&B)*
Payment: *Personal checks*
Children: *Welcome (cots and babysitters are available)*
Dogs: *Welcome with advance approval, and dog must sleep in a travel crate*
Open: *All year*

Darien is a little known hamlet along Georgia's coast, which most people bypass on their way to Little St. Simons or the Sapelo Islands. In all likelihood, what travelers miss will not be found in guidebooks, but only through information imparted by the locals, who will happily unlock the secrets of Darien and its environs for interested visitors.

Carolyn Hodges, owner of Open Gates, is one of these well-versed locals. She not only knows the interesting history of the area, but also leads tours throughout the region. She often takes visitors to see the picturesque shrimp boats, 18th-century forts and rice plantations, pointing out quiet restaurants that feature local seafoods and delicacies. Although Carolyn is originally from the Northeast, she has been a resident here for the last eighteen years. The house, however, has been around far longer than Carolyn. It was originally built in 1876 by a timber baron who not only survived the war between the states but also prospered in the years subsequent to that war.

Today, a rural route leads from the highway to Darien's Vernon Square, where guests will find the Open Gates Bed & Breakfast. This B&B stands with other lovely antique homes and a pair of churches which, together, encircle the town common. At the center of the common is a fountain framed by immense shade trees dripping with moss. A low white picket fence tops the brick wall that runs along the front of the B&B's property. In the 1930s, the man who owned the house put the fence up to discourage the neighborhood pigs from rooting around his lawn. Today, there are no signs of pigs, just the resident dog, Trotter, who can often be found resting in the shade of the porch's rocking chairs. The exterior of the house is awash with color, with the planter boxes, placed about the porch, overflowing with an array of annuals. Even the wrought iron sign marking the entrance has a basket of vibrant impatiens hanging from it.

The interior colors make an equally strong impression on most guests. The charming foyer has been painted a wonderful deep green, and the white trim of the archway almost creates a frame for the lovely antique writing desk just beyond. Some might be tempted to follow the elegant staircase to the upper floor of bedrooms; however, most are first drawn into another intriguing chamber—the living room. It has been painted a salmon bisque and furnished with an array of family heirlooms, antique furnishings, and portraits inherited by Carolyn. Some of the standouts are the 200-year-old Sarouk rug, baby grand piano, a pair of wing chairs and a camel back sofa, all of which are set around a most inviting fireplace. One of the more eye-catching items is an antique hair wreath, made by Carolyn's great grandmother in 1881, which is now encased in glass and framed.

The elegant counterpart to the living room, in both color and design, is the dining room, which is nearly filled by a pedestaled table and a Sheraton sideboard. Here, guests will discover numerous other family heirlooms, including silver, china, and crystal. Mornings, breakfast is presented either in the dining room or out on a table in the breezeway. The meal varies, but guests may expect to dine on either plantation pancakes, shirred eggs, or buttermilk waffles. These might be accompanied by baked apples, sugar figs, or fresh breads that may be topped with any of the homemade preserves that fill Carolyn's extensive collection of jam pots.

Of the B&B's four bedrooms, only the Timber Baron's Room is located on the first floor. This cozy chamber is furnished with an 1840 Victorian-style mahogany sleigh bed set amid an assortment of the family's wedding momentos. As with most of the other guest rooms, there are framed family photographs, collections of books, antique lamps, and clocks resting on old bureaus. The second floor Botanical Room contains a collection of books and artwork on nearby flora and fauna, which hints at Carolyn's love of biology, fostered during her undergraduate days at Middlebury College in Vermont. Down the hall, the royal blue Nanny's Room contains an antique washstand and a family baby basket. There are also an assortment of children's books that Carolyn has collected and placed around the room. These upstairs chambers share a bathroom.

The combination of an outside garden entrance and lots of space makes the Quilt Room ideal for anyone traveling with a dog. True to its name, it is dominated by a menagerie of colorful antique quilts from Pennsylvania. The quilts stand out sharply against the red fir-colored walls and hardwood floors. The king-size bed is draped with a star quilt, and the others are placed in a painted chest resting at the foot of the bed. Painted furnishings coupled with bold red curtains and colorful area rugs make this a delightful chamber in which to spend a few days.

At this intimate B&B, there are plenty of ways for guests to enjoy themselves. Many like to sit by the swimming pool, which is quite private with all of the surrounding magnolia, palm, and pecan trees. Others might prefer to borrow a book from Carolyn's collection and cuddle up in the hammock amid the tranquil surroundings. Some of the more interesting reading selections focus on the local history, which includes stories about the glory years of the 1800s, when this region of Georgia yielded huge crops of rice and cotton, along with vast amounts of timber. In the evening, guests often gravitate to the study, which is set in a private section of the house overlooking the pool. Here, they might browse through the wall of books, play backgammon, or enjoy the views through the wall of windows.

During the day, visitors usually like to investigate the now deserted rice islands. Walking through Vernon Square and along the side streets will yield a rich architectural history for the human travelers, and an interesting open space for Bowser. Visitors may also want to consider taking the Sapelo Island tour; Carolyn can often make the arrangements. Visitors must travel to the island by private boat. Once on the island, they will visit an old cotton plantation, now owned by R.J. Reynolds. Nearby Blackbeard Island is a national preserve, also accessible by private boat, offering trails to follow and a wildlife sanctuary to explore. When making reservations, let Carolyn know what you might be interested in doing, and she will come up with an itinerary that is just right for you and your canine cohort.

Dillard House

P.O. Box 10
Old Dillard Highway (Rte 441)
Dillard, Georgia   30537
(800) 541-0671 in Georgia, (706) 746-5348, Fax (706) 746-3344

Manager: John Dillard Jr.
Rooms: 50 doubles, 3 suites, 4 cottages
Rates: Doubles $55-95 (EP). Suites $75-130 (EP), Cottages $80-150 (EP)
Payment: AE, DC, DSC, MC, and VISA
Children: Welcome (cribs, cots, and high chairs are available)
Dogs: Welcome for $5 per day in all of the units except for the suites
Open: All year

Blink, and you might miss the sleepy village of Dillard, population 200. It is set into the northeast corner of Georgia, backed by the Blue Ridge Mountains and surrounded by farmlands. Pay attention when driving along the Old Dillard Highway, so as not to miss the road to the Dillard House, as it, too, is unobtrusive. After making the turn off the main road, guests will soon pass by a white kiosk, set behind a rock wall brimming with perennials and surrounded by shade trees. A little further on is the Dillard property itself, containing the original Dillard House containing a reception area and dining room. The cottages, pool, and tennis courts are grouped together, and just beyond the parking area lie a series of old-fashioned motel-style accommodations, Henry's Playhouse (for large gatherings), the stables, and the petting zoo. Over the years, the accommodations and amenities have been expanded and nicely updated, but the heartfelt southern hospitality is reminiscent of another era.

The Dillards first discovered this lovely region during the Revolutionary War, when a soldier named John Dillard dreamed of someday raising his family in this bucolic valley setting. He was finally able to act on these dreams in 1894, when he brought his family to Rabun County. John could not have realized what a tradition he would start, as the Dillard family has remained in these parts for over 200 years. More recently, they built a year-round resort, which allows them to share their legacy with visitors from around the world.

With almost as many types of accommodations as there are types of guests, families, couples, and singles all feel equally comfortable in these relaxed environs. The one constant in the accommodations is the decor, which varies little throughout the resort. The Old Dillard House offers rooms on the second floor. Period furnishings are intermixed with a simple yet appealing country decor, making these chambers especially appropriate for families or groups of friends. As much as we liked these rooms, we felt the single-story units and cottages were most appropriate for those traveling with a dog. For those who do not need the spaciousness of a cottage, the single-story units are perfectly adequate. Although they resemble a motel from the exterior, they are far more appealing once inside. Fully carpeted and furnished with reproduction American antique beds and Chippendale style armchairs, these units offer a comfortable and welcoming country decor. Coordinated floral fabrics are used for the comforters on the queen-size beds and for the full-length draperies framing the sliding glass doors. Cable televisions, air-conditioning, and modern bathrooms complete the list of modern amenities. We especially liked the pleasant pastoral and mountain views that could be enjoyed from either inside the room or from the rockers on the private patios.

On another part of the property are Helen's and Eddie's cottages, grouped together next to the expansive North White House and South White House, a separate building which is essentially a duplex. We liked Helen's Cottage, which is a quaint, gray-stained clapboarded building fronted by a small porch bedecked with rocking chairs. Once inside, guests will see that it has a large living room furnished with several armchairs and accented with country collectibles. A woodstove is as attractive as it is useful on cool nights. There is the modern convenience of a television; however, there are no telephones. The adjoining dining and kitchen areas are brightened by light streaming in through the bowed window. This cottage sleeps from 2-8 people in the two bedrooms, one of which contains a pair of queen-size beds and the other a pair of twin beds. Ceiling fans in each of these bed chambers are especially nice in the summer months. We thought the neutral color scheme and subtle floral wallpapers made this cottage very homey and comfortable. Eddie's Cottage is somewhat smaller, accommodating 2-6 people. It too has a living room with a fireplace and two bedrooms, but is also equipped with a Jacuzzi in the bathroom. The South White House is small, which is perfect for a couple traveling with a dog. There is a sitting room adjoined by a small sun room, a separate bedroom, and an efficiency kitchen. Finally, there is the North White House, which is not only the largest of the four but is the most nicely decorated and furnished.

Guests do not need to leave the property to find some interesting country collectibles and souvenirs for their friends back home. The gift shop is filled with assorted local wares, knickknacks, and an array of Dillard House farm products. To the rear of this building, guests will find the light and airy dining room, which is brightened by the expansive greenhouse addition. Most are drawn, though, to the massive stone fireplace that literally comprises much of one of the dining room walls.

We enjoyed the relaxed atmosphere in here, with natural pine board walls, ceiling fans, and a family-style configuration that makes for a most convivial dining experience. We know that many of the cottages have kitchens, but these are superfluous because the Dillard House turns out exceptional, old fashioned southern-style cooking. Patrons will discover there are no menus here, just trays of fried chicken, ham, and ribs coupled with corn on the cob, biscuits, hush puppies, beans, and potatoes. This is obviously not a spa menu, and guests seem to relish every hearty bite.

With filling meals such as these, it only makes sense to take advantage of the recreational options offered at the Dillard House. The stables are open to guests, providing everything from children's pony rides to trail rides for novices and experts. The youngsters will also enjoy both the playground and the petting zoo, where they can meet donkeys, goats, ponies, turkeys, and sheep. The swimming pool and pair of tennis courts are also quite popular with children and parents alike. In the evening, some head over to Henry's Playhouse, where a host of diversions ranging from bingo nights and bluegrass bands to square and clog dancing are offered. Nearby, visitors will also find white water rafting, boating, fishing, golfing and, in the winter, skiing. While most of these activities are people-oriented, Bowser will surely enjoy exploring the property, along with the forests, parks, and lakes dotting the region. Just south of Dillard, visitors will find the Tullulah Gorge State Park, where a sheer 1,000-foot crevice provides a spectacular setting for the waterfalls and lush greenery. In the 300-acre preserve, visitors will find some great trails for walking with Bowser, along with tennis courts, a playground, and a beach. Near Clayton, there is also the Black Rock Mountain, which offers 1,500 acres of hiking options.

The Helendorf

P.O. Box 305
Route 75
Helen, Georgia 30545-0305
(800) 445-2271, (706) 878-2271

Innkeepers: Richard and Barbara Gay
Rooms: 97 doubles
Rates: $45-95 (EP)
Payment: DC, MC, and Visa
Children: Welcome (cribs and cots area available)
Dogs: Welcome in specific rooms, with advance reservation and a $10
nightly fee
Open: All year

The small hamlet of Helen lies just south of the scenic 750,000-acre Chattahoochee National Forest, an enormous wilderness area with virtually unlimited recreational opportunities for visitors and their dogs. While there are plenty of things to do in this region, it is Helen that has the most interesting history. The town has always been closely tied to the timber industry, processing the trees brought in from the surrounding forests. Unfortunately, by the late 1960s, it had become a defunct lumber community. Local lore has it that when a Bavarian traveler first visited Helen around this time, the sight of the town nestled into the surrounding mountains so reminded him of his homeland that he began buying up property. With the help of the area's merchants, Helen soon became a replica of the man's native Bavarian village. Today, visitors will discover an Alpine village complete with red roofs, murals, flower boxes, and colorful flags. There are also a number of shops, outlet stores, restaurants, and amusements to keep visitors entertained during their stay in Helen.

The Helendorf is set in the center of town, putting it within easy walking distance of any of the local attractions. As guests pull up to the inn's entrance, they will see that the stuccoed exteriors are painted with charming murals. One is of a boy catching a butterfly, another of children dancing around a maypole, and a third of a girl resembling Rapunzel, whose long yellow braid is streaming down from a tower window. Once inside the reception area, guests will find themselves in the cozy beamed-ceiling sitting room, which is comprised of a pair of sofas flanking the raised fireplace.

There are various types of bedrooms available to guests; however, all have been furnished and decorated in a similar style. Most offer a pair of queen-size beds with fitted floral spreads and a whimsically painted dresser, upon which is set a television. Some rooms provide the convenience of a kitchenette and a small dining area. Although the Bavarian decor is not elaborate, it is quite appealing, especially when coupled with enchanting surroundings. The accommodations of choice offer balcony views of the Chattahoochee River. In these rooms, guests will enjoy listening to the soothing sounds of the rushing river, as well as the visual beauty of the lacy dogwood trees and lovely plantings that line its banks. Anyone who is not traveling with a dog may wish to inquire about the large riverside suites, which offer amenities like Jacuzzis, fireplaces, and complete kitchens.

One of the newest additions to The Helendorf is the indoor swimming pool, which guests enjoy using when the weather is a little on the cool side. Others may prefer to take Bowser for a walk through the village. There are several good restaurants nearby, which is helpful because the inn does not have dining facilities on the premises. During the year, there are plenty of organized events that draw visitors to this unique town. Hot air balloons are frequently seen drifting through the sky, and once a year there is the Helen-Atlantic balloon race. In the fall there is the ever-popular Oktoberfest, which follows the Munich tradition of providing lots of beer, music, singing, and dancing. The month of December brings the special Christmas festival, where the town is resplendent in lights and decorations, and visitors come from all over to enjoy an array of holiday festivities. It is important to travel beyond the boundaries of the village in order to connect with the natural attractions that for years have lured visitors to this picturesque region. Bowser might enjoy investigating some of the river-oriented activities, such as canoeing, swimming, or fishing for a few of the stocked trout. Golf and tennis facilities are available locally, as is horseback riding. While the Moccasin Creek offers 32 acres of recreational opportunities, and Vogel Recreation Area another 250 acres of hiking, fishing, and swimming, it is the Chattahoochee National Forest that attracts the most attention. The Cohutta Wilderness offers excellent hiking and fishing. The Anna Ruby Falls are two scenic waterfalls that also draw visitors, as well as hikers who are interested in exploring the nearby trails with their dogs.

Villas by the Sea

1175 North Beachview Drive
Jekyll Island, Georgia 31527
(800) 841-6262, (912) 635-2521, Fax (912) 635-2569

General Manager: *Edward Brophy*
Rooms: *176 one- to three-bedroom villas*
Rates: *$75-175 per day (EP), $475-1050 per week (EP)*
Payment: *AE, CB, DC, DSC, MC, and VISA*
Children: *Welcome; under 16 are free of charge (cribs, cots, and*
            high chairs are available)
Dogs: *Smaller pets are welcome (fee depends upon the unit)*
Open: *All year*

Jekyll Island was first discovered by Spain in the 16th century. The small chain of islands of which it is a part (including Sea Island and St. Simons Island) was given the name the Golden Isles. Then, in 1885, several millionaires decided that Jekyll Island would make a terrific hunting preserve and family retreat. Before long, the Goodyears, Goulds, Morgans, Rockefellers, and Pulitzers collectively purchased the island and created an expansive resort called the Jekyll Island Club. This aspect of the island's history is fascinating, because the net worth of the club's total membership represented almost one-sixth of the world's wealth. But other aspects of the story are equally riveting. In 1910, the first version of the Federal Reserve Act was drafted here. Subsequently, in 1915, the first transcontinental telephone call was made from the island. Despite all the privacy and exquisite accommodations, the subsequent generations of these millionaires were not interested in maintaining the club. Finally, in 1947, the island was sold to the state of Georgia, which eventually turned it into a state park. Today, visitors who wish to drive onto the island must pay a $2 entrance fee. While the aforementioned millionaires are long gone, several of their "cottages" still remain, as well as 10 miles of sandy beach, extensive bicycle trails, terrific golf courses, and wonderful ocean waters for swimming, boating , and fishing.

The best way to stay on Jekyll Island is to choose a place that is accessible to the island's diversions, but slightly removed from the main flow of activity, to maintain privacy. We thought the Villas by the Sea fit these criteria quite well. Located near the northeastern tip of the island, this is a good-sized resort comprised of 17 buildings situated on nicely landscaped grounds along the beach. Each of these buildings is named after a famous island personality, e.g. Getty, Rockefeller, Morgan,

Fitzgerald. Ten of the buildings overlook the large dunes lining the sandy beach, and thus offer optimum water views. As new arrivals walk about the property, they will discover a variety of grassy areas between the buildings and the dunes. These spaces have been reserved for such activities as volleyball, badminton, horseshoes, shuffleboard, and croquet. From here, five lighted wooden walkways rise over the lush foliage covering the dunes and lead out onto the wide sandy beach.

As one might imagine, in a complex of this size there are an assortment of accommodations available to guests. These range from mini-suites to one-, two-, and three-bedroom villas. The mini- suites contain a living room that connects through a short hallway to the bedroom. In between the two main rooms are a modern bathroom and a kitchenette outfitted with a refrigerator and microwave. The one-bedroom villas are very similar to the mini-suites, except the living room has been expanded to accommodate a dining area and a larger kitchen. We liked the private outdoor patios in these units, as well. To the rear of the villa is a master bedroom with a private bath and lots of closet space. The two- and three-bedroom villas, on the other hand, are not only more spacious but also more luxurious. These contain larger living and dining areas, as well as fully-appointed kitchens. They are perfect for families with either lots of children or additional family members, as there are multiple bedrooms affording guests a great deal of privacy. The general configuration here is that the living room, dining area, and kitchen are located to the rear of the first floor, while a queen-bedded chamber is situated off to the side of the front entry. The other bedrooms and bathrooms are located upstairs.

The decor is similar from one unit to the next and consists of off-white walls that are accented with framed prints of seaside or bucolic settings. Seashell lamps, dried flowers and wreaths, and potted plants and ficus trees add a warm, homey touch to each of these chambers. The Berber carpet is perfect for the seashore, as it wears well and doesn't show the sand that sometimes makes its way inside. We especially liked the lightness of these spaces, created by the white wicker furniture combined with the bleached pine and light oak furnishings. Vaulted ceilings and plenty of glass further enhance the sense of openness. In addition to central air conditioning and heat, guests may expect to find ceiling fans, cable televisions, and stereos. Given the similarity among the interior spaces, prospective guests need only decide on their view — dunes and ocean or intimate courtyards. Some might give up a water view in exchange for closer proximity to the expansive swimming pool and Jacuzzi.

When guests don't feel like cooking, they need look no further than the informal Crackers Restaurant, which serves a Continental cuisine. Its royal blue walls and lattice accents provide a charming backdrop to a menu that includes everything from hamburgers to an array of local fish specialities. Those in search of more athletic diversions will be pleased to find that there are several golf courses and an excellent tennis facility nearby. Others may prefer to take Bowser out to follow some of the extensive bicycling trails that encircle much of the island. Water enthusiasts will be happy to know that the marina offers rental jet skis and sailboats, along with para-sailing and fishing charters. Horse-drawn carriage rides and picturesque nature trails are also available; and panoramic views may be had from the airplane tours. Bowser will surely enjoy the miles of beaches (he should be leashed), as well as the interesting walks through Jekyll Island's historic district.

Burnett Place Bed & Breakfast

317 Old Post Road
Madison, Georgia   30650
(706) 342-4034

Hosts: Leonard and Ruth Wallace
Rooms: 3 doubles
Rates: $75-80 (B&B)
Payment: MC and VISA
Children: Welcome
Dogs: Welcome
Open: All year

To truly get the feeling for rural and historic Georgia, we recommend spending a few nights in one of its small hamlets, set well off the more traveled roads. Ideally, it is best to stay in an historic Bed and Breakfast, in order to fully appreciate the experience. One of our favorites is situated in the little town of Madison, about an hour outside of Atlanta. Originally incorporated in 1809, Madison was a prosperous community, whose residents included wealthy merchants and growers. They erected lovely Federal, Victorian, and Greek Revival houses, which today are fine examples of quintessential antebellum homes. These houses managed to survive the Civil War, when many other towns were burned, thanks in part to the efforts of former Senator Joshua Hill. He convinced General Sherman's Union forces to spare Madison and luckily, Sherman did just that, choosing to destroy only the railroad station. Today's visitors should be thankful, because Madison is a sleepy village of historic homes and churches surrounded by tree-lined streets and picturesque gardens.

Situated in the heart of the historic district is the Burnett Place, an elegant Federal-style home just a block off Madison's main street. Originally built in 1830, the white clapboard building is surrounded by large shade trees, mature plantings, and lovely formal gardens tucked into several nooks around the property. After parking the car, we noticed a small garden off to the side of the house where daffodils, azaleas, and dogwoods were in various stages of their spring bloom.

We walked up the front path to the columned front porch and found Leonard saying goodbye to a departing guest. He brought us inside, and we were immediately struck by the wonderful hues of yellow used throughout the foyer. Colorful quilts hang against the pale yellow walls and drape over the banister of the front staircase. We were struck as well with the aroma of potpourri wafting through the warm spring air. In the formal dining room, a few guests were still lingering over their morning coffee and another was inspecting the handcrafted corner hutch. An Oriental rug protects the hardwood floors in here, cushioning the two-pedestal table set in front of the fireplace. We found out that the hearty, full breakfasts vary daily and range from scrambled eggs to pancakes, accompanied by more traditional southern-style side dishes. After breakfast, the beautifully appointed and comfortable sitting room, just off the foyer, is an inviting chamber to relax in. Many like to read the paper as they sit nestled in one of the overstuffed yellow and blue chintz covered chairs that are arranged around the fireplace. We don't play the piano, but it caught our attention, as it was positioned near a pair of windows. There are a number of appealing antiques and collectibles in here as well, ranging from pillar and scroll mantel clocks to good-sized model ships.

As we walked through the house with Leonard, he gave us a short history lesson on Madison. He also informed us about the two years of restorative work that he and his wife completed on the house. Not only did he utilize his interior design skills, but he also sought the aid of the Madison Historic Preservation Commission to ensure that the home would retain its authentic historic character. We ascended the gracefully curving front staircase, where we saw still more quilts on display. One guest room, just off the landing, has a four-poster bed covered with a traditional white cotton spread. The blue and white period wallpaper and antique furniture enhance the natural character of the room. The windows are shuttered, the fireplace original, and the restored hardwood floor is covered with an Oriental rug. Another bedroom has cream colored walls, accented by burnt red trim. A pair of four-poster beds are placed next to one another. Windows surround the intimate sitting area that fills in another corner of the room, near the fireplace. Unlike the authentic bedrooms, the private bathrooms are modern, outfitted with white tile shower/bath combinations, and decorated with marbleized wallpaper. A third bedroom is located in the new addition. It, too, has a four-poster bed, but instead of hardwood floors, it has wall-to-wall carpeting. This bedroom may not have a fireplace, but the oversized bathroom is appealing, with its pickled floors and Jacuzzi bathtub.

We found Madison and the surrounding area to be great for dogs. There are a number of quiet side streets, perfect for enjoying long walks with Bowser. Hard Labor Creek State Park is located in nearby Rutledge, just ten miles from Madison. Here, visitors can golf, fish, swim, or follow the many nature trails that wend through the park. Lake Oconee, set on over 19,000 acres, has similar offerings and a little more space to enjoy them. Madison is set midway between Atlanta and Augusta. Some people may want to visit the revitalized city of Atlanta, or the sites and complexes built for the 1996 summer Olympics. And travelers will certainly want to visit Augusta, which not only has historic merit, but also hosts the world renowned Master's golf tournament. Regardless of one's recreational and/or cultural leanings, just about anyone will be impressed with the lovely accommodations, intimate B&B atmosphere, and truly affable hosts at the Burnett Place B&B.

The Swift Street Inn

1204 Swift Street
Perry, Georgia 31069
(912) 988-4477

Hosts: Dennis and Carolyn Lovejoy
Rooms: 4 doubles
Rates: $65-90 (B&B)
Payment: AE, MC, and VISA
Children: Most appropriate for children over the age of 12
Dogs: Welcome, with prior approval (an outdoor kennel is also available)
Open: All year

The small town of Perry is less than a 30-minute drive from Macon. Travelers searching for a relaxed Bed & Breakfast experience need look no further than The Swift Street Inn. The single story, coastal plantation-style home, was built in 1857 by Judge William Tyre Swift. It lies in a quiet residential neighborhood near the center of town. The dove gray clapboard home is easy to spot behind the low hedges, which, for most of the year, are accented by colorful, perennial gardens. A car port to the rear of the property is an ideal spot for unloading travel bags. Guests will also notice a small cottage, fronted by a fenced-in yard, where we found several couples playing lawn darts. Equally appealing, though, was the thought of whiling away some time by reading a book in the hunter green rocking chairs.

As we made our way up to the back door, we were greeted by Dennis, a robust man who couldn't have been more pleasant. He brought us in through the bright, modern country kitchen, which, as it turns out, is also the informal nucleus for the house. Guests are always wandering through here, not only to visit with their hosts, but also to nibble on any of the baked goodies or fruit that are usually set out to help satisfy hunger pangs. From the kitchen we headed into an elegantly furnished corner dining room, which is an especially cheery place for the morning meal. This hearty and healthy Continental repast usually includes muffins, fresh fruit, granola, and yogurt. Those who would prefer a hot breakfast need to provide their hosts with a little advance notice. It is from the dining room that we first spied the outdoor kennel, where the Lovejoy's dog, Muffin, was taking a mid-morning nap.

Walking down the wide, main hallway, we passed a wall of books that made us pause. There were many enticing titles and we were tempted to pick one up and relax in one of the comfortable, burgundy or navy blue wing chairs. Instead, we continued on to one of the bed chambers, the cozy Peach Room. In here, a four-poster maple bed rests on a colorful rag rug, which happens to nicely complement the peach-colored walls. The Rose Room, nearby, has two double beds covered with floral quilts. We thought the antique writing desk and the pair of wing chairs flanking the fireplace enhanced the antique feeling of the room. Pale blue walls, high ceilings, and windows framed by sheer lace curtains brighten the Dogwood Room. A country decor works well with the brass bedstead. The claw-footed tub is certain to beckon those who are in need of a little rejuvenation. The largest and most impressive chamber is the Magnolia Room, which is accessed through a pair of French doors. Hunter green walls surround an array of antiques. We also liked the charming foot stool that guests would probably need to climb into the high king-size bed. The loveseat placed in front of the fireplace is a perfect place to relax after a long soak in the double Jacuzzi. Or guests may be just as content to enjoy the lovely surroundings wrapped up in the robe that has been thoughtfully provided.

Regardless of which room guests ultimately select, most are certain to find that the high ceilings, beautiful appointments, and sense of spaciousness combine to create a unique and appealing B&B atmosphere. We also appreciated the subtle and tastefully presented modern conveniences, such as the air-conditioning, ceiling fans, and televisions. While the telephone is shared, we discovered that most guests preferred it this way, so as not to interrupt their vacation. An additional television and VCR are located in the common room, for those who might enjoy watching a videotape.

After Bowser has romped around the backyard a bit, guests might like to take him for a walk to the town center. The nearby Camellia Gardens are also quite lovely in season; once a month, visitors may enjoy visiting the Southeastern Antiques and Collectibles Market to search for treasures. Golf and tennis are available at the Houston Lake Country Club. Day trips, with Bowser, might lead north to Macon, where there are an abundance of historic landmarks and antebellum mansions. Travelers visiting in mid-March should check out the more than 300 events centered around the Macon Cherry Blossom Festival. Other outdoor adventures include a trip to the Oconee National Forest, where there are hiking trails, nature preserves, and the Ocmulgee River. South of Perry lies the 1,300-acre Georgia Veterans Memorial Park. This historic site sits on the banks of Lake Blackshear. Visitors can easily spend a few hours enjoying the lake, park, and historic aspects of the area.

Bed & Breakfast Inn

117 West Gordon Street (at Chatham Square)
Savannah, Georgia   31401
(912) 238-0518, Fax (912) 233-2537

Hostesses: Sue Friedman and Pam Gray
Rooms: 14 doubles
Rates: $40-85 (B&B)
Payment: AE, DSC, MC, and VISA
Children: Welcome
Dogs: Welcome with prior approval
Open: All year

Set in the middle of Savannah's historic district, just a few blocks from renowned Forsyth Park, lies a charming hostelry called, simply, the Bed & Breakfast Inn. The historic homes and buildings lining Gordon Row lead to the inn. Set across the way from Chatham Square, this nicely restored, three-story brick rowhouse is built in the Federal style and dates back to 1853. Ascending the curving front steps, visitors are quick to notice the potted plants placed alongside the treads and the flower boxes set under the windows. The charming entry gives way to an elongated sitting room. This inviting common area is furnished with period pieces and a smattering of antiques. The hardwood floors in here are covered with Oriental rugs, but it is the brass chandelier that drew our attention to the high ceilings. From here, walk through the wide arch and into the adjoining dining room. A multi-pedestal dining room table, surrounded by Chippendale chairs, is the focal point for this coral pink chamber. The decorative fireplace is fronted by a basket filled with dried flowers, while period paintings grace the walls. The formal southern atmosphere of this room complements the traditional southern breakfast that is served each morning. Guests may also opt to dine outdoors, on the private back courtyard.

While there are a variety of charming bedrooms in the main house, Sue and Pam prefer that guests traveling with dogs stay in the private Garden Suites. These are set off the two brick courtyards, to the rear of the property. Guests may access the suites and courtyard through the house, by walking through the dining room and out to a small deck. Those with their dog in tow may prefer to enter through the street-side door, set back unobtrusively under the steps leading to the main entrance. Once through the door, a brick hallway leads past an antique sideboard and a pair of side chairs to one of the two charming exterior courtyards. In the first, we found a small fountain and pool filled with carp; in the second, we were able to observe brightly colored finches flitting around a small aviary. The lush plantings and trees give guests a further sense of privacy.

The single-story Garden Suite is accessed off the courtyard through sliding glass doors. Its original brick floors are covered with an Oriental carpet. A combination of brick and plaster create interesting walls that are accented by dove gray trim. A Japanese screen is an appealing decorative touch. Bookshelves are well stocked with a variety of interesting reading materials. But it is the sleigh bed that is most memorable. At its end sits a charming bench; yet more enticing still is the camel back sofa that is arranged with other furnishings to create an intimate sitting area. In addition to providing a full kitchen, this expansive suite also features a dining nook. Another suite comprises two floors of the original carriage house. The first floor contains a living room, with a kitchen located off to one end. Upstairs, hunter green walls and red floral curtains combine to add dimension to the roomy, beamed-ceilinged master bedroom. We liked the four-poster rice bed almost as much as the tiny private balcony off the bedroom. From here, we could relax and look out onto the courtyards. The adjacent courtyard has a carriage house suite, as well, which is practically a clone of the one just described. We especially appreciated the air conditioning, television, and private telephone found in each of the suites. In the evenings, mints on the beds are a welcome, after dinner treat.

Because the inn is centrally located, it is easy to walk to the multitude of restaurants and stores. First time visitors to Savannah will find many other worthwhile activities and diversions available in this charming city. Dozens of small squares are found throughout the historic district and these are certain to be appealing to Bowser. His human companions, however, may be more enamored with the wonderful old houses, lovely fountains and statues, and beautiful gardens. There are extensive walking tours available, as well as informative trolley tours and romantic carriage rides. We think the Bed & Breakfast Inn offers the right combination of a low-key B&B setting amid a charming historic backdrop, making it one of the more desirable B&Bs in the Savannah area.

Ballastone Inn

14 East Oglethorpe Avenue
Savannah, Georgia   31401
(800) 822-4553, (912) 236-1484, Fax (912) 236-4626

Owner: Richard F. Carlson
Rooms: 16 doubles, 6 suites
Rates: Doubles $85-200 (B&B), Suites $180-200 (B&B)
Payment: AE, MC, and VISA
Children: Most appropriate for children over 13 years of age
Dogs: Welcome with prior approval in the garden level rooms, for a $10 fee
Open: All year

Savannah was founded by General James Oglethorpe and his band of settlers in 1733. From a bluff overlooking the Savannah River, Oglethorpe decided to lay the city out into 24 distinct grids, placing a combination of commercial and residential buildings around the public squares. Savannah's port became an important link between England and America's south. As a result, the city was prosperous for the next century and a half. Local plantations produced record yields of both tobacco and cotton and shipped it out of Savannah. Then, in the late 1890s, the cotton market collapsed—and so did the city that was so strongly linked with it. Thus began a long, steady decline. In many cases, as a city disintegrates so, too, do its historic landmarks. Fortunately for Savannah, however, a group of concerned citizens formed the Historic Savannah Foundation, which had the foresight to preserve precious vestiges of the city's history. It wasn't until much later that these sections of the city could be restored and revitalized.

Today's visitors will see the results of the intense preservation efforts. Remnants of grander times are everywhere, and one of the more impressive reminders is the building containing the Ballastone Inn. Set just a few blocks from the Savannah River and Factors Walk, it dates back to 1838. The structure was built of ballast stones by George Anderson, a local merchant. Over the years the building has seen many owners and experienced an equal number of reincarnations, from boarding house to bordello to the regional headquarters for the Girl Scouts of America. Many people have tried to adapt the building to fit their needs. In 1980, Tarby Bryant purchased the landmark and, with the aid of a few partners, poured over $2 million into its restoration. Before the end of the decade, the property again changed hands, with Richard Carlson, the current owner, completing the refurbishment.

As new arrivals meander down the street, they might notice the charming garden courtyard set behind a black wrought iron fence. Lush plantings and a decorative fountain make this a little oasis, where guests often opt to enjoy their morning meal or an afternoon libation. Visitors can follow the curve of the iron railing leading up the front steps to the entrance, and step inside to the elongated foyer. A small gift shop is tucked into an alcove, although guests usually pass right by this on their way to the reception desk, which is nestled alongside the Queen Anne staircase. This is elegance, perfectly refined. Oriental rugs are laid over the lustrous hardwood floors and designer fabrics cover the antique chairs and sofas. Other areas are filled in with potted plants and fresh flower arrangements. An adjoining parlor, with yet another Oriental rug, contains an ornately carved harp and original paintings hanging against navy blue walls. We just wanted to sit for awhile on the overstuffed sofa in front of the fireplace, and take in the details of the room. Decorative china is displayed on the mantel, topped only by a gilt framed mirror. The brass chandelier, coupled with floor-to-ceiling windows, lightens what would otherwise be a rather dark room. In the afternoon, the sideboard boasts a basket of fruit surrounded by teas, coffees, pastries, and a decanter of sherry. As we meandered deeper into the inn, we came across the full service bar and lounge. This intimate room is a wonderful place to relax after a busy day exploring Savannah.

Guests traveling with a canine companion are welcome to stay in the guest rooms just off the courtyard. These rooms may be found by walking through the courtyard, and into a hallway, that first zigs and then zags before reaching the guest rooms. As with the other 17 individually decorated bedrooms at the inn, these five bedrooms are beautifully decorated with Scalamandre fabrics and authentic Savannah color schemes; they are also outfitted with a fine collection of Georgian reproduction and antique furnishings. The cozy Savannah Room combines coffee-colored walls with hunter green and floral accents that make for a striking effect. The comparatively spacious Tomochichi Patch has a burnt red wall treatment, which seems to accentuate the four-poster bedstead. A small sitting area, containing a pair of rocking chairs and a sofa bed, centers around the fireplace. Shutters frame windows that overlook the courtyard. Hannah's Room boasts a brass bed, while the Sorgum Cane Room has a double queen bed and a fireplace. The amenities are similar to those offered at a five-star hotel, including nightly turndown service, chocolates on the bedside tables, and terry cloth robes in the bathrooms. Televisions with VCRs are a pleasant distraction, and air conditioning is a given. Each morning, a silver breakfast tray is filled with fresh fruit, southern-style muffins and breads, and an assortment of juices, coffee, and tea. This may be enjoyed in the room or taken out to the peaceful and private courtyard.

After enjoying a sampling of this filling repast, your canine companion will probably be anxious for a walk. There are 2 1/2 square miles to explore in the National Historic Landmark District. Bowser will probably be most interested in the waterfront parks, or any of the smaller parks located in each of the 24 squares in Old Savannah. Guests may ask the concierge for more recommendations on what to do in and around this lovely old section of Savannah.

East Bay Inn

225 East Bay Street
Savannah, Georgia 31401
(800) 500-1225, (912) 238-1225, Fax (912) 232-2709

Innkeeper: Jean Ryerson
Rooms: 28 doubles
Rates: $89-135 (B&B)
Payment: AE, CB, DC, DSC, MC, and VISA
Children: Welcome; those under 12 years of age are free of charge (cribs,
*   cots, and babysitters are available)*
Dogs: Small dogs, preferably under 30 pounds, are welcome with a $25 fee
Open: All year

Savannah's semitropical climate and well-preserved southern history attracts visitors year round. During the course of their touring, everyone seems to make a point of visiting the historic waterfront. Although travelers may come primarily to shop, they have the opportunity to glimpse into the history of this once thriving seaport community. Some prefer Old Savannah, because of its multitude of picturesque squares and historic homes. Such visitors walk the city with map in hand, finding something new and appealing around each subsequent corner. Individual reasons for visiting Savannah may be varied, but the East Bay Inn provides travelers with lovely accommodations nestled right in the center of Old Savannah.

Originally constructed in 1853 as a cotton warehouse, this three-story brick building was converted into an inn by the early 1980s. Annuals, overflowing from the hunter green window boxes, are protected by the shadows cast from the awnings overhead. The spacious reception area and parlor, also decorated with deep green accents, are both furnished with Georgian reproductions. In the front parlor, pretty floral draperies frame the oversized double-hung windows and provide a nice complement to the cranberry-colored walls. Wing and Chippendale armchairs, along with camel back sofas, are set around butler's tray tables and single pedestal tables. Interspersed throughout are potted plants and fresh flower arrangements. Brass chandeliers and lamps illuminate the room in the evening, when sherry and wine are set out for guests to enjoy. Many of Savannah's historic inns do not have elevators; however, this one does, and it quickly whisks guests up to their bedrooms.

Besides not having elevators, historic inns tend to have quirky bed chambers. This is not the case, however, at the East Bay Inn, where most doors open to short hallways that lead to the bedrooms, giving guests even more privacy. The color schemes range from a warm camel and crimson to lime green and navy. These assorted hues grace the plaster walls, often mixing with the exposed brick walls to create interesting contrasts. Decorative plaster work drew our eyes to the high ceilings in these spacious chambers. Equally eye-catching are the long windows framed by full length, tie-back curtains. Four-poster rice beds and Georgian period antique reproductions are set either on Oriental rugs covering hardwood floors or on neutral wall-to-wall carpeting. Armoires conceal cable televisions, while telephones, coffee makers, and air conditioning round out the list of standard amenities. The modern bathrooms are equally well appointed, containing thick fluffy towels and an array of toiletries. As with most fine hotels, evening maid service is provided and chocolates are left on the pillows of the turned down beds. We especially liked the larger chambers, which featured lovely sitting areas, a private patio, and a view of the park. If we had to pick our favorites, though, they would be the corner rooms, with two walls of elongated windows that let in copious amounts of sunlight.

Each morning, guests are invited down to the café, where baskets of fruit, jars of cereals, and trays of muffins are laid out, buffet style, on a long table. This cozy room is located off the reception area, where a handful of tables are set between a wall of windows and a gleaming cherry wood bar. The inn also has a restaurant in the cellar. Skyler's offers a diverse selection of Continental entrées and a number of local, innovative seafood specialties.

As with other historic inns, it is easy to walk a dog in this area. Visitors are free to stroll down by the waterfront parks, shops, and array of eateries, or through the picturesque squares. Many visitors use the inn as a home base for day trips as well. Within 30 minutes of Savannah, there are a number of state parks that welcome dogs. One of the larger is Fort McAllister, which includes 1,700 acres of land. This historic site also has water access. Skidaway Island is under ten miles from the city and encompasses some 500 acres. Hiking trails, picnic sites, and fishing and swimming areas are all available here.

Joan's on Jones B&B

17 West Jones Street
Savannah, Georgia 31401
(800) 407-3863, (912) 234-3863, Fax (912) 234-1455

Hostess: *Joan Levy*
Rooms: *2 suites*
Rates: *$95-110 (B&B)*
Payment: *Personal checks*
Children: *Welcome (cribs are available)*
Dogs: *Welcome in the Garden Suite, with prior approval and a $25 fee*
Open: *All year*

Savannah offers travelers an array of lodging options, ranging from large hotels catering to business travelers to more intimate inns and charming Bed & Breakfasts, for those seeking a more personal experience. Joan's on Jones is one of the smaller and more intimate of the latter, and is certain to intrigue any B&B fan. This B&B offers two spacious, very private suites in a house located in a quiet, residential neighborhood. Best of all, Joan's on Jones is located right in the heart of Savannah's National Historic Landmark District. The B&B is housed in a lovely, three-story Victorian townhouse that dates back to 1883. The building has both a front staircase leading up to the Levy's residence and a street-level side door, which is the entrance to the front suite.

The day we visited, both Joan and her Cocker Spaniel were on hand to greet us. They took us to the street-side guest chamber, known as the Jones Street Suite, where we emerged into the spacious, crimson-walled front parlor. Pocket doors open to reveal the master bedroom, where we found a classic four-poster rice bed covered in a floral bedspread. In addition to the array of white wicker and the lovely, antique furnishings found throughout the suite, guests will also discover that the suite is equipped with a pseudo-kitchenette containing a refrigerator, microwave, and ice maker, along with a hearty assortment of "breakfast fixin's." This gives guests the choice of taking their morning meal when they are ready, not when the host has stipulated. Guests are thus free to catch a few extra winks; some even choose to breakfast in their pajamas. The good-sized modern bathroom is outfitted with black and white tiles and a pedestal sink.

Just beyond this room lies a second suite, known as the Garden Suite. Since this is the "doggie suite," guests usually enter through the walled, garden courtyard situated off Jones Lane, just behind the house. We especially liked the light and airy feeling in here, due mostly to the pastel yellow walls, doors, and windows opening onto the patio and garden. The sounds of water splashing from the fountain, coupled with the fragrant blossoms from the assorted plantings, combine to make this our favorite suite. The Garden Suite feels like one large chamber.

Most guests are surprised to discover that the room formerly served as the kitchen for the house. The huge, brick fireplace that dominates this space was once used to cook all the meals for the household. A queen-size iron bed is surrounded by formal antiques and other period furnishings. Oriental rugs cover the heart-pine floors, and lovely paintings and Queen Anne mirrors hang from the Savannah-gray brick walls. This suite also contains a kitchen that is fully-equipped for creating either simple or more complex meals. The bathroom in this room is similar to the one in the Jones Street Suite. Additional amenities found in both are the color, cable televisions and the individual climate controls. Best of all, when the two suites are combined, there is more than enough space to accommodate additional friends or family members; yet there is still a good deal of privacy, should guests desire a little time to themselves.

Because this is a residential neighborhood, Bowser can join the local doggy contingency for both evening and morning walks to the dozens of intimate squares and parks nearby. One popular day trip entails a drive south to St. Simons Island, which is a beautiful and affluent area just off Georgia's coast. On the island, visitors will find the Fort Frederica National Monument, marking the site where, in 1736, one of the most important British forts was built. Leashed dogs are allowed to explore the earthworks and ruins. There are also extensive bicycle trails that wend along St. Simons. These are well worth investigating. After a busy day enjoying the sights and attractions around the Savannah area, guests can return to the homey atmosphere of the B&B. Here, they will discover that Joan has thoughtfully left them a bottle of wine and an assortment of goodies, to make them feel all the more comfortable at Joan's on Jones.

Olde Harbour Inn

508 East Factors Walk
Savannah, Georgia   31401
(800) 553-6533, (912) 234-4100, Fax (912) 233-5979

Manager: Jean Ryerson
Rooms: 24 suites
Rates: $95-175 (B&B)
Payment: AE, DC, DSC, MC, and VISA
Children: Welcome (cribs and cots are available)
Dogs: Welcome with a $25 fee
Open: All year

The charming Olde Harbour Inn was originally constructed in 1892. Its primary purpose at the time was to house an oil company. Today's guests, however, would never sense this, as the inn has been completely refurbished to accommodate luxurious river view suites. Architecturally, the exterior is one of the nicest along the waterfront, with the cream colored walls showing off the carved stone beading and dentil moldings found along the top edge of the building. Windows on the lower floors are framed by gray shutters, while Palladian windows line the entire second floor. Black wrought iron railings form French balconies and line the front steps leading to the inn's entrance.

The public rooms and foyers of Olde Harbour Inn are pleasingly intimate. The two front parlors are furnished with a mix of Queen Anne and Chippendale-style reproductions, coupled with brass accents. Oriental rugs cover the darkly stained hardwood floors, but these spaces are hardly somber. Framed pastoral and nautical prints line the walls. In keeping with the seaside theme, there is the Marine Room, where guests are offered a substantial Continental breakfast each morning. Southern biscuits and homemade muffins are complemented by fresh fruit and cereals. It was not, however, the meal that captured our attention, but the surroundings. This space offers some of the best views of the river front, visible through the large dining room windows framed by jabots. Leather Windsor chairs placed around simple wood tables set the informal scene for this repast. In the afternoons, wine and cheese are set out for the guests to enjoy, and later in the evening, overnighters may retire to either of the front parlors for an after-dinner libation.

The upstairs bedrooms are similar in ambiance to the public rooms, except the layout in each varies substantially from one room to the next. The Studio Suites include a small sitting area, situated off to the side of a queen-size four-poster rice bed. The Living Room Suites expand on this configuration by offering an entirely separate living room. The Balcony Loft Suites feature private balconies providing some of the nicest river views, as well as a second story loft that contains a double bed set under skylights. The high end rooms at the inn are the Two-Bedroom Loft Suites. These expansive accommodations, located on the top floors of the building, have 25-foot high ceilings—which makes these chambers feel almost palatial. The queen-size master bedroom has the most commanding view of the river, although those sleeping in the loft's twin beds have the added benefit of skylights. The four-poster rice bed is a standard in most of these spaces, with both French and English reproduction furnishings adding still further to the formal feeling. The walls are a light cream color, while pale peach and green floral patterns and Bermuda plaid fabrics are used to cover the furniture. All of the beds have traditional quilted spreads and dust ruffles. Some of these have pastel color schemes; others use deep cranberry floral fabrics. Generally, jabots edge the windows, while lovely, framed prints and dried flower wreaths dress up the walls. Brass sconces and table lamps illuminate these chambers at night. The mahogany armoires conceal cable televisions, and pass-through windows make the fully-equipped kitchens even more accessible.

The inn is situated right along Factor's Walk on the edge of the Savannah River, in the heart of the city's historic district. This gives guests an array of opportunities for picturesque strolls around the city with their canine companions. Best of all, within a minute's walk from the inn are a number of activities along River Street. Here may be found a nice little park (which Bowser should appreciate), a variety of shops and eateries, and everything from riverboat rides to carriage tours. Those interested in venturing further afield will want to explore the many islands, nature preserves, and resort towns to the north and south of Savannah. Hilton Head is an easy day trip to the north, while the wilds of Jekyll Island lie off to the south. Whatever guests ultimately decide to do for fun, the centrally located Olde Harbour Inn provides not only spacious and elegantly appointed suites, but also views of the river that are hard to beat.

River Street Inn

115 East River Street
Savannah, Georgia 31401
(800) 253-4229, (912) 234-6400, Fax (912) 234-1478

Manager: Pamela Bradshaw
Rooms: 44 doubles
Rates: $69-140 (B&B)
Payment: AE, MC, VISA
Children: Welcome and free of charge under the age of 18, when staying
with parents
Dogs: Small pets welcome with prior approval
Open: All year

Located in Savannah's historic district are a handful of antique inns. One of the more intriguing is the grand old River Street Inn, which is set along the renowned Factor's Walk. Constructed in 1817, the building was formerly used for storing, sampling, grading, and exporting raw cotton. Unfortunately, at the time, the cotton industry was growing at such a rapid pace that the original ballastone and brick structure soon outgrew its usefulness. Because the merchants were unable to expand towards the river or out onto the bluff, they decided to add three more stories, providing access to each by way of bridges and walkways. Like other river front structures, this building was more recently abandoned and slowly began decaying .

When the area was revitalized during the 1980s, the entire building was converted into a wonderful waterside inn, housing dining facilities, spacious common areas, and a large number of guest rooms. Today, the beautifully restored facade is accented by authentic Savannah colors and illuminated by gas lanterns. Period furnishings—a mix of reproductions and antiques—fill the common areas and bedrooms. The centerpiece for the inn is the five-floor atrium. On each level, intimate nooks create natural sitting areas that have comfortable wing chairs, a smattering of antiques, impressive portraits, and potted plants. Throughout the rest of the inn, Oriental rugs cover the hardwood floors and traditional prints hang from the grass-papered walls. We enjoyed taking the brass elevator up to our bedroom's floor. The higher we climbed, the better the view of the waterfront through the elevator window.

Each of the guest rooms is unique, both in layout and in decorative style. The beds vary, from a four-poster canopied rice bed to a two-poster pine bedstead. Some rooms are quite light, with peach-colored walls accented by beautiful floral draperies and quilted bedspreads. Other rooms are more masculine in feeling, with exposed brick walls and hunter green, dove gray, or cranberry trim. Brass accents, coupled with nautical or hunt prints, complete the motif. Some chambers boast of fireplaces and large writing desks, while others contain decorative world globes and large, pine chests topped by ship's models. The corner rooms, located on the upper floors, held the most appeal for us, as they offered additional floor-length windows coupled with the 12-foot high ceilings. The combination of the two creates a sense of spaciousness, while also providing expansive vistas of the Savannah River area. Three-quarters of the rooms have views of the river, and the remainder overlook the park. French balconies, fashioned from black wrought iron, are one of the best places to take in the sights and smells of the river front. While the building is antique, the good-sized modern bathrooms are not. Each of these have Corian sinks fitted with brass fixtures, an assortment of toiletries, and soft cotton towels. Satellite televisions, private telephone lines, and individual thermostats are items found in most large hotels, and are welcome amenities for guests here as well. Each night the maid turns down the bed and places handmade chocolates on the pillows. The business traveler will also discover that everything from fax and copy facilities to secretarial services are available at the inn.

In the morning, guests are invited to partake of a Continental repast in Huey's Cafe. Most guests are happy to select a complimentary morning newspaper and just settle in for awhile. Anyone yearning for a more substantial breakfast will find a variety of eateries and restaurants from which to choose, all along Factor's Walk. While it might be a bit early for billiards, keep in mind that the inn does have a Billiard's Room. Less sedentary pursuits can be found in the nearby Downtown Athletic Club. Some enjoy taking their canine companions for a leisurely walk around Savannah's Historic Landmark District, which is comprised of cobblestone streets, historic landmarks, and an assortment of picturesque squares and parks. For humans, points of interest include City Market, The Sea Maritime Museum, and the Antique Mall.

The Statesboro Inn

106 South Main Street
Statesboro, Georgia 30458
(800) 846-9466, (912) 489-8628, Fax (912) 489-4785

Innkeepers: The Garges Family
Rooms: 12 doubles, 3 suites
Rates: Doubles $65-75 (EP), Suites $90 (EP)
Payment: AE, DSC, MC, and VISA
Children: Welcome, parents must be responsible for them at all times
(cribs, cots, and high chairs are available)
Dogs: Small, well-behaved dogs are welcome in specific rooms with prior
approval
Open: All year

The quiet town of Statesboro is situated near the eastern border of Georgia, approximately an hour's drive from Savannah and Augusta. Over the years, The Statesboro Inn has catered to all types of travelers, from parents visiting a student at the local Georgia Southern University to sports enthusiasts attending the annual Master's Golf Tournament in Augusta. Originally built in 1904, the inn was home to William Guy Raines, a local city councilman and hardware store owner. Mr. Raines added many of the fine finishing touches to the house, perhaps, as is generally believed, because of his connections with the hardware and lumber business.

The inn is visually appealing, even from the road, as it is set among large shade trees and mature plantings. It is also architecturally distinct, combining elements from many eras. Some call it Victorian because of the gables and bay windows, but they would be overlooking the Palladian window over the front door and the Tuscan columns supporting the wraparound front porch which give it a Neoclassical feeling. Whatever it is, it certainly is unique. A restful scene generally awaits guests, whether it be of people rocking on the expansive front porch, or gathered around the umbrella tables on the brick courtyard, to the rear of the house. The inn appears rather small from the street, however, upon further investigation guests will discover an additional wing that extends towards the back of the property.

From the moment we stepped through the side door, it seemed that our affable hosts were in constant motion trying to tend to their overnight guests and dinner patrons. Of course, we were visiting during one of the busier times of year, the week of the Master's tournament. The inn was full of guests who shared one common interest—golf, making for a most convivial atmosphere. Wherever we went, whether it was the charming sitting room or the pair of dining rooms, we could hear people talking about the Masters. The sitting room is very traditional, in every sense of the word. The hunter green walls are trimmed with dark wainscoting, while brass sconces and chandeliers illuminate this space ever so subtly. The hardwood floors are covered with area rugs. Wing and armchairs are centered around a sofa, covered in a floral fabric, that is brimming with teddy bears. A secretary stands in one corner, while a model train and a pair of duck decoys adorn the fireplace mantel.

The restaurant is also very intimate with dark paneling and boxed-beamed ceilings, accented with stained glass windows. The corner fireplaces and flickering candlelight cast a pleasant glow over the burgundy table cloths topped with white overlays. The restaurant has won a number of accolades over the years for its varied Continental fare. Appetizers usually include crabcakes served with a tarragon cream sauce, escargot, and shrimp cocktail. Entrée selections often focus on seafood, and the salmon filet topped with a creamy dill sauce, blackened Cajun style grouper, or scallops baked in papillote are favorites. Patrons who cannot make up their minds might opt for the surf and turf, or simply try the ever-popular filet mignon with a green peppercorn sauce.

Fortunately, the guest bedrooms are not far from the dining rooms, a fact which is appreciated after a wonderful meal. The bedrooms range in size from intimate and lovely singles to expansive chambers with fireplaces and whirlpool tubs. A comfortable and homey decor is the backdrop to the antique furnishings and thoughtful array of modern conveniences. One particularly noteworthy bedroom has 12-foot ceilings and salmon colored walls. A small corner sitting area is composed of white wicker furniture; occupying much of the the rest of the bedroom is a four poster queen-size bed. The large marble-tiled bathroom is equipped with a whirlpool bathtub. Another guest room we saw had a sitting area set with a combination of mahogany antique reproductions and rattan furnishings. The bed is placed unobtrusively in a windowed alcove, while a writing desk is surrounded by an array of Asian collectibles. Inns sometimes forego modern conveniences in search of historic accuracy; however, here the television, ceiling fan, and refrigerator are welcome additions. Some of the other guest chambers were furnished with white iron and brass beds or hand-carved headboards, and all presented an appealing decor, accented by an array of country collectibles.

It is easy to walk Bowser both inside and around the inn. Off-site excursions might include the George L. Smith II recreation area, with over 1,200 acres, or Magnolia Springs, a nearby nature area with just under 1,000 acres of land. In both places, visitors will find walking trails and more than enough open space to satisfy their canine companions. While in the area, some may enjoy a visit to the Bo Ginn National Fish Hatchery and Aquarium. On the Hatchery and Aquarium grounds, there are over 20 ponds displaying a wide variety of fish in various stages of growth, and there are an additional 20 acres for Bowser to explore as well.

Tate House

P.O. Box 33
Route 53
Tate, Georgia   30177
(800) 342-7515 in Georgia, (404) 735-3122

Hosts: Ann and Joe Laird
Rooms: 4 suites (B&B), 9 cabins (EP)
Rates: Suites and cabins $89-135
Payment: AE, DC, MC, and VISA
Children: Welcome; under 12 years of age are free of charge when sharing a
*   room with their parents*
Dogs: Welcome in the cabins
Open: All year except Christmas

Wending through the foothills of the Blue Ridge Mountains, picturesque sights abound. One of these treasures, hidden amid all this natural beauty, is the Tate House. A massive, pink marble mansion, the Tate House sits alongside an English garden and manicured lawns encircling a fountain. Huge trees shade the house and a portion of the long, formal drive that leads to the rear of the 27-acre estate. As guests approach the house, they will come to a set of stairs that encircle yet another fountain.

Once inside, new arrivals may be overwhelmed by the impressive foyer, fashioned with marble floors and a hand-painted mural adorning the wall. This chamber then opens into a series of large, high ceilinged rooms that are equally well appointed. Unfortunately, guests traveling with a dog are not allowed to stay in the bedrooms located upstairs; however, a tour of these beautiful spaces is a must. A winding staircase leads to the magnificent guest rooms, which have been individually decorated and furnished with a variety of impressive antiques. One large corner room is outfitted with a green and coral color scheme, with Oriental accent pieces. Another bedroom contains a king-size finial bedstead, placed in the midst of several mahogany antiques and reproductions. The fireplace is an added benefit. A third chamber is also furnished with a king-size four-poster bed, although the antique, tall case clock is one of the more notable focal points. While the fireplace is appealing, our attention was focused instead on the lovely tapestry draperies that frame the picturesque garden views. Upon arrival, anyone staying in the house is treated to champagne and, in the morning, a full breakfast. In addition to the exquisite guest bedrooms and common areas in the main house, there are also a restaurant and bar on the first floor, located behind a large atrium. At the time of this writing, the restaurant was closed to the general public, but was still available for special functions or events.

During our tour of the mansion, our hostess revealed some of the fascinating history surrounding it. The land was purchased by Samuel Tate in 1834, although the mansion was built much later, in 1923, by Mr. Tate's grandson, Colonel Samuel Tate. Colonel Tate and his father played an integral role in this region's marble mining operations. During his lifetime, the Colonel discovered some rare Etowah pink marble that was being extracted from the quarry behind the eventual house site. Colonel Tate set aside for his personal use some of the nicest pieces, later drawing up plans for the construction of this mansion. The mansion was completed in 1926, but the Colonel lived in it for only 12 years before he died. Unfortunately, over the next 36 years it was sorely neglected. Besides falling into total disrepair, the house was ravaged by looters, and the grounds were left to go wild. Ann Laird discovered the disheveled estate back in 1974 and began a series of painstaking restorations to the building and the grounds. Today, its former grandeur has been restored. Undoubtedly, this would make Colonel Tate a proud man.

Walking around the property, guests will come across a swimming pool and tennis court, before arriving at the more recently constructed log cabins. The nine spacious cabins form a semi-circle that overlooks one of the larger, sprawling lawns. We found these buildings to be very attractive and appealing, both inside and out. Contained within these log walls is a large living room, with a set of stairs that climb to a lofted bedroom. A stone fireplace is the focal point for the living room, which is furnished with a pair of couches and chairs, along with the convenience of a television and a wet bar. The cabins are well designed, having windows wherever possible, which makes the honey-colored pine-walled rooms seem all the more open and airy. The lofts are surprisingly spacious and bright as well, with enough room for the king-size bed, a writing desk, and both arm and rocking chairs. The bathrooms are located on the first floor, along with hot tubs, which are placed in the corner of the living room. Brass lamps supply the light, and air conditioning cools the air. The rather simple decor and comfortable furnishings make these nicely furnished accommodations an inviting option for travelers and their canine companions.

In addition to the expansive grounds and woods and rural surroundings, there are a number of wilderness areas that will appeal to guests and their dogs. Just outside of Jasper are the Amicalola Falls, which are part of a 1,000-acre scenic preserve. Here, visitors will find picnic spots and hiking trails, along with an assortment of fishing opportunities. By far the biggest natural attraction is the Chattahoochee River National Recreation area with over 4,000 acres for visitors to explore. There are a wealth of things to do here, some of which include boating (rentals are available), hiking, picnicking, and even nature programs. The Tate House is an easy drive from Atlanta, but seemingly hundreds of miles from the hustle and bustle of civilization, making it a terrific destination for anyone wanting to truly get away from it all.

Susina Plantation Inn

Box 1010, Route 3
1420 Meridian Road
Thomasville, Georgia   31792
(912) 377-9644

Owner: Anne-Marie Walker
Rooms: 8 doubles
Rates: $125-175 (MAP)
Payment: Personal checks
Children: Welcome
Dogs: Welcome with prior approval
Open: All year

South of the historic Thomasville area, just a few miles from the Florida border, is a wonderful antebellum plantation house that has been transformed into a terrific southern-style inn. Originally built in 1841 by noted architect John Wind, the 6,000-square foot mansion was part of a prosperous cotton plantation. At one time, over 8,000 acres of land were being worked; but over the years the acreage was slowly sold off, ultimately reducing the overall property to its present level of 115 acres. We would have to say that the overall setting is not only bucolic, but also impressive. The approach to the Susina Plantation Inn is beautiful, with a long drive that leads past sprawling lawns dotted with lovely magnolias and majestic oaks dripping with Spanish moss. The mansion seems truly out of a southern novel. The two-story portico is supported by four massive Ionic columns, while expansive verandas lie off both sides of the house. Above the pair of front doors, a French balcony is fastened. To us "Northerners," this was just about as close to Gone with the Wind's Tara as we would probably ever get.

The interior is equally impressive, dominated by a freestanding, curved staircase that is a stately reflection of old world craftsmanship. Nothing is overdone, but it is all perfectly delightful and very inviting. The hardwood floor is covered with an Oriental rug runner, and walls are lined with period antiques and a pineapple motif wallpaper. Just off the foyer is a spacious, high-ceilinged living room. The pink-colored walls beckon guests to spend a little time relaxing in any of the comfortable sitting areas that are around the fireplace, the piano, and array of impressive antiques. To the rear of the living room is an elegant corner dining room. The light pours in through the wall of high windows, which are framed with sheer fabric and draped in a festoon and jabot arrangement. The high boxed-beamed ceilings, walls papered in an English floral print, and brick fireplace set the formal tone for this room. The mahogany, two-pedestal dining room table is surrounded by a set of Chippendale chairs. Off to the edge of the room is an antique sideboard, where tea can be served. This is also the setting for the full country breakfast and the five-course gourmet dinner that are served to guests each day. The ever changing dinner usually begins with a seafood appetizer, followed by a lovely salad, a vegetable soup (such as asparagus), and then the main course, which ranges from grilled quail to filet mignon. In addition to a dinner beautifully prepared and presented, guests are also offered a fine selection of wines to complement their meal. A wonderful assortment of homemade desserts follows, capping off a most delightful dining experience. Besides entertaining guests of the inn, Anne-Marie also stays very busy organizing business meetings, hosting weddings, and preparing elaborate murder mystery weekends.

As with the gracious common areas, each of the guest rooms exudes an old world ambiance that Anne-Marie has carefully cultivated. As one might imagine with a house of this size, the bedrooms are all very spacious, filled with antiques, and offer pleasing views of the grounds. One of our favorites is a corner room, which has been painted a hunter green and furnished with a four-poster canopy bed set opposite a fireplace. Just out the door lies one of the inn's porches. Another chamber, set across the hall, also contains a four-poster bed, but the walls are lined with grass paper. This room, and all the others on the right side of the house, have access to an expansive veranda overlooking the swimming pool and tennis court. Another guest room, painted an olive green, has a double bed placed between two windows. This heavy Empire mahogany bedstead rests on an Oriental carpet, and a mirrored dressing table has been placed alongside the decorative fireplace. Whether guests are relaxing with one of the inn's many good books, or just taking a long hot bath in one of the claw-footed bathtubs, they are sure to feel relaxed amid these tranquil surroundings.

During their stay, most people and their canine cohorts are more than content to spend their time on the plantation. This self-contained inn has most everything one might need right on the premises. Off to one side of the mansion are a tennis court, swimming pool, and single-story house, where the former owners used to stay during the colder off-season. The plantation also has a formal croquet course, as well as a stocked fish pond. Bowser will certainly enjoy exploring the assorted walking trails that cut through the property. A short drive west of Thomasville will bring visitors to the Earl May Boat Basin and Park in Bainbridge, where there are walking trails, along with fishing, swimming, and boating opportunities. Luckily, Thomasville was not burned or destroyed during the Civil War. In the years following the war, Northerners traveled here by train in the winter months to escape the cold weather. These were affluent folks, who built their own "plantations" for hunting purposes, not for the growing of cotton. The region is still renowned for its excellent duck, deer, quail, and turkey hunting. Those who visit during the right season might be interested in experiencing one of the local events, ranging from Mule Day and a rattlesnake round-up to a rose festival and assorted tobacco auctions. At day's end, return to Susina Plantation Inn, slip out onto the veranda, and enjoy a refreshing glass of lemonade or iced tea.

Evans House Bed and Breakfast

725 South Hansell Street
Thomasville, Georgia   31792
(800) 344-4717, (912) 226-1343, Fax (912) 226-0653

Hosts: Lee and John Puskar
Rooms: 1 single, 4 doubles
Rates: Single $65-95 (B&B), Doubles $70-115 (B&B)
Payment: Personal checks
Children: Most appropriate for children over the age of 12 (babysitters are available with advance notice)
Dogs: Welcome in the Regency Room, with advance notice and prior approval, provided the dog is crated when left alone.
Open: All year

Thomasville is a lovely, well-preserved, southern community that was somehow overlooked as the Civil War progressed and various portions of the south were torched. Both before and after the Civil War, the region was renowned for its fertile soil and ideal growing climate. Over the years, 70 plantations sprang up all around the small town of Thomasville. Today, the town not only boasts of seven historic districts, but also maintains a southern lifestyle that is reminiscent of another era. We have always felt that in order to gain an insider's perspective on a given region, it is important to stay in a small Bed and Breakfast, rather than a more impersonal motel. Because there is such close interaction between the guests and their hosts, it is far easier to gain an appreciation for the area's attributes. This is certainly the case at the Evans House, situated in the Parkland Historic District and just across the street from the 27-acre Paradise Park. The Victorian/Neoclassic-style house dates back to 1898, when it was built by Robert R. Evans. His wife added a second floor to it a few years later. After a fire in 1907, there were extensive repairs made to the house. Since that time the house has remained relatively intact, despite a few extensive renovation projects.

We arrived one sunny spring afternoon, to the serene setting of moss-draped shade trees and gardens in full boom. As we headed up the back walk, we encountered two resident cats surveying the action at the assorted bird feeders placed about the backyard. Lee greeted us at the kitchen door, and then gave us a tour of the first floor. Along the way, she explained that whichever room guests ultimately select, vases of fresh flowers and plates of homemade cookies will await them, as well as crisp linen sheets that are always turned down at night.

Our first stop was the Library bedroom, which, true to its name, contains a wall of built-in shelves filled with an interesting array of books. Off to the side is the Mission-style oak bed covered in a simple, white Bates spread. Like the other bedrooms, this one boasts of 12-foot high ceilings and an assortment of either turn-of-the century furnishings or more elegant antiques. Lee told us that many of their guests are intrigued with the claw-foot tub and its European hand-held shower head. On the other side of the hall, we came upon the Regency room. This is the most appropriate guest room for anyone traveling with a dog, as there is only a short distance from the bedroom to an outside entrance. We really liked this good-sized bedroom, especially since it was filled with a number of antiques. The king-size bed and writing desk are two of the more noteworthy highlights. Several brass lamps supply the subdued lighting, both around the bed and in the small sitting area. One of the room's more whimsical features is in the bathroom, where guests will discover an endearing stained glass window featuring a teddy bear.

Further down the hall, through the office, lies the coziest bedroom— the Rose Room. When we were visiting, this room was in the process of being modified and was slated to be finished soon. Up the staircase, past another appealing stained glass window (this time containing a rose), lies the Imperial room. This expansive corner room can be connected to the Blue Sitting Room to form the Imperial Suite. Aside from providing the most private accommodations in the house, these rooms are blessed with a good deal of afternoon sun. Lee told us about a newlywed couple who spent the first night of their honeymoon in this chamber. Lee's husband John, who has a large collection of puzzles, was busy working on a recent acquisition when the newly wedded husband wandered downstairs. He was so intrigued and engrossed with the puzzle that he and John ended up working on it for the better part of the night. It was not until the wee hours of the morning that he finally found his way back upstairs, finding his bride in a deep sleep. The house has always been a special spot for honeymooners, going back to Mrs. Evan's lifetime. Evidently, as her brothers and sisters married, they would come to live in the house and she would charge them rent to help make ends meet. Mrs. Evan's children used to call it "Honeymoon House on Paradise Park," a description that would be equally appropriate today.

Every morning, guests make a point of getting up for the gourmet breakfast. It is served in either the dining room or the expansive breakfast room. The menu varies with the day; guests should stay a full week for a sampling of all Lee's treats. One morning, she might prepare a baked grapefruit with brown sugar and cinnamon, followed by strawberry crepes topped with an orange sauce and yogurt. This may be accompanied by country ham or bacon and an angel food strudel. Another day, fresh fruit salad is followed by John's infamous Cuckoos Nest, an egg casserole with sausage, ham, or bacon, and spiced cheese. A homemade nut roll or strawberry jelly roll rounds out this dish. Eggs Benedict on a croissant or the fresh apricot or raspberry French toast are two other delightful options. Since an authentic southern breakfast should be experienced, at some point, during anyone's visit, we recommend trying the eggs and country sausage, accompanied by the grits and buttermilk biscuits.

After a meal like this, it's important to take an invigorating walk. The park is just across the road. Upon returning, some enjoy relaxing on the expansive, columned front porch and reading the morning paper. A little later, many guests venture down the tree-lined brick streets in the historic part of town, or they may head out to visit one of the numerous plantations in the area. One attraction that should not be missed is the well-preserved Pebble Hill Plantation, an exquisite southern shooting plantation. Some guests also enjoy driving west to the 600-acre Lake Seminole, where there are a variety of swimming and boating options available to visitors and their dogs. North of Thomasville, vacationers will find the Reed Bingham recreation area, with over 1,600 acres of land—ideal for hiking, swimming, boating, and picnicking.

Florida

★ Fernandina Beach

★ Ponte Vedre

★ St. Augustine

★ Flagler Beach

★ Apalachicola

Inverness ★

Orlando ★

★ Kissimmee

Brandon
Madeira Beach ★ ★ Treasure Island

★ Lake Wales

Longboat Key ★

★ Siesta Key

Stuart

Palm Beach ★

Boca Grande ★

Captiva Island ★ ★ Sanibel

Delray Beach ★

Ft. Lauderdale ★

Naples ★
Everglades City ★

Bal Harbour ★
Miami

Florida

Key West ★ ★ Marathon

The Gibson Inn

100 Market Street
Apalachicola, Florida   32320-1776
(904) 653-2191

Owner: Michael Koun
Rooms: 28 doubles, 2 suites
Rates: Doubles $55-80 (EP), Suites $80-110 (EP)
Payment: AE, MC, and VISA
Children:Welcome (cribs, cots, and high chairs are available)
Dogs: Welcome
Open: All year

Apalachicola isn't easy to spell, or to pronounce—nor is it easy to find, since it is well off the beaten path that Florida's tourists usually follow. We recommend, though, that guests take a chance and travel north by northwest, away from the Keys, Miami, the Gold Coast, and Disney World—and keep driving until they eventually reach Florida's Panhandle. This diverse coastline is edged by sleepy southern-style towns and cities that have generally escaped the hand of the resort developers. To better understand the area and its populace, it is first important to become acquainted with its history.

First there were the Seminoles, whom the Spanish conquistadors tried to displace in the 1600s. (They were mildly successful.) The next group of interlopers had far more luck. These were the plantation owners from the bordering southern states, who realized that the rich soil was perfect for growing cotton. While most of the cotton was grown inland, tiny Apalachicola turned out to be a natural seaport for shipping the cotton. Most of it was shipped by boat from Alabama and Georgia, down the Apalachicola River. The cotton boom was over at the end of the Civil War, but the port remained open, as cypress was now the raw material of choice being shipped down the river. This was a short-lived period in the town's history, however. Since then, the town has become more dependent on the ocean, not the river, for its livelihood. Today, the bulk of the country's oyster beds lie just off Apalachicola's shore, and some of the 2,600 people who live here either work the beds or fish the coastal waters.

In addition to the cotton and cypress coming from the north, crushed quartz also ran out of the Appalachian Mountains down the Apalachicola River, forming the white powdery sand beaches that now line the Panhandle's coastline. The combination of white sands and turquois waters are being rediscovered once again, but this time people are coming to simply enjoy the area's natural beauty—not to exploit it. This was certainly the case for two brothers, Michael and Neil Kouhn, who bought the Gibson Inn in 1983, restored it, and opened its guest rooms and restaurant to the public. Life here has not been the same since. The inn, once known as the Franklin, was built in 1907 by James Fulton Buck of South Carolina. It must have been resplendent in its day; however, the building went through a long period of neglect before the Kouhns found it. From what we understand, the place was well built and the interior spaces and detailed woodwork have managed to survive over time.

It is easy to find the Gibson Inn; just look for a rambling Victorian building, topped by tin roofs and a cupola. The cypress shingles are painted blue, and two floors of wraparound porches provide crisp white accents. Wide steps lead to the first veranda, where guests walk past old-fashioned rocking chairs, through a pair of doors, and into another era. The black cypress beams and hardwood floors serve as strong reminders of life at the turn of the century. The craftsmen who originally built this place could not have known how beautifully the paneling, moldings, and wainscoting would mellow with the years. The most obvious example of their work is in the handcrafted staircase that rises to the second and third floors.

The only similarity among the bedrooms is the fact that they are located off a central hall. Otherwise, each is distinctive. Most are furnished with turn-of-the-century antiques, such as white iron and brass or four-poster, carved wood bedsteads covered with soft sheets and comforters. Some chambers have antique armoires containing televisions, while others are fashioned with writing tables and armchairs. The bathrooms are private, and guests may expect to see pedestal sinks set alongside claw-footed tubs. The fixtures are often original brass and porcelain pieces. Guests may request a corner room, where multiple, double-hung windows open to let in the cooling Gulf breezes. Or, when the day is still, they might turn on the paddle fans instead. Hardwood floors are still in good shape and are often protected by dhurrie or braided rugs. This place is not at all overdone. In fact, some of the furnishings look as if they have experienced some good use, which give them, and the inn, all the more character. Modern concessions are few, except for air conditioning, cable television, and telephones.

While the overnight accommodations are terrific, they are not necessarily the Gibson Inn's most noteworthy feature. It is the dining room that shares the accolades. In here, the original beams and tongue-and-groove paneling helped us to gain a better sense of the inn's historic authenticity. Off-white walls and original globe lamps further enhance the ambiance. Just as the inn rooms are reasonably priced, so is the gourmet fare that is presented each night. Unless guests are allergic to oysters (and there is a warning on the menu), this is the place to try them. They are served raw, or cooked as oysters Rockefeller or Remick. Some people enjoy them lightly fried; others prefer them in the seafood sampler, which combines Gulf shrimp, scallops, stuffed crab, and the fresh fish of the day. Oysters Remick may also be ordered as an entrée off a special menu. The oysters are first poached and then topped with a horseradish and chili sauce. Swiss cheese is grated over the top and the entire concoction is baked. Another delicious option is the shrimp, scallop and crab Dijon, a platter that is sautéed with mushrooms and shallots in white wine and butter. It is then placed in a puff pastry, topped with provolone cheese and Dijon butter, and baked. Those who are not fish fans may prefer to indulge in the equally tantalizing filet mignon, prime rib, or chicken Cordon Bleu. Most meals include the perennial favorites: hush puppies. It won't be easy, but guests should save a little room for the chocolate bourbon pecan pie, Key Lime pie, or the Mississippi mud pie. They won't regret it.

Afterwards, guests may want to go get Bowser and take a quiet evening walk—and just enjoy the feeling of being in a small, friendly southern town. This may be Florida, but the azaleas, camellias, and Spanish moss dripping from the trees certainly make people feel as though they are somewhere else in the deep south. While this is technically a seaport, it is a quiet one that has plenty of character. The inn is actually four blocks from the water, but guests will still have the feeling of being right on the Gulf coast. In recent years, the beaches around here have gotten plenty of publicity, because they are still relatively unspoiled. Just off Apalachicola, there are a few barrier islands, some of which have been left in their natural state. As visitors will notice, there are thousands of acres of state and national parks in Florida, but very few of them allow dogs on the beaches. The beautiful island of St. George does allow canines, and visitors should take advantage of it. There are 1,800 acres out here, consisting of white sandy beaches and dunes, hiking trails, and areas for bird watching. The staff at the inn highly recommends this adventure, and so do we. Another place worth investigating is Cape Sandblast, just across from Port St. Joe. By the way, the staff members are animal people and are also quick to provide additional suggestions for other out-of-the-way spots to visit with a canine companion. Lastly, we should say that guests don't need to worry about mispronouncing Apalachicola—Apalach will do just fine.

Sheraton Bal Harbour

9701 Collins Avenue
Bal Harbour, Florida 33154
(800) 325-3535, (305) 865-7511, Fax (305) 864-2610

General Manager: *Joe Terzi*
Rooms: *615 doubles, 53 suites*
Rates: *Doubles $110-260 (EP), Suites $285-500 (EP)*
Payment: *AE, DC, DSC, MC, and VISA*
Children: *Welcome; those under 17 years of age are free of charge when*
staying in rooms with their parents (cribs, cots, high chairs,
babysitters, and extensive children's programs are available)
Dogs: *Those under 20 pounds are welcome*
Open: *All year*

The Sheraton Bal Harbour provides the experience of a private and exclusive community within the equally exclusive city of Bal Harbour. The hotel's facade tells little about its interior, but one step through the front doors and the elegant decor reveals itself. There are no sharp angles in the atrium foyer, just three tall stories of curved walls fitted with paned windows. Beneath the windows, facing the ocean, is a semicircular bar topped by waves of frosted glass, giving visitors an impression of looking out over frothy ocean waves. This private retreat is the perfect setting for enjoying an afternoon libation. Massive potted palms and other trees provide a lush canopy of green, both here in the foyer and throughout the expansive lobby. As guests walk across the lobby's marble floors over to the banks of elevators on the other side, they come across huge, elegant flower arrangements set upon verdigris and marble tables.

Various wings of the hotel house a multitude of guest rooms. Perhaps the best choice for those traveling with a dog are the Garden Villas. We took an elevator, unobtrusively set off by itself, to reach this wing of rooms located on ground level. These lovely suites contain a living room, a small dining nook, and a separate bedroom that is accessed through a pair of glass doors. Large windows in the living room overlook the swimming pools, as well as the ocean beyond. Although in some of the villas the furnishings are slightly dated, they are still very attractive, and nicely enhanced by the array of amenities. The living room and bedroom each have separate televisions. Each villa is also furnished with a clock radio, an in-room safe, walk-in closets, and a mini-bar. Gourmet coffee (Starbucks) is used for the in-room coffee makers. The rather small bathrooms are well stocked with toiletries, a hair dryer, and thick towels. A separate outside entrance allows ease of access from the villas to the sandy path that runs behind the dunes and along the beach.

The bedrooms in the main part of the hotel are quite different from the villas, although all have an unusual sense of spaciousness. Even the standard doubles have huge dressing rooms and walk-in closets that allow for additional privacy and storage. Some contain sleek, polished wood tables and chairs designed especially for the hotel; others are furnished with attractive, pickled wood bureaus, headboards, and desks. In most of the rooms, chairs with ottomans are well-placed by windows. In some, more elaborate sitting areas have been created with sofas and armchairs. Color schemes are light, with varying shades of green and taupe, flecked with maroon. Local Florida scenes are depicted in the artwork, with lithographs of a simple banyan tree, for example, or a grove of palms amid a beachfront setting. Some guest rooms have high ceilings and brick walls that have been painted out white, while others have private terraces and expansive ocean views.

This is a resort destination, which is expanding even as we write. We were impressed with the extensive amenities already available to hotel guests. For instance, there is the Camp Bal Harbour, designed for children ages 5-12. Children may enjoy a full schedule of activities, such as games, arts and crafts, volleyball, basketball, treasure hunts, swimming, and much more. By the beginning of 1996, the physical space for the children's camp and adult recreation center will have been completely redesigned. This is also true for the swimming pools, which is perhaps the biggest modification to be made to the hotel. A design firm that has created other elaborate resort water parks will spend over $12 million to dramatically alter the two existing pools. Large boulders will create a 17-foot waterfall (along with a couple of Jacuzzi waterfalls), which will lead to a water slide that will feed into a river running into the pool. Of course, all this would not be complete without the waterside tropical bar, where swimmers may enjoy their favorite libations before venturing out for a little more fun in the water. Another part of the resort complex that is being upgraded is the tennis courts. Currently, these are located on the rooftops of some low-lying oceanfront buildings, but a new 16,000 square-foot outdoor facility is being built.

Amidst all the changes, the white sand beach remains a primary draw for the resort. There are actually two parts to the beach: a wide, sandy jogging path (which serves as a type of secondary beach) lies at the edge of the hotel property; on its other side are low dunes, with the main beach and ocean just beyond them. Dogs are not allowed on the main beach, but they may walk for miles along the wide secondary beach. We saw runners, walkers, and plenty of dogs enjoying this scenic oceanside setting, where water views appear at the breaks in the dunes. Guests and their dogs may also enjoy a leisurely stroll through the adjacent downtown section of Bal Harbour, which still maintains its

Old Florida feeling. Just across from the hotel are the exclusive Bal Harbour Shops, located in an outdoor atrium mall. Here, Gucci and Chanel boutiques peacefully coexist beside F.A.O. Schwartz and the Banana Republic. There are also a few stylish outdoor restaurants that are as popular with the locals as they are with the hotel guests. Those who prefer to stay home for meals will find a number of casual and exotic eateries right on the premises. The Garden Café serves a buffet style Continental fare, intermixed with a few à la carte dishes. This is an ideal option for families, as the children can eat at a reduced price. The more formal restaurant is also undergoing renovation and will reopen as Al Carbones, specializing in Mediterranean cuisine. Eventually, there will also be the Ocean Grill, which will draw people as much for its food as for its outdoor terrace seating supplying unobstructed views of the ocean.

The Sheraton Bal Harbour is well situated, because it is close to Miami Beach, without being too close. Vacationers who yearn for a beautiful stretch of relatively quiet beach front, who want to feel comfortable going walking in the streets, and who enjoy a little touch of Old Florida mixed with New Florida sophistication, should definitely consider investigating this lovely hotel.

Bay Harbor Inn

9660 East Bay Harbor Drive
Bay Harbor Islands, Florida 33154
(305) 868-4141, Fax (305) 868-4141 ext. 602

Owners: *Sandy and Celeste Lankler*
Rooms: *22 doubles and 14 suites*
Rates: *Doubles $60-116 (B&B), Suites $80-225 (B&B)*
Payment: *AE, CB, DC, MC, and VISA*
Children: *Welcome (cribs, cots, and high chairs are available)*
Dogs: *Welcome in the Creekside Building, for a $12 daily fee*
Open: *All year*

Miami is a cultural melting pot, with as ethnically diverse a population as can be found just about anywhere in the United States. Hotels and inns distinguish themselves by the clientele they attract, with some catering to the hip Eurocrowd, others to old-world eastern Europeans, and still others to the South Americans. The Bay Harbor Inn seems to attract all types. Perhaps guests are drawn to the blend of old

Miami—found in the original 1940s inn—and new Miami, represented in the more contemporary Creekside Building. These two facets integrate well to form a small enclave on the Bay Harbor Islands. Perhaps, too, the reason people especially enjoy the inn is the staff, who treat guests like long lost friends. Staff members are both friendly and accommodating, even chatty. We don't claim to understand the strong appeal, but whatever it is, it works.

Guests' first impressions of the Bay Harbor Inn are of the peach stucco inn. A short, semi-circular drive leads under an awning, where there is always someone available to help off-load luggage and park the car. Two pairs of flanking doors, topped by Palladian windows, lead guests into the high-ceilinged lobby. The naturally-stained hardwood floors are set with formal wingback chairs and oak Victorian sofas and tables. Paddle fans gently circulate the air. The suites and bedrooms that lie upstairs have carpeted floors, instead of the hardwood found in the lobby. They also offer a mix of traditional Georgian antiques and Victorian oak, which give these spaces their distinctive personalities. These accommodations, while very nice, are not appropriate for people traveling with a dog. Instead, Bowser is invited to stay in the rather contemporary Creekside Building, which lies kitty-corner and across the street from the inn.

Very often, when an inn becomes well known and the owners need more bedrooms, they will build fairly nondescript motel units somewhere else on the property. These usually lack the charm of the inn, but they do aid in accommodating an overflow of guests. This is not the case, however, at the Bay Harbor Inn, where accommodations in the two-story Creekside Building are perhaps even more desirable than those in the inn. These extraordinarily large spaces are furnished with streamlined contemporary furnishings that replace the eclectic collection of antiques and reproductions found at the inn. Sage green and peach are the colors of choice for the coordinated floral bedspreads and tieback draperies that frame the wall of floor-to-ceiling glass doors and windows. All the creature comforts people would expect from a full-service hotel can be found here: cable television, private telephones, air conditioning, refrigerators—even irons and ironing boards. Modern bathrooms are equally well appointed with soft cotton towels, blow dryers, and an array of toiletries. Most views from the Creekside Building are appealing; however, we would recommend reserving one of the bedrooms facing the Intercostal Waterway, where palm trees and water combine to create an exceptionally peaceful setting. Rooms that are considered "garden view" are located on the second floor and overlook the amoeba-shaped heated swimming pool, which is framed by still more palm trees and tropical foliage. This is truly a little oasis that constantly surprises guests, who are often used to the high-rise buildings in neighboring Miami Beach. Each morning, guests can rise early and step out to the private, tiled patio where it is fun to observe the activity on the waterway below. The ample Continental breakfast is served on the Yacht Celeste, which is tied up along the Creekside Building.

The Bay Harbor Inn is owned and operated by the Lanklers, and although they have only owned it for nine years, they have imbued the inn with a sense of tradition. One of these traditions is the Palm Restaurant, housed in the historic part of the inn. A green and white striped awning denotes the entrance to this restaurant, which is a spin-off of the original Palm Restaurant started in New York City in 1927. The atmosphere is reminiscent of an old-fashioned private club, where waiters wear starched white aprons, are exceptionally professional, and serve plentiful portions. Patrons are surrounded by caricatures of Hollywood stars and the politically famous, interspersed with an occasional stuffed sea turtle or some other marine creature. Many enjoy starting the meal by sampling the jumbo shrimp or crabmeat cocktails, or perhaps the clams casino. Guests shouldn't expect French sauces or Nouvelle Cuisine, but they may freely choose from the huge swordfish steaks, lamb chops, prime rib, or filet mignon, as well as the house specialty, the 32-ounce New York sirloin for two. Veal Piccata, Marsala, Milanese, or Parmigiana fill out the veal menu. Anyone who wants to enjoy an after-dinner drink, might head back over to the piano bar, which is filled with antiques from the Vanderbilt mansion in London.

There are a variety of diversions in the nearby area that Bowser will enjoy. The Bay Harbor Islands are on Biscayne Bay, slightly north of Miami Beach. The tiny enclave of Bal Harbour is just over the bridge. It has as a gorgeous beach, and even better shopping and people-watching alternatives. When conversing with the staff, we learned that some people come and stay at the Bay Harbor Inn because it is conveniently located next to the exclusive Bal Harbour Shops. Most leave their cars at the inn and walk across the short drawbridge to the shops, as parking there can be both expensive and difficult to come by. While some may not be interested in taking their canine companion shopping, the walk over to Bal Harbour is certainly a nice one. There are also a number of lovely side streets, as well as impressive gated residences and beautiful homes that are an appealing backdrop to walks with Bowser. We think one great expedition is out to the beach. Dogs are not allowed on the main beach, but they may enjoy the secondary sandy path that fronts it. Here, visitors are welcome to walk, jog, or play with their dogs.

We think the Bay Harbor Inn is a preferable alternative to the countless large hotels in nearby communities. The rates are reasonable and the staff is most affable, leaving us with a good feeling about this hidden oasis.

Gasparilla Inn & Cottages

P.O. Box 1088
Fifth Avenue at Palm Avenue
Boca Grande, Florida   33921
(813) 964-2201, Fax (813) 964-2733

General Manager: Stephen F. Seidensticker
Rooms: 140 doubles, 20 cottages
Rates: Social Season $160-218 (AP), Tarpon Season $112-148 (MAP), All
*   rates are per person*
Payment: Personal checks
Children: Welcome (cribs, cots, and babysitters are available)
Dogs: Welcome in the cottages only
Open: Mid-December through mid-June

To understand the appeal of the Gasparilla Inn, it helps to know a little something about Gasparilla Island. Fishing has always been an integral part of the culture, and fishermen were some of the first semi-permanent island residents, living on land they acquired through squatters' rights. They caught red snapper, grouper, yellow tail, and snook, as well as the famous tarpon. In the late 1800s and early 1900s, the island became well known to the country's industrialists, who were mining phosphate on the mainland. One of these phosphate mining concerns, the American Agricultural Chemical Company (AACC), needed a deep water port from which to ship its product to other parts of the country. Gasparilla Island was chosen as the port site. The chemical company acquired enough land to obtain railroad rights, then set about laying tracks that would carry the trains and the phosphate from the mainland to the port. The company later joined forces with a handful of wealthy industrialists to coordinate further development of the island. In 1911, the luxurious Gasparilla Inn was built to accommodate the well-to-do. The hope was that they would invest in the island by purchasing land and building houses.

Fortunately for today's residents, the grand plan failed. The island did attract a group of wealthy individuals who, preferring a low-key existence, quietly formed a small cottage community along the water. They also tried to limit commercial development on the island. These "beachfronters," as they were known, banded together in the mid-1920s to form the Gasparilla Island Association. They were "primarily interested in perpetuating [Gasparilla Island's] natural beauty and the charm of its individuality. The cottage colony at Boca Grande is expanding some each year, but it is still a small village and probably always will be." The Island Association literature continues by stating that "Boca Grande is entirely residential and there are no commercial activities—other than the village shops —within the community. Boca Grande was not affected by the Florida boom one way or the other. It has had no boom, will have no boom, and does not seek speculative investors." Today, walking through the tiny village of Boca Grande, it is apparent that there exists here the same traditional feeling that existed in the 1920s. There are few shops, except for the famous Loose Caboose ice cream store and The Patio, a general merchandise store that has all sorts of wonderful gifts, clothes, and necessities. Just a block away, and perfectly integrated into the community, is the Gasparilla Inn. The original inn was housed in a 20-room, box-shaped building, but after opening in 1912 it was quickly enlarged to look more like the inn we see today. The formal facade is accented with yellow clapboards and white trim. Columns rise three floors to provide the framework for a portico and a grouping of porches. The inn rambles off to the left and to the back, creating a cavernous hotel that exudes an old world charm.

We arrived during the height of the social season, when well-behaved children seemed to have the run of the place. As their parents and grandparents looked on (this is a multi-generational spot), we found the youngsters making themselves at home in the formal Pelican Club, with its pecky cypress walls, a pocket billiard table, and inviting leather chairs and sofas. A set of alligator jaws are displayed in here, along with a stuffed Florida panther. Shells combed from the beaches are displayed in cases all over the room. The huge living room is equally appealing. A grass-green ceiling is framed by white boxed beams. The many private sitting areas in here are set with comfortable sofas, chintz covered armchairs, and white wicker tables. Lovely chintz fabrics are draped over round tables and stitched into balloon shades framing the elongated windows. During the cool months, a fire is lit in the white brick fireplace. Some guests enjoy playing the grand piano set at the end of this inviting salon, or they retire to one of the several enclosed porches for a game of bridge or backgammon. Visitors should look carefully at the backgammon tables, because rather than containing the usual triangular points, these handmade wooden boards are inlaid with periwinkle shells. The upstairs bedrooms are all oversized, a bit dated, and furnished in a style similar to that of the public rooms.

Guests traveling with a dog stay in the cottages set on streets adjacent to the inn. The cottages blend right in with the neighborhood; in some cases, we had to look twice to be sure we were in the right spot. The cottages are miniature versions of the inn and are built in the Old Florida style, with interesting eaves, double hung windows, and, in some cases, Palladian windows. Guests may reserve a standard bedroom or request a bedroom and parlor. Most have screened-in porches that provide even more living space, and some contain kitchenettes. Old

Florida ambiance prevails inside as well, with attractive wicker and rattan furnishings setting the tone. Beds are usually higher than the norm, and backed by yellow or white lacquered headboards. The bright tropical pattern spreads do much to enliven the spaces. French doors open to the porches or parlors, providing extra space that guests undoubtedly appreciate and use. Visitors can step out the door onto lawns that lead to sidewalks lined with black iron gas lamps. At night, the path to the inn is well lit, guiding guests to and from their dinner.

During social season, all meals are taken at the hotel. The main dining room is reminiscent of The Cloister, another formal southern hotel on Sea Island, Georgia. Many of the inn's staff have worked here for years. In fact, the maître d' has been overseeing operations for over 25 years. The bright yellow walls and lime green chairs seem just as ageless, lending a certain charm to the dining room. The menu changes daily and is just as traditional as its surroundings. An appetizer of shrimp or smoked salmon is accompanied by the crudité tray, juices, and homemade breads. This is followed by the hot consomme, jellied bouillon, or gazpacho. Main courses might include the fresh pompano, filet mignon, osso bucco, or sautéed lump crab on a bed of spinach. The strawberry shortcake, ice cream cake with a black rum sauce, and homemade ice creams are just a sampling of the assorted desserts. Coat and tie for men is still required in the evening, but during the day the dress is casual, especially at the Beach and Tennis Club. This is beachside dining at its best, as guests enjoy a buffet lunch on the porch overlooking the sparkling blue waters of the Gulf of Mexico. Golfers may wish to dine at the Pink Elephant restaurant, after playing on the gorgeous 18-hole course adjacent to the inn. Croquet is also available on three different professional courses. Children will get their fair share of exercise in one of the two heated swimming pools—one at the beach, the other on the children's playground adjacent to the cottages.

Bowser should not feel left out of the action, as this is an extremely dog-friendly community. The old railroad tracks may be gone, but a terrific jogging path runs along the former rail bed. Those who prefer pedaling may rent a bicycle from the inn and take Bowser for a run around the island. Equally appealing, and far less strenuous, are the lovely walks through this quiet, picturesque community. Many of the side streets are lined with banyan trees and, in some cases, the branches have grown together to form a lush, green tunnel over the road. Grab Bowser, head down to the docks, and take the boat over to Cayo Costa for the day. This island is lush with vegetation, but even better are the pristine beaches that everyone, including dogs, can explore together. Bowser will also certainly enjoy walking on the incredibly soft, white sand beaches, which are as great for shelling as they are for aimless wanderings. Gasparilla Island is truly a small piece of paradise, one that the locals try to keep as private and as peaceful as possible.

Behind the Fence

1400 Viola Drive @ Countryside
Brandon, Florida 33511
(813) 685-8201

Hosts: Larry and Carolyn Yoss
Rooms: 1 single, 1 double, 1 suite, 1 cottage
Rates: Single $45-55 (B&B), Double $55-65 (B&B), Suite $65-75 (B&B),
    Cottage $65-75 (B&B)
Payment: Personal checks
Children: Welcome (high chair and cot are available)
Dogs: Welcome with a $10 fee in the cottage rooms
Open: All year except in July

"Behind the Fence," the name of this cozy Bed and Breakfast, derives from the proprietor's Amish heritage, and has a meaning not immediately apparent to visitors. Amish communities have a strong religious base that stresses simplicity and self-reliance. In the purest orders, farming is done without chemicals or modern machinery, and everything is literally made by hand. Amish people are self-sufficient individuals who have tried to peacefully coexist with the modern world. As the years progress and Amish children grow into adults, it is becoming increasingly difficult to keep the next generation on the farm. Carolyn and Larry Yoss know all about this dilemma, as Larry grew up in a predominantly Amish community in Ohio and the Yoss's son-in-law, who has also left his home community, was raised Amish. Anyone who leaves the Amish community is called a "fence-jumper"—which is why the Yoss's felt it was appropriate to call their Bed and Breakfast "Behind the Fence."

The house and cottage at this B&B are historically accurate copies of an 1800s saltbox house and cottage. Set well off the road, under the canopy of massive oaks and pines, they appear to be the real thing. The exterior walls are only 20 years old, but much of the interior, including the doors, windows, stairs, paneling and molding, was crafted in the late 1800s. Carolyn told us that before their house was a B&B, whenever the area's historic structures were to be torn down, the Yosses were contacted; they would then go to the site, salvage appropriate pieces off these buildings, and add them to their own home. As a result, what is now the B&B has an array of historic features that are representative of Florida's architectural history. Equally authentic are the Amish furnishings, which the Yosses collected when they lived in Ohio. The culmination of their efforts were so stunning and unusual that the Brandon League of Fine Arts asked the Yosses to open their house to tour groups—partly as a fundraiser and partly because the house had historic and educational value. Once the Yosses started to share their home with the public, the next natural step was to permit overnight guests to immerse themselves in the ambiance of the place. In 1994, the Yosses finally decided to open their home as a B&B.

While the main house is the center of activity for guests, those staying here with a dog are asked to stay in the cottage. As it turns out, the two bedrooms in the cottages are not only our preferred accommodations, but they are also the most private. The cottage, built as an authentic reproduction, is surrounded by ferns, azaleas, and native wild flowers. Six-over-six double hung windows are framed by shutters, and interior walls have been made from white-washed boards that have small gaps between them. Antique beds, including a four-poster pencil post, are covered with soft linens that reflect traditional Amish colors. Decorative and antique baskets, wreaths, and mirrors add interest to the walls and tables. In one room, a ladder back chair and blanket stand are set against a wall, while in another, an antique blanket chest lies at the end of the bed. One bathroom has a claw-footed shower/tub, along with a pine chest for storing towels and sundries. An old wash basin containing a pitcher of flowers is an appealing touch. The cottage's porch overlooks the intimate swimming pool, which has been carefully designed to blend into its surroundings. Large, flat stones create the decking, but it is the pool's dark bottom, that makes the water appear a deep blue and truly enhances the already naturalized setting. The overall effect is of a quiet and secluded place that feels as though it is hundreds of miles from civilization.

A short walk from the cottage brings guests over to the saltbox for breakfast. This is served in the dining room, which overlooks the yard through a bow window. The patina of the window moldings provides a handsome contrast to the white plaster walls. Bunches of dried flowers and herbs hang from the rafters. A corner hutch and trestle table are just two of the many beautiful antiques found about the house. At breakfast, fresh fruit, cereal, and toast are accompanied by coffee and tea. However, most memorable are the homemade Amish sweet rolls, which come from the restaurant owned by the Yoss's daughter and son-in-law. With a little advance notice, breakfast trays will be brought to the bedrooms for a more private and leisurely meal. At some point during their stay, guests will want to explore the house a little more. One entire wall of one room is dedicated to old black and white photographs, outlined by burlwood frames as lovely as the pictures they hold. Beneath this display is an old wooden church pew, draped in a handwoven blanket. On the pew are seated a doll and several antique handcrafted stuffed bears. There is a treasure in just about every corner, which makes this charming B&B seem more like a living museum than an intimate hostelry.

The town of Brandon may not be a premier tourist destination, but it is close to many of the more notable attractions of the area. Set on the outskirts of Tampa, it is only a short trip to Lake Wales, and to Braedenton, the citrus capital of the state. Two small parks, Hillsborough River State Park and Lake Manatee State Park, are within easy driving distance. For a longer outing, guests may choose from among the beaches off St. Petersburg or drive south (one of our favorite adventures) to the keys off Sarasota. From Boca Grande, day trip over to the Cayo Costa nature area where there are acres of trails and beaches that allow Bowser. This entire region has been called Florida's nature coast. To find a little bit of that nature, guests may also visit the park next to Behind the Fence, where there are nature trails to explore and tennis courts to play on.

'Tween Waters Inn

Box 249
Beach Road
Captiva Island, Florida 33924
(800) 223-5868, (941) 472-5161, (941) 472-0249

Manager: Jeff Shuff
Rooms: 65 doubles, 14 apartments, 47 cottages
Rates: Doubles $135-230 (EP), Apartments $170-250 (EP),
*   Cottages $80-270 (EP)*
Payment: DSC, MC, and VISA
Children: Welcome; children under 12 are no charge (cribs, cots-$5, high
*   chairs, and babysitters are available)*
Dogs: Welcome in select units, for $8 a day, provided they are leashed when
*   on the property.*
Open: All year

Anyone who has the impression that coastal Florida is made up of densely packed high-rise buildings and very little open space should take a closer look at its southwest coast. The islands of Sanibel and Captiva are the antithesis of their east coast counterparts. There are thousands of acres of natural preserves; calm, turquoise-blue Gulf waters; and soft, white sandy beaches topped with an array of exotic shells. Houses and small resorts are discreetly tucked behind lush foliage, and even the complexes of boutiques and restaurants are often difficult to see from the main road. A causeway links the mainland to

Sanibel and, further up the road, the two islands are joined at Blind Pass by a short bridge.

The 'Tween Waters Inn lies just north of the bridge between Sanibel and Captiva. After crossing the bridge onto Captiva, the road appears to narrow considerably as the jungle of foliage closes in on the strip of pavement. Look closely and drive slowly, so as not to miss the inn. The 'Tween Waters Inn rests on a strip of land separating the Gulf of Mexico from the Pine Island Sound. Given the number of storms that have blown through here, it is remarkable that the inn has remained intact for over 60 years. Actually, the resort as we see it today originated from one cottage built by a Virginia couple. They and their children added to the property until 1969, when it was sold to investors. The investors' "enlightened" concept was to bulldoze the entire place and turn it into a condominium complex. Fortunately, the idea never came to fruition and another group of investors from upstate New York purchased the resort in 1976 to preserve "a bit of island history and nostalgia." The Shuffs have been here ever since, successfully maintaining the inn's traditions and adding a few modern touches.

Visitors staying at 'Tween Waters should know they are in good company. Some of the inn's more notable guests have included Anne Morrow Lindbergh (who wrote *A Gift from the Sea* while staying here), Canadian wildlife artist Robert Bateman, and the renowned New York Times cartoonist and conservationist J. N. "Ding" Darling. (Darling also worked to help establish the 5,000 acre J.N. "Ding" Darling National Wildlife Refuge on Sanibel.) For many of these famous guests, the cottages became their temporary home away from home.

People staying here with a dog are welcome in select cottages, set on different parts of the property. Unfortunately, the cottages allowing dogs do not offer water views; however, they do make up for that with their character. The exterior colors are yellow and white or pale salmon, and the architecture is truly Old Florida. Our two favorite cottages are numbers 105 and 106, which are tucked just back from the main road in a stand of pine trees. Number 105 is a one-room cottage, containing a double and a twin bed, along with a cozy kitchenette. The two screened-in porches provide a little extra outdoor living space. The cottage next door is substantially larger, with two bedrooms, a kitchenette, and a living room with a brick fireplace. The decor varies, depending upon the cottage and when it was last updated. Most of the floors are tiled and, in some cases, the spaces are brightened by pickled wood walls. Furnishings are generally a mix of naturally-stained rattan sofas and chairs set alongside glass-topped tables. A small formica table, fine for casual breakfasts and lunches, suffices nicely, with most guests opting to eat in one of the local restaurants for dinner. The amenities are well conceived, although not overwhelming. All the accommodations have a refrigerator, a safe, a cable television, and a private telephone.

The other cottages that accept dogs are placed along one edge of the property, close to the swimming pool. Unfortunately, there are fewer plantings and trees around these buildings, but as a result, the cottages allow more light inside them. The most spacious are numbers 138 and 139. These are the cottages closest to both the beach and the road. We have been told that the road noise can sometimes be bothersome. Toward the rear of the property there are more one-room cottages, which appealed to us because they are quieter and have small private patios. The decor in these is similar to that of the other units. Anyone who happens to be here without a dog can stay in the larger, two-story buildings that face either the Gulf of Mexico or the sound. These are modern units that are carpeted, attractively decorated and, most importantly, have nice water views.

Guests will find plenty to do at the inn. This is a supremely casual spot, yet there exists a level of refinement that makes it seem like a private club. The charming lanes that wend around the cottages are unpaved, the paths are made of sand, and the wooden boardwalks are linked by rope handrail—but all this merely adds to the low-key atmosphere of the place. To the rear of the property there is an Olympic-size swimming pool, where guests will find plenty of deck space, chaise lounges, and even a few thatched huts. One of these huts contains the No Se Um Pool Bar and Poolside Grill, which serves lunch and an assortment of refreshing libations. Adjacent to the pool are three tennis courts. There is also a marina where Hobie Cats, motor boats, or canoes may be rented to explore the backwaters of the sound. Upon request, the staff will secure fishing guides, provide bait and tackle, or recommend the best areas for shelling. There are also shuffleboard and bocci courts on the premises. But the most popular place of all is the beach, where cabañas and umbrellas are set out to protect people from the hot sun. Of course, the warm waters are always appealing, as is a stroll down the five-mile beach.

The most famous restaurant on the property is the Old Captiva House, which has won many awards over the years for its fine cuisine. The physical space is intimate and surprisingly formal, with walls of French doors opening to an outdoor terrace framed in white lattice and topped with flower-draped trellises. The elongated dining room is broken up by pillars and small tables covered with coral-colored overlays. Appetizer selections include everything from escargôt and an oyster cocktail to clams casino and marinated grilled shrimp. The Captiva bisque is one of the favorites, though, loaded with shrimp and flavored with brandy and fresh herbs. The seafood entrées range from grouper baked in parchment paper with herbs, white wine, and Dijon mustard to the seafood carbonera, consisting of scallops, mussels, and clams served on saffron vermicelli. Another favorite dish is the char-grilled tuna, topped with a tomatillo corn salsa and served on a bed of fried plantains. Duckling, Tournedos St. Germain, and Veal Oscar complete the varied menu. Those who want to save the Old Captiva House for a special occasion will be pleased to know about the more casual Canoe Club (next to the marina) and the Crow's Nest pub, which serves drinks and light fare throughout the afternoon and evening.

Bowser , too, will find plenty of things to occupy him during the vacation. Dogs are technically not allowed on the beaches in Lee County; however, during our visit we noticed a fair number of these furry creatures out strolling with their owners. Evidently, there is a fine issued to those walking their dogs on the beach. Still, there seems to be a certain tolerance for it as well, particularly early in the morning and later in the evening. We cannot recommend that people break dog laws. Nonetheless, we feel it is important to understand what the accepted practice is among the locals. There are also twenty miles of bicycle paths on Sanibel that are great for riding, walking, or in-line skating with a canine companion.

The Colony

P.O. Box 970
525 East Atlantic Avenue
Delray Beach, Florida 33447
(800) 552-2363, (407) 276-4123, Fax (407) 276-0123

Owners: *The Boughton Family*
Rooms: *103 doubles*
Rates: *$110-150 (MAP)*
Payment: *Personal checks*
Children: *Welcome — 2 and under $20 per day (MAP); all others are $40 per day (MAP), (cribs, cots, and high chairs are available)*
Dogs: *Welcome at $20 per day ("EP")*
Open: *December to April*

Imagine combining the cool summers of coastal Maine and warm winters on Florida's exclusive Gold Coast into one successful business. Since 1935, the Boughton Family has managed to do this with their two Colony Hotel properties. Their hotel in Kennebunkport, Maine has always been a standout in our New England travel guide, and we are pleased to add their sister hotel in Florida to the pages of our Southeast book. Both Colony Hotels are charming, as much for their idiosyncrasies as for their strong link with the traditions of the past when people "summered" in Maine and "wintered" in Florida. Today's guests will undoubtedly enjoy the thought of being able to cross over the threshold of either hotel for a step back into time.

The Colony of Delray Beach is situated in the old section of town, where small storefronts bring to mind an idealized main street from decades ago. Permanent awnings shade the sidewalks, and shopkeepers and their patrons are on a first name basis. While the twentieth century has left its mark on the area encircling this enclave, The Colony and its adjacent stores have somehow retained their Old Florida ambiance. The Colony's 1920s hotel building is still quite striking, with its Mediterranean facade highlighted by two central domes, red tile roofs, and camel-colored stucco walls. Little wonder that it is listed on the National Register of Historic Places. When the weather is warm, pedestrians walking by the hotel will find guests congregated on the front porch, either playing cards or quietly rocking in the hotel rocking chairs. In the evening, the mood changes as live jazz is performed on the porch, guests sip vintage wines, and others dance, either on the porch or on the sidewalk, it does not seem to matter. Pairs of French doors, normally propped open, seem to beckon people inside.

We found The Colony an appealing place, in many ways reminiscent of The Colony in Maine. The lobby and living room have an inviting summer house ambiance, with an abundance of white wicker furniture bedecked with peach, green, and yellow chintz cushions. Yellow walls and white trim are brightened by sunlight streaming in from the overhead skylights. This is an expansive room, with multiple sitting areas tucked in among white pillars and potted palms. Each grouping has a different focus. In one, a set of chairs encircles a table covered with a partially completed jigsaw puzzle. Another sitting area faces the white brick fireplace and built-in bookshelves, where guests tend to congregate on the cooler days and nights. Afternoon tea is served in here as well; quite a civilized way to renew one's energy for the evening hours. There are no televisions in the rooms, and few are air conditioned; the one modern concession is the television room that is located just off the lobby. We loved the physical layout of the hotel, especially the old-fashioned front desk, where we half expected to see a switchboard operator plugging in calls to the bedrooms.

Upstairs guest rooms are reached by an elevator, looking very classic, that hums its way up to the upper two floors of the hotel. There are few suites here, just plenty of adjoining bedrooms. Hallways are long and rather dark with exposed pipes. Behind the bedroom doors, guests will find a funky decor that appears as old as the building. Like the building, though, everything is still very clean and in good shape. More recently decorated rooms have brighter color schemes and contemporary bedspreads. Regardless of which rooms guests ultimately select, inside them they will find old-fashioned jalousied windows, which are usually left open to take advantage of the cool breezes. The bathrooms, too, are reminiscent of another era. We stepped up into one, where a combination bathtub/shower sported a bright tropical fish shower curtain, but the rest of the features and porcelain fixtures were pleasantly antiquated. An eclectic array of naturally-stained wood bureaus and tables are intermixed with rattan and other traditional Florida style pieces. Most everyone would agree that the overall effect of this casual formality is very appealing. We hope it will remain much the same for another fifty or sixty years.

Formality comes into play during dinner, when appropriate attire is still suggested for the evening meal. We thoroughly enjoyed the dining room, where paddle fans turn, and breezes drifting through the Palladian windows cause the potted palm fronds to flutter and the tablecloths to sway. The pale pink and white color scheme is a soothing contrast to strong Florida sunlight. The menu changes daily; while it is not considered Nouvelle cuisine, it is very good. Diners may start with an appetizer of chilled strawberry soup or fresh fruit topped with shaved coconut. After the salad course, striped bass with a spicy salsa or the breast of chicken stuffed with wild rice are options. Simple desserts top off the meal, ranging from ice cream or sherbet to a chocolate brownie à la mode. What makes the meals (and the entire stay) extra special is that the staff knows all of the guests by name, along with their culinary likes and dislikes.

After dinner, many people retire to the living room for a brisk game of cards or simply to visit with other guests. The comfort level is high among the patrons at The Colony, for many reasons. The staff treats everyone as though they are part of an extended family, and in many ways they are, as most of the guests have been coming here for decades. We recently talked with Justena Boughton, who is the acting president of the Colony Hotel Corporation, and she tells us the clientele has changed dramatically over the last five years. These is nothing staid about this group; they are active, energetic, and have infused The Colony with renewed life. Guests who have been coming here for years, and those who are part of the new era, create a wonderful mélange of people, all of whom assimilate well into this traditional environment. This quick assimilation is usually due to the efforts of the social director, who easily arranges golf or tennis outings and coordinates games for both children and adults. Although the hotel is not on the beach, it is just a leisurely ten-minute walk to the water. The Colony's private beachside club, the Cabaña Club, is a five-minute shuttle bus ride from the hotel. From its waterside setting, guests will enjoy not only the picturesque surroundings, but also the sense of exclusivity it offers. The large, heated saltwater pool is surrounded by neatly manicured hedges, ensuring the utmost privacy. Multiple chaises and a handful of umbrella tables are placed around the deck. There is also a covered, oceanside patio, which is accessed by walking through the cabaña. The Cabaña Club is the center of activity during the day, where most guests are happy to lie in the sun and take an occasional dip in the pool. Lunch is also served here, so there is little reason to venture anywhere else.

Bowser, too, will feel like a privileged guest while staying at The Colony. Dogs are not allowed on the beach at the Cabaña Club, but a ten-minute drive to Boynton will bring visitors to a wonderful "doggie beach," where canines are allowed to frolic, swim, and socialize to their hearts' content. Another favorite jaunt is the short walk through the old section of Delray Beach to the water. Along the way, visitors will pass by an array of classic edifices that have retained their vintage 1920s look. Once near the water, there is a sidewalk that follows along the ocean's edge, passing through the more exclusive residential neighborhoods. Delray Beach is also fairly close to the exclusive Boca Raton area, where not only is there excellent shopping, but also two great oceanside parks —the Red Reef Park and Spanish River Park.

Rod and Gun Club

200 Riverside Drive
Everglades City, Florida   33929
(813) 695-2101

Owner: *Martin Bowen*
Rooms: *17 doubles*
Rates: *Doubles $50-75 (EP)*
Payment: *Personal checks*
Children: *Welcome; 5 years of age and and under are free of charge*
Dogs: *Welcome*
Open: *All year*

In order to understand the present day Rod and Gun Club, it is important to first grasp the history of the club and Everglades City. Go back 1000 years to the area's first inhabitants, the coastal mound dwellers, and continue through history to the Spanish and Seminoles, finally stopping for a brief moment with Barron Collier. For those unfamiliar with the story, Collier was an immensely wealthy industrialist who strongly influenced the development of southern Florida in the early part of this century. He built roads, bridges, and railroads, hoping to attract others to "his" part of the world. At one point, he decided Everglades City would be the perfect county seat for the newly formed Collier County, which had recently separated from neighboring Lee County.

It was during Collier's life that Everglades City went through its boom period. He invited wealthy industrialists to fish and hunt in southern Florida, but needed a place to entertain them. Collier took over the W.S. Allen estate and converted it into a private club where his friends, most of them politicians and dignitaries, could stay. The impressive list of guests, both in Collier's day and beyond, includes United States Presidents Teddy Roosevelt, Dwight Eisenhower, and Richard Nixon. But the Rod and Gun Club's most auspicious moment was when Harry Truman visited in 1947 to sign the document creating Everglades National Park. Unfortunately, once Collier died, the town and the club went into a steady decline.

Mother nature compounded this downward spiral with Hurricane Donna, in 1960, which damaged not only Everglades City, but also the Rod and Gun Club. Then, in 1969, a fire pretty much finished the job by destroying its outbuildings and motel rooms. Somehow, the mansion endured, and for that we are thankful. This is a homestead built for a hot southern climate, with huge screened-in verandas and wide porches overlooking mangrove swamps. Step inside to equally cavernous spaces, made all the more appealing by the lustrous cypress walls. The hunting lodge feeling is further enhanced by a collection of wall-mounted game fish, small animals poised on mantels and positioned in the corners of the rooms, and a stuffed bear set atop the telephone booth. Most striking is the eight-foot alligator hide splayed out on a wall next to the billiards table. In the middle of it all is an enormous brass fireplace, and off to the side, an unobtrusive front desk. The tiny wood-paneled room, containing an intimate bar, was one of our favorite spaces. Just opposite this are two huge dining rooms, both with 20-foot ceilings. The food is what continues to attract people to the main inn, as the upstairs guest rooms were closed years ago.

Given the choice, we would choose to dine on the veranda, which looks across the water to the "hammocks" or islands of trees and sawgrass. There is an old-fashioned air of civility about the club, which still caters to the sportfishing and hunting crowd. Some people arrive with their own fish, which the chef will gladly sautée, grill, or blacken for them. Everglades City is also where the majority of Florida's stone crab claws are off-loaded and sent to market. This is therefore the prime spot for savoring fresh stone crab claws, in season. Not interested in crab, then maybe the conch fritters or clam chowder would be more appealing. The "turf" offerings are limited; it is clear that seafood is the favored food around here. Shrimp steamed in beer, delicate *fruits de mer* served over fettucine, and grilled deep sea scallops are fresh and delicate. The seafood platter is an excellent choice for those who are having a tough time deciding. We smiled at the idea of "swamp" and turf—deep fried frogs legs and a New York steak. We recommend saving a little room for the southern peanut butter, pecan, or Key Lime pies which top the dessert menu.

As we mentioned, the overnight accommodations are no longer in the hotel, but are situated in small stucco and clapboard cottages grouped around an expanse of grass. These are simple buildings with tin roofs, tiny porches, and jalousied windows. Cottages numbered 34, 35, and 36 are closest to the water and most desirable, but once inside, it becomes very difficult to tell one from another. Hardwood floors are about as exotic as these places get, with standard motel-type beds and bureaus serving as the main furnishings. The cottages are exceptionally clean, though, and reflect some of the old-fashioned charm of the club. Separate outside entrances lead directly to the greenery of the parklike grounds.

This is a great place for walking with one's dog, as it is flat and serene, with paths leading along the docks and into the village. Guides leave from the Rod and Gun Club to take interested adventurers out among the Ten Thousand Islands for sport fishing or exploring. This is a place where even the most able guides can get somewhat disoriented, so don't even think about exploring these waters without one. The Everglades National Park manages most of the land and conducts boat tours as well. Dogs are allowed in the park, but are restricted to dog walk areas. Because the Everglades is ecologically sensitive, they cannot venture on the nature trails or go into the back country. They can be walked around the visitors' areas, the campgrounds, and generally anywhere that isn't considered a trail. Upon returning to the club, most people like to cool off in the pool, which is totally enclosed by screening, to keep away the voracious bug population.

The Phoenix' Nest

619 South Fletcher Avenue
Fernandina Beach, Florida 32034
(904) 277-2129

Hostess: *Harriett Johnston Fortenberry*
Rooms: *5 suites, 1 cottage*
Rates: *Suites $70-95 (B&B), Cottage $95 (B&B)*
Payment: *AE, MC, and VISA*
Children: *Not appropriate for children under 12 years of age*
Dogs: *Welcome*
Open: *All year*

We were truly pleased to have discovered The Phoenix' Nest, but were also a little hesitant to let the word out about such a unique Bed and Breakfast—for fear it would become "discovered." The Phoenix' Nest is a true hideaway, lacking even a sign to differentiate the house from any of the others that line the beach road. Guests have to look carefully for the picket fence, which fronts the weathered, two-story Colonial style house. It is set across from an open stretch of beach and dunes, which is frequently windswept and quite deserted.

To understand The Phoenix' Nest, it is first important to know a little about Harriett. She told us that in 1989, which was a difficult time for her personally, she retreated to this place by the sea. The idea of a B&B didn't really occur to her until friends, and friends of friends, began to drift in for a day—or two, or three—to share this peaceful spot with her. Harriett found she enjoyed creating an environment where her guests could completely unwind. Before too long, the thought of operating a B&B was suggested and the rest is, as they say, history. Harriett has carefully created a distinctive mood for each suite; collectively, they are overwhelmingly beautiful and serene.

The day we arrived we found Harriett tending to her flower gardens. We talked for awhile as she watered her plants and then took us on a little tour. We soon discovered that the furnishings and knickknacks in each suite, and especially the cottage, are an amalgamation of items Harriett has collected over the years. As we opened the door to Moriah, we were drawn in by the rich color scheme created with the use of sophisticated and elegant fabrics. Harriett loved the colors and the textures in one of these designer fabrics so much that she searched long and hard to find others to match. Luckily, she found both fabrics and wicker furniture at a Ralph Lauren outlet. Loving the furnishings, too, she bought all 20 pieces and placed them throughout the guest rooms. While Moriah is an expansive space, we were drawn to the three windows, where we could bask in the breathtaking ocean views. At that point, if the door had accidentally shut and locked for a few days, we would have been quite content.

Just next door, we found the romantic Pelican suite. A natural wicker bed, draped in a floral quilted bedspread is situated near a pair of French doors. The doors open to reveal an intimate deck and views of the sparkling water. A smaller space to the rear can be used as a bedroom, but most use it as a sitting room. Wherever we ventured, we found intriguing collectibles and a host of little treasures. Manatee is entered through the gardens at the back of the house. Harriett calls the decor "mature." We thought the word "masculine" might apply as well, since the chamber is fashioned with handsome teal and cranberry colors commingling with camel hues. In the tiny kitchen, where china and glassware are usually set out on the breakfast table, we found a bust resting atop an antique wooden refrigerator. Without exception, each suite is awash with color, pattern, and texture. This is not the highly coordinated look of a decorator; it is the work of an artist trying to create a mood through the use of tranquil colors and careful placement of beautiful furnishings. One of the more whimsical features was a wooden fellow whom we nicknamed the "walking toilet paper guy." He was perched over the toilet paper, and as the paper was pulled, his little feet would start to move.

This sense of whimsy is perhaps even better expressed in the Coconut Hut, a separate cottage located behind the main house. Harriett told us that she had been saving things in her attic for years, ultimately hoping to create a wonderful space for her grandchildren, who could come to play dress-up, make music, or discover the past. Unfortunately, she ended up moving before her grandchildren could enjoy her attic's treasure trove. Luckily, she brought the collection with her and set it up in the cottage. What a treat! One guest, who thought he was being relegated to the garage (this was never a garage, always a cottage), was even more upset when he saw what was displayed inside. Grass hula skirts were laid on wooden chests, along with feather boas, dress-up clothes, stuffed animals, and an extensive collection of hats. Harriett suspected that once left alone, this guest, like many of the those who had stayed here before him, would get into the spirit of things. This was confirmed when she walked in one morning to find a purple feather boa draped around one of the stuffed dogs. The next day the same dog was sporting a little sequin number. Guests are often delighted with this chamber, which also contains a 50-year-old collection of records and a phonograph to play them. A rainstick, a guitar, a thumb harp, a mandolin, an accordion, morracas, and even a washboard all enable guests to accompany the old recordings. The king-size bedstead is luxurious, but the carved coconuts sort of topped it off for us. In here, as in the rest of the suites, there are a television and VCR. Harriett has an enormous collection of videotapes that range from black and white classic movies to Paul Simon concerts and gorillas communicating through sign language. The collection is eclectic and thought provoking—just like the rooms and the hostess.

Harriett is the sort of person we could talk with all day, and we almost did. However, she also has a great respect for her guests' privacy. Breakfast baskets are delivered to the suites each night, filled with all sorts of fresh baked goodies, juices, and other treats to be enjoyed the next morning. Even if the suite does not have a full kitchen, guests may expect to find a microwave, refrigerator, coffee maker, and toaster. Many early risers enjoy taking their canine cohort over to the beach across the street. Walk over the dunes and down to the soft sand, where everyone will appreciate the surf and sun sparkling off the water. Behind the Phoenix' Nest are 200 acres of forests that are also fun to explore. Others may prefer just to stroll along the quiet back streets lining the beautiful residential areas in the 50-block historic section of Fernandina Beach. A host of shops line these quaint brick-lined streets, and are worth investigating. On the waterfront, visitors can watch the shrimp boats as they come in to off-load their catch. There are plenty of ways to enjoy Amelia Island and Fernandina Beach; however, we wouldn't be surprised if guests decided to limit their activity to the beach and The Phoenix' Nest—our idea of the perfect sojourn.

The Topaz

1244 South Oceanshore Blvd.
Flagler Beach, Florida   32136
(904) 439-3301

Owner: Paul Lee
Rooms: 8 hotel doubles, 40 motel rooms
Rates: Hotel Doubles $56-140 (EP), Motel Rooms $46-71 (EP)
Payment: AE, DSC, MC, and VISA
Children: Welcome; under 12 years of age are free of charge in the same
room as their parents (cribs and cots—$5)
Dogs: Welcome in the motel rooms with a $25 deposit, $10 non-refundable
Open: All year

Seasoned travelers making the trek along I-95 have perhaps seen the sign for Flagler Beach, but few can say they have been there. The residents of Flagler Beach call it the "peaceful beach"—and they intend to keep it that way. Flagler Beach is a relaxed, unspoiled Atlantic seaside community tucked between quiet and historic St. Augustine and the more frenetic Daytona Beach, a car racing and spring break hot spot. We approached Flagler Beach from the north, along the scenic oceanside highway. We were treated to views of unspoiled beaches and saw very little commercial enterprise. The only exception is the quiet, old-fashioned Marineland, which was the world's first oceanarium, that looks as though it intends to move into the 21st century with its original character intact.

Flagler Beach isn't a lot different, well settled into the simplicity of the 1950s with just a smattering of surf shops, gas stations, and a few old motels and restaurants set along the shore road. When developing the coastline, somebody seems to have forgotten about this beach. We couldn't be more pleased, as it gave us a sampling of what Old Florida must have been like several decades ago. Just beyond the center of town we found The Topaz, which is a small complex that combines an antique building, a great restaurant, and a pair of modern motel wings. In general, we steer away from detailed descriptions of motels because there is rarely enough noteworthy information to pass on to our readers. However, every once in a while we can make an exception, and The Topaz is one of them.

The main hotel, built around 1925, is a two-story building with an appealing combination of Spanish tile roofs and walls made of white shell stone, commonly called coquina. Three arches mark the entrance to the intimate hotel. Upon entering the foyer, guests are immediately thrown into a kind of time warp, as a vast collection of Americana is revealed in the museum-like setting. Two rooms contain old-fashioned Lionel trains, a red Western Flyer bicycle, and an assortment of antique tin and metal toy cars. The latter are just smaller replicas of the "real" car collection housed to the back of the property. Placed in nooks along the walls are the original toy characters from several Disney films, including Snow White and the Seven Dwarfs. Some of the hotel's silver, reputedly used by Charles Lindbergh, is also on display. A small back room contains glass display cases that hold most of the smaller items, but the space seems larger, due to the huge antique mirror set against one wall. As we re-entered the main lobby, we saw that it was also packed with oddities. The many small tables are illuminated by Victorian lamps, while a player piano stands at the ready in the corner alongside an authentic Victrola. We could have spent hours checking out all the knickknacks. It wasn't easy to get beyond them, but try we did; and so we discovered beautiful hardwood floors, intricate cornice moldings and plasterwork, as well as a curving staircase. Just off the lobby are three antique bedrooms. These are not appropriate for Bowser, but they are definitely worth a peek. We were most impressed by the cavernous Jacuzzi Room, especially with the ornate plasterwork on the 20-foot high ceilings. The oversized canopy bed and Victorian antiques would overwhelm most bedrooms; but not so in this space, which is almost fit for royalty.

Anyone in need of a reality check can step outside to the motel units. These are some of the nicest motel rooms we have seen in years. Each has been recently redecorated and updated with teal green carpeting, attractive floral spreads on the pairs of queen beds, and coordinated draperies framing the windows. The best units, having unobstructed ocean views, are on the second floor, but all offer amenities similar to one another. Cable television with free HBO movies, telephones, air conditioning, and reproductions of 1920s-style radios are all standard features. Each unit has off-white walls which, combined with the sliding doors and windows, make them quite light and airy. The bathrooms, too, are modern and exceptionally clean. Guests who are staying longer may wish to consider the modern efficiencies with full kitchens that are an attractive blend of white cabinetry and wood paneled doors, plus a small formica island for serving or eating meals. Those needing even more space may wish to reserve an efficiency with one bed and a pullout sofa. Of the two wings of rooms, we prefer the one on the left. The rooms there appear a little more modern and offer private balconies and sliding glass doors, which allow even more of the ocean breezes to permeate these spaces.

In the center of it all there is a great swimming pool, which seems to be just as popular as the beach. We also appreciated the fact that dogs, provided they are leashed, are allowed on the beach here—a rarity throughout most of the state. Even after walking for what seemed like several miles, we encountered few people and plenty of wildlife. In some ways we were reminded of portions of the more remote sections of North Carolina's Outer Banks. Many people like to take their dogs for a short stroll to town, where they can check out the surf report with the locals.

In the evening, we recommend trying out the hotel's restaurant, called the Topaz Café. The café has long been offering fabulous, yet simple meals served on a patio overlooking the ocean. Here, white iron tables and chairs are placed under whirring paddle fans. The menu changes daily and is displayed in the beak of a pink flamingo sign board that stands in front of the hotel. Some of our favorite appetizers are the lobster tortoloni—an herb pasta filled with lobster, shallots, and spinach served over a saffron chardonnay shrimp sauce, or the roasted Vidalia onion stuffed with feta cheese, pinenuts, oregano, and Greek olives. Look for the sweet and spicy grilled shrimp and bananas, with a watermelon salsa and Thai curry sauce. Fish is usually the basis of the entrée menu. One favorite is the sea scallop and jumbo shrimp brochette with scallion-sundried tomato couscous, saffron shrimp sauce, and basil pesto. The grilled local fish may be ordered with a choice of Dijon-dill butter and capers, garlic herb butter and sautéed mushrooms, or ginger. The restaurant's famous "smashed" potatoes accompany the filet mignon or the chicken marengo. The free-range, organic-raised veal is served with avocado, eggplant, tomato, and field mushrooms over angel hair pasta. A true taste sensation is the bourbon and molasses glazed tenderloin of pork with a cheddar cheese grits cake and cider-apple pork jus. The restaurant has been named one of the top 200 in the state of Florida, quite an accomplishment for a small, out of the way place like this.

The Topaz is a decidedly casual place, where the beach beckons, dogs are welcome, the food is fantastic, and the guest bedrooms are memorable—even the motel rooms. Little else matters here; few people know about the place, and those who do try to maintain it as a well-kept secret.

Westin Hotel
Cypress Creek

400 Corporate Drive
Fort Lauderdale, Florida   33334-3642
(800) 228-3000, (305) 772-1331, Fax (305) 491-9087

General Manager: Mark Spadoni
Rooms: 260 doubles, 33 suites
Rates: Doubles $99-219 (EP), Suites $209-419 (EP)
Payment: AE, DC, DSC, MC, and VISA
Children: Welcome (cribs, cots, high chairs, and babysitters are available)
Dogs: Under 20 pounds are welcome
Open: All year

We try to provide a mix of accommodations in our books, to cover the needs of most travelers,   We occasionally include hotels located near major metropolitan areas, for those who are in town on business, on an overnight stop between flights, or enroute to a long-term vacation destination. Cypress Creek is one of those centrally located destinations, situated just off I-95 and close to the Fort Lauderdale Airport. Rest assured, it is not a typical airport hotel. Instead, the Westin Cypress Creek is housed in a beautiful office park amid lagoons and plenty of green space. This makes it fairly easy to bring a dog here, as there are plenty of places to walk it around the hotel.

Cypress Creek is one of the nicer hotels in the Westin chain, built with reflective glass in a style similar to other buildings in the office park. We entered the expansive complex and drove to the hotel, past open, grassy areas and mature trees. While Cypress Creek is big by most people's standards, the designers have managed to make the interiors feel quite intimate. A three-story atrium lobby is divided into small sitting areas by massive columns and large potted ficus trees. To the rear of the building, there is a small step-down bar and the Fountain Café, one of the hotel's two restaurants. The lagoon and its various fountains line the back edge of the property and provide a visual coolness.

A pathway lined with mature plantings wends along the lagoon and emerges at the large W-shaped swimming pool and Jacuzzi. The waterfall is pretty, and also provides melodious background sounds that serve to cover up the less agreeable sounds coming from the Interstate. The Health Club building, with its attractive shrubs and trees is also well sited to ensure privacy. Anyone who wants to work out, instead of relaxing in the pool-side chaise lounges, will find a full complement of equipment in the Health Club. Nautilus machines, Lifecycles, a whirlpool and sauna are terrific, but it is the massage therapist who truly works out the kinks. Bowser may prefer the Timber Challenge par course, which begins at the hotel and provides guests with another effective aerobic routine. It is suggested that the course only be used between dawn and dusk, as it is not lit at night and may not be safe during these off hours.

After a day in the sun, sleep comes easily. The end rooms held the most appeal for us, as they contain interesting curved walls and more window space. Teal and cream colors are soothing to the eye, especially when used in the striped wallpaper and as matting around the botanical prints. Furnishings are good, quality reproductions of English Georgian-style antiques. A full complement of room amenities are certain to enhance most guests' traveling experience, including a mini-bar concealed in the bureau, ironing boards and irons tucked away in the closet, and an extensive list of travelers' services. The tiled bathrooms have almond- scented Caswell Massey soaps, shampoos, and creams, as well as blow dryers. Coffee makers and a good supply of coffee help get the morning off to a good start, although there is also 24-hour room service available. Larger rooms offer good-sized tables for working or dining and all of the upper floors have nice views of the surrounding landscape.

The hotel has two restaurants, with The Fountain Café being the most informal of the two. We happened to visit the hotel on a Sunday, when the expansive buffet was laid out. It was difficult to choose from the selections that included sushi, smoked salmon with capers, Eggs Benedict, trays of tropical fruits, and all sorts of pastries. The more formal Cypress Room is a dinner-only restaurant offering an award-winning cuisine. The night of our visit, the steamed grouper with corriander pesto wrapped in rice paper and drizzled with a ginger persimmon sauce sounded appealing. Of course, the seafood scampi was also quite exotic, and included fresh water clams, New Zealand mussels, shrimp, scallops, angel hair pasta, and tobico caviar. The most unusual award would have to go to "from the wildside" where patrons could choose between the tournedos of Texas antelope and grilled buffalo rib-eye steak. Filet mignon and a Black Angus porterhouse steak completed the evening's menu. The excellent food is enhanced by the abundance of dark wood and leather, and first rate service from the wait staff.

The Westin Cypress Creek is not a long-term destination for anyone traveling with a dog, since there are not an abundance of doggie activities; but for guests who want to stay in the Fort Lauderdale area for a night or two, it is a good place to know about, offering exceptional accommodations and service, along with a host of four-star amenities. Those who end up closer to Ft. Lauderdale's beaches during their visit might like to know about a recently opened beach area for dogs—albeit limited. There are 100 yards of beach, just off Sunrise and A1A, that are available to dogs on weekends between 5-9 p.m. Unfortunately, in these densely populated areas, canines and their owners will have to be content with the what little beachfront they can find.

Crown Hotel

109 North Seminole Avenue
Inverness, Florida 34450
(904) 344-5555, (904) 726-4040, Fax (904) 726-4040

Owners: *Mr. and Mrs. Nigel Sumner*
Rooms: *2 singles, 30 doubles, 1 suite*
Rates: *Singles $40-60 (EP), Doubles $55-75 (EP), Suites $110 (EP)*
Payment: *AE, CB, DC, MC, and VISA*
Children: *Welcome (cribs, cots, high chairs, and babysitters are available*
             with advance notice)
Dogs: *Welcome with prior approval, for a $10 fee (per pet per night)*
Open: *All year*

With the exception of Orlando, Florida's interior remains relatively undeveloped and is usually overlooked by tourists. Visitors who step off the beaten track can obtain a sense of Old Florida, far from Disney and even more removed from the famous white sand beach communities. We enjoyed the drive into Inverness, which took us by rambling horse and cattle ranches, citrus groves, and through pretty wooded areas. Inverness, with its quaint old main street, is still a quiet town with an abundance of lakes and pristine land surrounding it.

The town appears to have changed very little since it was founded in 1868, except in its name, which was changed early on from Tompkinsville to Inverness. The hotel is more like a cat, however, that has exhausted its nine lives, and then some, having gone through many different incarnations over the years. In the 1890s it was a general store, but it was soon moved and renamed the Orange Hotel. At some point, the two-story building was divided in half, moved again to Seminole Avenue, and placed on top of a one-story foundation. It was then renamed the Crown Hotel and has remained firmly affixed to its foundation ever since. The same cannot be said however, for the hotel's completely redesigned interior. As different owners tried to make the hotel profitable, it went through various stages of repair and disrepair. Eventually, in 1979, a British man bought the Crown Hotel and poured two and a half million dollars into it. As a hotelier, though, he was only mildly successful and went through some fairly difficult years. Finally, the Sumners bought the Crown Hotel in 1990 and have remained here ever since.

From the exterior, the Crown Hotel is very appealing, set on a quiet street lined by huge shade trees and a scattering of palms. Gables, eaves, and awnings overhanging the windows add character to the roof line of the long building. We walked in through leaded glass doors, emerging into a room lined with glass display cases, whose contents glittered under the light from the crystal chandelier. The cases housed authentic reproductions of the Royal Crown Jewels, assembled under the authority of the Queen of England. Jeweled sword sheaths, staffs, crowns, and tiaras fill the cases, along with other British Royal memorabilia. The free standing staircase spirals up to the second floor, where we expected to find guest rooms reflecting the formality of the lobby. Although the bedrooms have been individually furnished and decorated in keeping with Victorian England, the accommodations are decidedly understated. Victorian light fixtures illuminate the chambers, where brass beds, muted floral wallpapers, ornately carved Queen Anne armchairs and wing chairs are the standard. Some bedrooms have hardwood floors, whereas others are fully carpeted. An old-fashioned pedestal sink is placed directly in the bedroom, whenever the bathroom is too small to accommodate it. The antiques are authentic, although well worn. These guest rooms feel like a favorite tweed jacket — a bit threadbare, yet classically comfortable.

Churchills, the hotel's dining room, is an excellent choice for dinner. Popular not only with the guests, it is also a favorite with the locals, who are happy to have a fine restaurant in town. Before sitting down to dinner, many guests first visit the English pub, complete with its copper bar, handful of tables, and dart boards. Later, when they walk into Churchills, guests are certain to feel that physically, it has less British charm than the pub. The menu is primarily Continental, but those who want to sample authentic English fare might order the steak and kidney pie, chicken and mushroom pie, or the roast of the day. Lighter and more local offerings include the shellfish Caribbean with shrimp, scallops, peppers, and red onions or the sole served with artichokes, capers, palm hearts, garlic, and lime. The sole is finished with an herb wine sauce. There is also a shrimp dish that is sautéed with mangoes and a spice rum.

This is not a resort, but there is a very private swimming pool located toward the rear of the hotel. It is surrounded by white walls rimmed with pretty plantings and shaded by large trees. Most enjoy relaxing in the old-fashioned wood chaises before and after taking a dip. Bowser will like the long walks along the quiet residential side streets near the hotel, or strolling the other way toward town and the Whispering Pines Park. One of the more appealing aspects about the area is the number of lakes in the immediate vicinity, such as the Tsala Apopka Lake, Big Henderson Lake, and Big Spivey Lake. Nearby, there is also the Fort Cooper State Park , which had been a military outpost during the Seminole War. Here, visitors and their dogs can explore the fort site, along with nature trails that crisscross the area. The Lacoochee River flows through this region, and visitors renting a canoe will not only enjoy the lovely surroundings, but also the intriguing wildlife. After a busy day, it is always nice to return to the hospitality and comfort of the Crown Hotel.

Center Court
Historic Inn & Cottages

916 Center Street
Key West, Florida 33040
(800) 797-8787, Telephone/Fax (305) 296-9292

Innkeeper: *Naomi Van Steelandt*
Rooms: *4 doubles, 3 cottages*
Doubles: *Doubles $118-138 (B&B), Cottages $138-308 (EP)*
Payment: *AE, DSC, MC, and VISA*
Children: *Welcome in the cottages (cribs, cots, and babysitters are available)*
Dogs: *Welcome in the cottages, with advance notice and prior approval, along with a $50 fee*
Open: *All year*

Before visiting Center Court, we spoke at length with Naomi, who just recently finished a complete renovation of the property. She is quite a perfectionist, and has spent countless hours redesigning and refurbishing the historic group of cottages. Center Court has already won numerous accolades for the renovation and preservation of the buildings, which also include restoring the original well and cistern. After talking with Naomi, we became intrigued with the inn, and, upon visiting it, we knew we had discovered something completely unique.

First-time visitors to Key West will easily find Center Court, as it is just a half block off Duval Street. Anyone familiar with Key West knows that Duval Street can also get noisy, yet Center Court is seemingly immune to the commotion. The cottages lie behind a white picket fence, in a residential neighborhood of tiny bungalows and beach shacks that have somehow escaped the recent "upgrading" of Key West. From the street it is difficult to see the extent of the renovation work that has been completed at the Center Court, but as guests walk down the narrow brick path it all becomes visible. The Main House was built by a ship's captain in 1873 and has been converted to accommodate four bedrooms and a living area. We first investigated the bedrooms, which were decorated in varying shades of peach and Key Lime green. White wicker headboards combine with floral bedspreads to further enhance the festive feeling. In the Main House, and throughout the complex, there is also original artwork produced by talented locals, adding to the Caribbean flavor of the place. The bathrooms are all new and tiled and fully stocked with amenities usually reserved for five-star hotels. Soaps, shampoos, and creams, as well as hair dryers, are complemented by the soft thick towels for bathing and beach. Guests in the Main House also have use of the white tiled living room and kitchen, where a buffet breakfast awaits them each morning. The extensive repast includes fresh fruits, cereals, muffins, and the house specialty: a gourmet blend of exotic coffees. Once again, Naomi has combined pale peach colors and off-white floral fabrics, this time on the couches and walls, to create a lovely setting. Soft music and tropical breezes make it easy to linger over breakfast.

The living area in the Main House opens directly to a covered patio, set with tables. The patio, in turn, flows out to an oval shaped, heated swimming pool. Just opposite is a small cottage, called Cistern House, which was actually built over the original cistern. Inside are a bedroom, kitchenette, and bathroom, where the Caribbean color scheme makes up for the diminutive dimensions. The triangular windows in the eaves let in plenty of natural sunlight. From this charming abode, guests step up another level to find the two story Family House and Cottage. Most will notice the square-headed nails that were used to frame this house and the Cottage back in the 1880s. The Family House is aptly named because it sleeps up to six people. Bleached hardwood floors and the walls' pale colors keep the interior light, particularly on the first floor. The living and dining areas are interconnected with the kitchen to create an open space that flows together beautifully. Meals can be enjoyed around the butcher block table or from the caned stools set along the kitchen's countered island. The living room is outfitted with a television, VCR, stereo system, and a queen-size sofa bed. A spacious bathroom is also found on the first floor. The master suite, furnished with a king-size water bed, and a double-bedded room, are located on the second floor. Peach and turquois are used as subtle accent colors throughout the house. Most of the living in Key West occurs outside, and Naomi has made certain to maximize every corner of outdoor space. The Family House has a private porch with a grill, an outdoor shower, and a covered front porch lined with white wicker chairs.

A couple desiring the ultimate in privacy, and who want more space than is found in the Cistern House, should reserve the Cottage. Wooden decks lead past the fish and lily pad pond to this separate building. Once again, this is a totally redesigned space, with a living room and small kitchen on the first floor and a master bedroom upstairs. We should note that the bathrooms in here and the rest of the outbuildings are as well appointed as those in the Main House. The furnishings are also similar, with an appealing combination of lightly stained wicker and oak, coupled with cotton fabrics. The enclosed patio off the living room further enhances the feeling of honeymoon-style privacy, making the *Cottage* one of our favorite finds.

Guests may also wish to try out the small exercise pavilion that Naomi has equipped with a full complement of machinery, such as a Stairmaster, stationary bicycle, free weights, and a Soloflex machine. Of course, others might prefer to relax and just hang out on the European-style sun deck or perhaps take a dip in the Jacuzzi. All of the accommodations have air conditioning and ceiling fans, along with remote control televisions, telephones, and irons and ironing boards. Guests may also take advantage of the laundry service, without charge. Naomi and her staff are exceptionally gracious and are well equipped to set up reservations for anything from dining to diving. They even make their international guests feel comfortable, as they speak German, French, Italian, Spanish, and some African languages.

Because Center Court is ideally situated in the center of Old Town, there are an array of interesting walks to enjoy with a canine companion. One walking adventure might include a visit to the Fort Zachary Taylor State Historic site, which consists of a Civil War fort and acres of land that a leashed Bowser may enjoy exploring. The general rule concerning dogs in Florida state parks is that they must be on a six-foot leash and cannot walk on any of the bathing beaches. Unfortunately, the nicest beach in Key West is located on these state grounds. Hopefully, Bowser will be able to pass up the sand for a walk back into the town. Guests may want to pick up a couple of fruit smoothies from one of the sidewalk vendors and share them with Bowser before returning to the inn.

Chelsea House

707 Truman Avenue
Key West, Florida 33040
(800) 845-8859, (305) 296-2211, Fax (305) 296-4822

Innkeepers: Jim Durbin and Gary William
Rooms: 13 doubles, 2 suites
Rates: Doubles $75-115 (B&B), Suites $165-260 (B&B)
Payment: AE, DSC, MC, OPT, and VISA
Children: Not appropriate for children
Dogs: Welcome , with advance notice and prior approval
Open: All year

Land is a rare commodity in Key West, particularly in Old Town. Everyone—from the owners of the most stately homes to those occupying the smallest guest houses—maximizes their privacy and minimal acreage by creating lush tropical gardens. The Chelsea House, built in 1870, is unusual, because the two antique homes that comprise it lie on a rather expansive two-thirds of an acre. This was the first guest house we visited in Key West, and we had no idea its extensive gardens were so unique. We were, however, impressed with the historic mansion from the very start. Visitors step inside, past the shutters flanking the front door, into a cavernous formal foyer dominated by an elegant curved staircase. We weren't sure if it was the high ceilings and open doors or the sherbet green walls that gave us instant relief from the tropical heat.

As we walked around the first floor of the mansion, we met many of the guests who were staying here. This is an establishment primarily geared to adults, where children would feel out of place and uncomfortable amid the quiet surroundings. On the other hand, the Chelsea House is very appropriate for anyone traveling with a dog, since there are a number of rooms that open directly to the outside, making it easy to come and go without disturbing the other guests. The spacious chambers are furnished with Victorian oak and wicker antiques; however, the wall treatments are strictly Key West. Varying shades of pastel peaches, greens, and yellows not only enliven each of the rooms, but also provide a festive basis for the traditional decor and array of interesting knickknacks.

Our first-floor favorites are Rooms 1 and 2. Both are immense and contain wonderful architectural features such as hardwood floors, 14-foot high ceilings, detailed woodworking, and an occasional stained glass window. As with most of the other bedrooms, these chambers provide easy access to the out of doors. In Room 2, guests will find a marble-topped coffee table and wicker day bed set in front of a bay window, with sheer white tie-back curtains filtering the sunlight. The king-size bed is covered with a pretty floral spread. The only drawback to these two rooms is that they face the road and can be a little noisy at times. Some of the quieter rooms are found on the second floor, to the rear of the mansion. Couples traveling together might consider reserving Rooms 11 and 12, which share a balcony. Both have hardwood floors and queen beds; however, Room 11 has a French Provincial theme, which derives, in part, from its sofa and selection of antiques. Room 12 contains an antique writing desk, a love seat, and a Colonial headboard. Modern amenities mimic those found in many first-class hotels, with in-room safes, color cable televisions, private telephones, and alarm clocks. Bathrooms have blow dryers. Early risers can brew their own pots of coffee and snack on their private stash of refrigerated goodies, while waiting for the Continental breakfast to be set out. Of course, air conditioning is a welcome feature during any hot spell, although we preferred the gentle breeze provided by the ceiling fans.

The three bedrooms in the Pool House are a little less private and lack some of the intrinsic details found in the mansion's bedrooms, but they do open directly onto the pool area and the intimate Chelsea Café and gardens. Of the three, we prefer Chelsea 7, which has a nice mix of French antiques and contemporary rattan, along with both a queen-size bed and day bed. Tiled floors are cool to the touch, even on the warmest days. Anyone requiring more space should consider the two suites in the house facing quiet Elizabeth Street. The pale, coffee-colored exterior matches that of the main house. French doors lead from the balconies into the contemporary living room/dining room combinations. The first-floor suite offers a huge entertainment center with a television, VCR, and radio. In both suites the furnishings are fairly contemporary, but are nonetheless quite lovely. The hardwood floors of the upstairs suite led us from the living and dining rooms, past a very modern and fully-equipped kitchen, to the two bedrooms. We liked the combined effect of the tropical-patterned bedspreads and the rattan bureaus and bedside tables. The French doors off the bedrooms open to reveal lovely garden views.

Guests may be as private or as social as they please. One natural spot to which people gravitate is the library, which is located to the rear of the mansion. Choose a book off the shelf and relax on the comfortable sofa. The sliding glass doors, leading to a terrace and good-sized pool (by Key West standards), are generally left open. More informal sitting areas are created by the foliage, which provides a kind of privacy screen. It was on our tour along these brick walkways that we picked up one of the resident dogs, Cicely, who was out nosing around a bit. We found the open air cabaña and patio, where fresh fruits and juices and sweet breads and muffins are served every morning. Those who enjoy relaxing in the buff will appreciate the private clothes-optional sun deck. In addition to the benefits of a full body tan, the deck offers easy access to Duval Street. There are bicycles for rent or guests may walk to town, but we recommend leaving cars behind in the small private parking lot.

The main road that runs by the guest house is usually busy, but Elizabeth Street may be taken for a stroll into the quieter, more residential neighborhood. One of the more notable dog-oriented walks leads guests along Elizabeth Street to Angela and Margaret Streets, where the famous Key West cemetery is located. While some might think this rather morbid, others, especially dog fanciers, may find it intriguing. Besides looking for whimsical quotes on the above-ground tombs of the famous (and not so famous) who are interred here, visitors may also check out the number of dogs who are buried with their human companions. Others may want to forgo that tour and head out on a diversion without the dog. This might include kayaking at Big Pine Key, a tour on a glass bottom boat, or a visit to the Audubon House and Tropical Gardens.

Courtney's Place

720 Whitmarsh Lane
Key West, Florida 33040
(800) UNWIND-9, Telephone/Fax (305) 294-3480

Owners: Chuck and Linda Krumel
Rooms: 6 doubles, 2 suites, 6 cottages
Rates: Doubles $59-129 (B&B), Suites $79-139 (B&B),
      Cottages $99-169 (B&B)
Payment: AE, DSC, MC, and VISA
Children: Welcome, children under 12 years of age are free of charge (crib,
      cots, and babysitters are available with advance notice)
Dogs: Welcome in the first floor rooms and cottages, no charge
Open: All year

There are very few guest houses left in Key West that are truly tucked away from the action, as tourists seem to permeate just about every facet of life in Old Town. Courtney's Place is one of the exceptions, as it is set on a quiet residential street, with only a small portion of the pale peach, gingerbread exterior appearing outside the stone walls. A gate opens to reveal an intimate courtyard backed by the historic main house, a small swimming pool (about the size of a Jacuzzi), and a handful of the cottages. Our unannounced arrival seemed to momentarily surprise Linda, a high-energy redhead who was catering to a full house of college kids on spring break. As we watched her, it became clear that she had a wonderful way with people—light-hearted and convivial. Guests seemed equally at ease with her, chatting non-stop as they helped themselves to a Continental breakfast of homemade muffins and banana bread, fresh fruits, and juices.

While we waited for a moment with Linda, one of the guest dogs wandered in with its owners to say good morning. This was our kind of place, as Linda was as kind to the dog as she was to its human companions. It turns out that her family used to breed dogs in upstate New York. Linda owns both a chocolate and a yellow labrador retriever who go by the names of Mr. and Piedmont. They did not accompany us on the tour of the property, content instead to rest in the shade. As we meandered about the grounds, Linda gave us the background on Courtney's Place. Named after her daughter Courtney, the inn has an intriguing history. The cottages were built in the late 1800s on the highest point in town—18 feet above sea level. Evidently, pirates also saw this as a desirable location because they used to bury their bounty here—sometimes permanently—often forgetting its exact location, or perhaps unable to return for it. Linda told us a story, which she also mentions in her literature, about a neighbor who was digging a pool and found gold coins valued at $10,000. The only treasure today's guests are likely to find, however, are the cottages and bungalows scattered about this historic property.

Each of the six cottages is slightly different from the others, architecturally; however, they are all extremely attractive and exude an old Key West flavor. The hardwood floors are perfect for the climate, as they remain cool and impervious to the tropical moisture. Some of the cottages have large kitchens and living rooms with adjacent eat-in areas, while others combine tiny kitchenettes with equally cozy sitting areas. The kitchens are fully equipped with modern conveniences, such as microwaves, complete sets of pots, pans, and flatware, and, of course, the obligatory blender for creating exotic liquid concoctions. Chefs can tend to their cooking either in the kitchen or on the outdoor barbecue.

The bedrooms may not be expansive, but they are pretty—with beds backed by wicker or oak headboards, topped with bright tropical spreads that are set alongside matching bureaus. The furnishings might include rattan sofas and chairs fitted with festively patterned cushions, or perhaps overstuffed sofas and light oak Windsor chairs. There are plenty of paintings and framed posters on the walls, depicting typical Key West scenes. We liked the private patios that allow guests to extend their living space to the outside. One cottage, which we thought especially appropriate for families or for two couples traveling together, contained a small kitchen and living area, and a pair of bedrooms situated off a long hallway. Guests who do not need as much living space should consider one of the first-floor bedrooms in the main house. These are as well-appointed as the cottages, individually furnished, and private. It is difficult to describe the overall decor and furnishings at Courtney's Place, because each room is so unique. Guests can depend on the fact that rooms are attractively furnished, comfortable, and clean, making them very appealing.

We also noticed that this seems to be a place where guests feel they can sleep late, eat breakfast at their leisure, and not worry about the details of the day. But don't expect guests to stay up late partying, as Linda very clearly states that there must be quiet after 10:00 each night. Although the inn's swimming pool is tiny, guests do have beach and swimming rights at the Reach Hotel, which happens to be on a coveted strip of private sandy beach. Others may just enjoy taking Bowser for a leisurely walk along the quiet side streets around Courtney's Place. Bowser will find plenty of animal life in the neighborhood, as there are almost as many dogs, cats, and birds here as there are people. An early morning walk to town—a mere two blocks—is always delightful, because this is when many of the locals venture out for their paper or coffee. We saw one man with a parrot on his shoulder and a pair of dogs at his side, all taking their morning constitution together. There are bicycles available for rent at Courtney's Place, making it easy to head out for explorations of the area. We recommend leaving Bowser home during the heat of the day, and perhaps taking a short trip to the reef for some snorkeling. Linda and Chuck are also good informational resources. After living here for over 25 years, they can recommend an assortment of hidden spots in Key West that seemingly remain as off the beaten path as Courtney's Place.

The Cuban Club

1108 Duval Street
Key West, Florida 33040
(800) 432-4849, (305) 296-0465, Fax (305) 296-0475

Owner: Fred Salinero
Rooms: 8 doubles , 8 suites
Rates: Doubles $70-140 (B&B), Suites $150-300 (EP)
Payment: AE, MC, and VISA
Children: Welcome
Dogs: Smaller dogs are welcome, pet deposit required
Open: All year

Before we visit dog-friendly accommodations, we do a lot of background research to develop our list of possibilities. We try to be thorough, but occasionally we miss something special and only learn about it once we start poking around a particular area. We discovered The Cuban Club by accident, not during our preliminary research. It is a relative newcomer to Old Town's lengthy list of accommodations, with the suites having just been converted from long-term rentals to short-term rentals and overnight accommodations. Travelers who decide to book a suite or bedroom here are in for a real treat.

First a little background. The club is in an area that once held many of the cigar manufacturers' warehouses. Many of these structures were damaged or destroyed in 1886, when a fire blown by high winds and fueled by tinder dry roofs devastated much of this section of Old Town. Even if Key West's only fire truck had not been out of commission, the town would not have been equipped to handle the emergency. It was after this fire that all buildings were required to install the tin roofs that are so prevalent today. The club itself was built a few years later in 1900, as a gathering place for Cuban families who were still involved in Key

West's cigar industry. Here, they could visit with other Cubans, dance to Cuban melodies, and generally revive their lost sense of culture in a foreign land. Dues were minimal, ranging from fifty cents to a dollar, but were substantial enough to erect and maintain these buildings. The buildings have not escaped fire or decay, having endured a couple of small fires and some years of neglect.

Fred Salinero is responsible for the recent renovations and resurgence of The Cuban Club. The result is so striking and authentic that the Historic Florida Keys Preservation Board and the Chamber of Commerce each bestowed top honors for the restoration of the buildings. The two-story, white clapboard facades are enhanced by first- and second-floor wraparound porches, dotted with antique Cuban rockers. This was formerly a club with cavernous rooms, so it should not come as a surprise to learn that each suite is between 900 and 2,000 square feet. In addition to the sheer size, these chambers also have interesting architectural details, such as cathedral ceilings, bulls-eye moldings around the doors, and two-story Palladian windows to maximize the natural light. As we climbed the staircase leading to the entrance of the first suite, we were both startled and captivated by the deep lemon yellow walls and tropical green stair treads. Stepping through the door, the white walls, white tile floors, and pale fabrics on the assorted couches and wicker chairs provided a stark contrast to the bold colors on the other side of the door. A staircase leads to the loft bedroom, which is furnished with a king-size bed covered in a lively, tropical-patterned spread.

Another suite we visited faces Duval Street, and has French doors opening to a long balcony. To call it a suite is actually a misnomer; this is an apartment. A small foyer leads to the enormous living room. The deeply hued hardwood floors create a certain warmth in here, with the neutral fabrics merely enhancing the overall effect. The enormous cherry armoire contains a television, but it seems dwarfed by the cathedral ceilings. There are two bedrooms, one in the private loft, and another off the living room. The simple fan-shaped headboards and matching bureaus add to the Caribbean feeling. There are very few decorative items or pieces of art displayed on the walls, but we think the architectural design elements speak for themselves and need little enhancement. We were also very impressed with the state-of-the-art kitchens in both the suites. The tiled bathroom in this one consists of a long powder room that has a separate door leading into the toilet and shower area. Caswell Massey soaps and shampoos are set out alongside the two sink basins. Finally, there are the eight Bed and Breakfast accommodations, which are available in another house just off Duval Street. These are similar in style to the suites, but on a smaller scale and without the kitchens. They are perfect for travelers who don't require much space and are looking for more of a guest house feeling.

The Cuban Club is a terrific find, particularly for anyone who wants luxurious surroundings and plenty of independence. This is an easy spot for entertaining, preparing meals, and generally settling into the Key West lifestyle. It is also just far enough from the center of town that it remains fairly quiet, yet is within easy walking distance of the more noteworthy restaurants and beaches. A group of specialty shops, found on the first floors of the buildings, are also intriguing. Guests interested in a leisurely stroll with their canine in tow may wish to try the short three-block walk to the Southernmost Point, or perhaps a fifteen-minute trip to the Fort Zachary State Park. Bowser will probably also like investigating the pretty residential neighborhoods that surround the Club. Those who are interested in learning a little more about Key West's history and famous sights can hop on the Conch Train for an hour and a half tour of the town. Don't laugh, we actually learned a lot of fun facts from these informative guides. During a passing rain storm they even brought out the ponchos so that we could stay dry and still enjoy the remainder of our tour.

Douglas House

419 Amelia Street
Key West, Florida 33040
(800) 833-0372, (305) 294-5269, Fax (305) 292-7665

Innkeepers: *Robert Marrero and Andrew Davies*
Rooms: *7 doubles, 8 suites*
Rates: *Doubles $88-128 (B&B), Suites $118-178 (B&B)*
Payment: *AE, DC, MC, and VISA*
Children: *Infants and children up to the age of 3 are appropriate, as are children over the age of 12. (Cots are available)*
Dogs: *Welcome with a $50 refundable dog deposit*
Open: *All year*

The Douglas House is comprised of two small Victorian-Bahamian style houses set on a quiet side street, just a quarter block off Duval Street. These quaint, gray-stained antique homes are accented with white pillars and linked by porches and gates. Their appealingly simple facades are deceiving, however, because as guests pass through the gates and down the narrow paths leading between the houses, they emerge into a lush tropical jungle of plants, flowers, and palm trees. We took the path that revealed one of the hidden courtyards. Here we found a small cabaña, where guests were casually enjoying their Continental breakfast while perched on stools next to the counter. A good-sized heated pool, inset with a Jacuzzi, is nearby, and even though it was still relatively early, there were a few people enjoying a morning dip. We crossed over a wooden footbridge to find a second pool (unheated) situated alongside a bungalow. The bungalow is decidedly one of the more charming and secluded accommodations. Although this accommodation is usually reserved well in advance, it is worth inquiring into its availability. The lush foliage around the bungalow and the pools create many intimate spaces, exuding the feeling of being in a Japanese tea garden. Around one corner we came across a tiny pond; around another was a small seating arrangement, perfect for two people.

At the Douglas House there are a variety of accommodations to choose from. Room 9 is one of our favorites. In here, two queen-size beds sit in a bedroom with eight windows, allowing for a wonderful combination of refreshing breezes and plenty of sunlight. The huge living room, situated just off the bedroom, has plenty of sofas and chairs. The hardwood floors in this suite lead to the private deck. We also like the Honeymoon Suite, which feels somewhat like a secluded treehouse, as it is located on the second floor and has a deck partially obscured from view by trees. We walked into a cozy living room and kitchen combination that looked as though it had been recently renovated. We climbed a steep set of stairs to the intimate loft, which is brightened by pickled wood walls and a skylight. The cathedral ceiling and open railing across the loft make this cozy chamber seem almost spacious. A tiled modern bathroom is equipped with a good supply of towels, as well as fragrant botanical soaps and shampoos.

Guests and their dogs who need to be more grounded will appreciate the wide variety of first-floor guest rooms. We happened to see one conveniently located off a path leading onto the property. This room is somewhat darker than the others because it is tucked into a protected part of the building. Nonetheless, we still found it appealing. In it, a small sitting room combines with a good-sized kitchen to form a single large space. Folding doors open to reveal the bedroom, which is dominated by a queen-size bed backed with a fan-shaped headboard. Muted colors have been used for the floral bedspread, as well as for the sofa in the sitting room. Other bedrooms have more lively Caribbean color schemes, as well as a variety of endearing built-in features, such as stained glass windows, interesting alcoves, and interior shutters. Guests who would like to entertain while in town may reserve a suite with a formal dining room—complete with an Oriental rug and crystal chandelier. The houses may be historic, but they also contain an array of modern conveniences, including modern kitchens, air conditioning units, cable televisions, and private telephones. Given our options, we prefer the bedrooms on the upper floors overlooking the gardens, or the bungalows in back. Whichever room guests ultimately select, they may expect private patios or decks that overlook the lush greenery or colorful flower gardens. Although the Douglas House may not be one of the more well-known guest houses in town, it is usually very busy, through word-of-mouth recommendations alone. This inn is one of the better kept secrets in Key West, and one worth considering when looking for a great home away from home.

Once again, we would like to point out that it is easy to walk a dog in Key West. It is only a few short blocks to the Southernmost Point, and a somewhat longer walk to the outdoor shopping areas and bars down by the town square. We want to stress that this is a terrific place for canines, as they are an integral part of this eclectic community where visitors can easily become a part of the multi-cultural backdrop that makes this island chain so intriguing.

Eden House

1015 Fleming Street
Key West, Florida   33060
(800) 533-KEYS, (305) 296-6868

Innkeeper: *Mike Eden*
Rooms: *29 doubles, 11 suites*
Rates: *Doubles $55-125 (EP), Suites $90-250 (EP)*
Payment: *MC and VISA*
Children: *Welcome, but there are no special amenities available for them*
Dogs: *Under 20 pounds are welcome*
Open: *All year*

When Mike Eden purchased the Eden House in 1975, he inherited an informal, European style pensioné. Furnishings were at a minimum, and bathrooms were scarce. This is one of the original Key West guest houses, where patrons, in the 1960s, could sleep comfortably for under $10 a night. To say that the atmosphere was relaxed is an understatement—this was the quintessential hippie retreat. Over the years, the place has significantly changed and become more upscale, in keeping with the rest of Old Town. To many of the locals and old-timers, the town has lost a little of its relaxed island feeling, but to the well-heeled who continue to flock here, it offers a full spectrum of intimate guest houses, fine restaurants, and art galleries.

The Eden House is within easy walking or bicycling distance of the shops in Old Town. It is tucked into a quiet, mostly residential neighborhood, filled with other historic Key West homes. Its 1920s Art Deco-style facade makes it unusual, with a pale green stucco exterior and covered porch that extends over the sidewalk. Inside the lobby, the paddle fans stir the warm air while guests relax in their wicker chairs. It was hard not to flash back to the movie Casablanca as we stood there taking in our surroundings. We soon learned that this was just a prelude to what we would find within the labyrinth of buildings known as the Eden House.

During Mike's 20-year tenure here, he has slowly acquired the other historic buildings adjacent to the original hotel and created a lovely compound. The rear building was his home for many years, before he converted it into apartments and suites. One of our favorite chambers is actually Mike's old apartment. This space, complete with a screened porch, has rustic pine walls but is modern in every other sense of the word with a fully-equipped kitchen and a good-sized bathroom. Our tiled bathroom was as large as our bedroom, with a shower running the length of one wall. An array of toiletries and lots of thick towels were thoughtful additions. The Effie Perez House was another building that Mike decided to buy and restore. It was in such a state of disrepair that the town used it as a haunted house one Halloween. Now, the nooks and crannies of this gray clapboard house are accented by crisp white trim and French doors opening to private balconies or decks. Suites and apartments are either tiled or carpeted and are filled with rattan furnishings. The fabrics are fairly neutral in color, but come in an array of tropical patterns. Some suites contain circular staircases leading up to the bedrooms. Paddle fans slowly move the air, although the addition of air conditioning is welcome on especially hot nights. Additional amenities in the apartments and suites are the cable televisions, refrigerators, and in many cases, kitchens. These houses are joined to the main hotel by extensive decking interspersed with lush tropical plants. A small waterfall and fish pool lie between the hotel and the Effie Perez House. In the afternoon, guests enjoy a complimentary happy hour, poolside. Most of the bedrooms overlook the pool and Jacuzzi, but, surprisingly, it is usually very quiet and guests have a feeling of complete privacy.

Although people traveling with a dog cannot stay in the original hotel, it would be remiss of us to overlook its Key West charm. The rooms in here are quite simple, with only a bed and a dresser furnishing these small chambers. Brass hooks serve as impromptu closets; there are no televisions, and rarely a private bathroom, in fact there are very few amenities at all. These clean and attractive bedrooms are appealing and inexpensive (by Key West standards), attracting guests who choose to spend their time exploring Key West and not their room.

Some people come to the Eden House to completely unwind, and feel little desire to leave the property. Fortunately, they can enjoy wonderful meals at Martin's Café which is an open air dining room tucked behind the hotel. The restaurant and its chef have German roots; however, the menu is a mix of Continental favorites. Their breakfasts are outstanding, with four types of Eggs Benedict topping the menu. Indulge in the classic, vegetarian, shrimp, or veal versions, or sample the delicate crèpes instead. The crèpes can contain Gulf shrimp or chicken and are topped with a Riesling sauce. Dinner is by candlelight, with selections such as escargôt in a garlic herb butter or the German potato soup as a first course. Entrées include filet mignon topped with a bernaise sauce, yellowtail served with a caper lemon butter, and a traditional wiener schnitzel.

Those who choose to travel beyond the confines of the property should be sure to examine the Eden House's brochure on Key West before they leave. We tried a few of the suggestions and were always pleased with the results. Their comments below the restaurant name, such as "Good Stuff" or "Worth the Trip", also come in quite handy. Guests can rent bikes at the Eden House, making excursions to town all the more fun and convenient, given the very limited parking near the stores. Because small dogs are preferred at the Eden House, we can safely say that it is simple to pop Bowser in the ample basket on the front of the bicycle and he can enjoy the leisurely adventure, as well. Walking Bowser from any of the suites or apartments is easy to do, as he can slip in and out through a locked gate and explore the quiet side streets whenever you feel the urge.

The staff is very accommodating and is always happy to direct guests to appropriate dining and late night entertainment. We loved the personalized attention and low-key atmosphere at the Eden House. This is not an overdone guest house filled with contrived guest rooms and an array of knickknacks. Instead, it is a lovely mix of old Key West and Europe, providing guests with both an intimate and informally delightful vacation experience.

Southernmost Point Guest House

1327 Duval Street
Key West, Florida 33040
(305) 294-0715, Fax (305) 296-0641

Hosts: Mona and Sandy Santiago and son
Rooms: 3 doubles, 3 suites
Rates: Doubles $55-110 (B&B), Suites $75-150 (B&B)
Payment: AE, MC, and VISA
Children: Welcome (crib and cots —$5 per night)
Dogs: Welcome
Open: All year

The Victorian-style Southernmost Point Guest House is striking with its gingerbread molding, wraparound porches, multiple gables and roof lines. The mansion was built in 1885 by the then-famous cigar manufacturer, E.H. Gato Jr. He was either a perfectionist or an eccentric (we suspect a bit of both) for, at some point, he had the house moved across Duval Street and turned so that his favorite porch received optimal sun time. Today, the house stands firmly on its original foundation; but it is a reminder of an era when Key West's cigar and sponge industry were at its peak and its inhabitants were enjoying the financial benefits. The opulence of this period is reflected in many of the expansive 1800s homes, which have endured throughout Key West's boom and bust times.

Visitors will discover that, true to its name, the Southernmost Point Guest House stands close to the famous Southernmost Point of the United States. The latter is marked by a huge buoy and plaque, which just about every tourist feels obligated to visit—but usually leaves wondering what all the hoopla is about. The guest house, while less well-known than it's namesake, is far more endearing. Surrounded by palm trees and tropical foliage, the informal grounds have a relaxed Key West feeling to them. The same can be said for the mansion. The parlor gave us a feeling for what we might find in the guest rooms, as it is filled with Victorian collectibles and an assortment of unrelated knickknacks. Since it was morning when we visited, the Continental breakfast was laid out on tables throughout the room. Breads, muffins, donuts, and other baked treats were placed on one tray, multiple boxes of cereal filled another, and a third held baskets brimming with fruit. Coffee was also supplied, along with a selection of international teas. While in the parlor, we had a chance to look at letters from previous guests that were taped to the windows and displayed about the room. After reading them, it was obvious that this place had left a lasting impression on its guests.

We met Mona, who is energetic, enthusiastic, and imbued with almost as much character as the guest house. She loves this place, and is proud of her association with it. We were given the grand tour of the mansion, where all of the guest rooms are accessed by separate outside entrances. Each has been individually furnished in an eclectic fashion. A first-floor room has ceilings that appear to be almost 18 feet high. The furniture, in here as in the rest of the house, looks like a collection of interesting hand-me-downs acquired from many generations. Some are antiques, others are vintage 1950s pieces. Linens are frilly, towels don't necessarily match, and bedsteads are well worn but very comfortable. Some of the beds are covered with floral prints, others with cotton spreads resembling zebra stripes. One of our favorites was Suite 5, not so much for the room as for the veranda, where guests have glimpses of the ocean through the palm trees. One bedroom has white tiled floors covered with assorted cotton rugs, while others feature original hardwood floors or are fully carpeted. Private bathrooms have been retrofitted to the guest rooms, which range from tiny to tremendous. The most spacious accommodation is a third-floor suite, with a master bedroom containing a king-size bed, a separate living room, a kitchen, and a private sun deck. Other guest rooms often contain a pair of double beds, along with a sofabed and a full kitchen.

For all its individuality, there is a certain comforting continuity that prevails at the Southernmost Point Guest House. Paddle fans circulate the tropical air, air conditioning vanquishes the heat, and refrigerators keep drinks and snacks for another day. Thoughtful extras, such as mints, fresh flowers, and baskets of toiletries, may be little touches, but they are nonetheless appreciated. The televisions are remote controlled, telephones are private, and the coffee makers are new. The inviting atmosphere allows guests to feel comfortable kicking off their shoes and relaxing in one of the lounge chairs. Best of all, Mona loves to have dogs around. In fact, she informed us (with a smile) that she sometimes prefers dogs to some of her guests. Oh yes, one final tidbit: the guest house even offers off-street parking—which is highly unusual, as parking in Old Town is virtually nonexistent.

The Southernmost Point Guest House is within a half block of tiny South Beach, located at the end of Duval Street. Some may prefer to rent a bicycle next door and ride out to the better beach found at Fort Zachary Taylor State Park. Bowser can come and enjoy most of the state park, but will have to stay off the beach. Guests who come back later, *sans* dog, are free to enjoy the snorkeling, swimming, and sunning available at this appealing strip of imported sand. At the end of the day, the barbecue awaits, allowing guests to create their own casual meals and relax on their private porch or in the gardens. Let the rest of the tourists watch the sunset festival at the north end of Duval Street, leaving the southern end in relative quiet. This makes after-dinner walks with Bowser, through the surrounding neighborhood, all the more appealing and pleasant.

Incentra Carriage House Inn

729 Whitehead Street
Key West, Florida 33040
(305) 296-5565

Innkeeper: Marianna Mike
Rooms: 5 doubles, 1 suite, 2 cottages
Rates: Doubles $59-125 (B&B), Suite $120-175 (B&B),
Cottages $135-290 (B&B)
Payment: AE, MC, and VISA
Children: Welcome
Dogs: Small dogs are welcome with prior approval
Open: All year

The Incentra Carriage House Inn is literally a block from the famous Hemingway House. If guests need any further evidence of its proximity to the great writer's home, they will see it in the six-toed cats that frequently stroll the grounds. The cats seem comfortable calling the inn's lush gardens their home —as do the free-ranging chickens and roosters that roam the property. Although the street in front of the Incentra Carriage House Inn is not one of Key West's most scenic, the historic 1870 Bahamian-style house is certainly lovely. The inn was originally owned by a prominent African American family, the Flemings, who operated a livery from this location. Today, the well-kept house is dressed up with white shingles, green shutters, and a small veranda. Guests will pass through a gate and under a small portico to enter the inn's very private gardens.

The property has over 100 varieties of tropical plants, creating a lush setting that extends almost to the next block. Meandering brick paths lead through the property: under a banyan tree, for example, around a lychee tree, then past a sapodilla. All of the trees seem to predate the three cottages situated on the property. The scent of jasmine fills the air, and the dense foliage makes people feel as if they are the sole occupants of this secluded oasis. The focal point for the inn is a large swimming pool, which provides a great way to ease the effects of the tropical heat.

As we were walking to one of the cottages, we noticed a rooster scratching in the dirt. We were told that the wandering fowl tend to dig up the small plantings just as soon as they are put in the ground. We did not see any signs of this, however, just plenty of well tended gardens. Our first stop was at the Villa/Samaritan Lane Cottage, which is a long, white, one-story cottage fronted by a covered porch. The pillars supporting its roof are enhanced by gingerbread molding corner pieces, while its base is trimmed with white trellis. Double hung windows and French doors make the bedrooms in this cottage open and airy. Guests may reserve the entire cottage, consisting of three bedrooms, a kitchen, and two baths, or any combination thereof. Here, as in the rest of the inn, the furnishings are an eclectic mix of antiques and rattan or wicker. Nothing is overdone, and it all blends together to create a pleasing, low-key decor. Each bedroom opens directly onto a patio or veranda, with the end rooms being the most desirable, as they afford an additional degree of sunlight and privacy. A narrow hallway wends through the cottage, tying the three rooms together. Our favorite bedroom has natural board walls painted out white, a huge wicker bed, and tables draped in yellow chintz. Guests needing use of the kitchen will find it to be fully stocked, although somewhat small. The rather funky bathrooms are also exceptionally clean.

The most requested accommodation is the Carriage House, which is set opposite the pool. It, too, has a small covered porch on the front, but the real living space is located toward the rear of the house. Here, the private patio is surrounded by walls covered with bougainvillaea that appear to be in perpetual bloom. The combination of the living room's cathedral ceiling and its walls of French doors opening onto the patio contribute to the generally spacious feeling of the cottage. White wicker and naturally stained rattan furnishings—combined with captain's chests, sisal rugs, and colorful botanical prints—comprise much of the rather Spartan, but very comfortable, furnishings. Guests are enamored with the beautiful backdrop of tropical foliage that may be enjoyed through the wall of windows and French doors. A futon provides an additional bed, although most people clearly prefer the comfort of the king-size bed in the separate bedroom.

As guests retrace their steps to the front of the property, they will come back to the Bahamian house. Those on a tight budget, and who don't mind a miniscule bedroom, may choose from one of the four guest rooms on the first floor of this house. On the other hand, the expansive upstairs room (referred to as the Treehouse) is a converted attic space that is accessed by way of an outside staircase. The deck is especially inviting, with a hammock that is perfectly sited to take advantage of this tranquil setting. Just inside is one elongated room set under the eaves. Two double beds and a futon will easily accommodate a group of friends or a family. Here again, an interesting mix of Caribbean and Floridian furnishings fill this chamber. We liked the green and gold paint-splattered effect on the wood floors. Paddle fans recirculate the cool sea air, but just in case it gets hot, air-conditioning is available as a backup. The kitchen in here is well equipped. We found that the only drawback to the Treehouse was the teeny tiny bathroom that seemed to have been added as an afterthought.

In the morning, guests may partake of a Continental breakfast set out on the shaded terrace behind the Bahamian house. Some choose to enjoy this meal at one of the small tables, while others bring it back to their rooms. It is easy to have a dog at the Incentra Carriage House Inn, as just about every bedroom (with the exception of the four first-floor Bahamian house chambers) has private, outside access. We recommend walking in the direction of the Hemingway House, then heading toward Duval Street. From there, there are plenty of great back streets to explore. In the evening, dogs can really have fun. Many people and their dogs stop by the special dog beach, adjacent to Louie's Backyard. While their owners enjoy a tropical libation, the dogs cavort with one another, and everyone has a fine old time. Another good option is a walk down Duval Street, where dogs are frequently found in the sidewalk cafés, sleeping at their owners' feet. First-time visitors to Key West will undoubtedly be surprised by just how much their canine friends blend into the fabric of the community.

Merlinn Guesthouse

811 Simonton Street
Key West, Florida 33040
(305) 296-3336, Fax (305) 296-3524

Innkeeper: Pat Hoffman
Rooms: 1 single, 10 doubles, 2 suites, 5 apartments
Rates: Single $36-50 (B&B), Doubles $67-100 (B&B), Suites $115-150
(B&B), Cottages $100-135 (B&B)
Payment: AE, DSC, MC, and VISA
Children: Welcome in the apartments only (a crib is available)
Dogs: Welcome in the apartments and cottages, with a one-time $10 fee
Open: All year

Meandering along the quiet back streets of Key West's Old Town, it is easy to walk right by the Merlinn Guesthouse. We did—and had to backtrack to find it. The inn is easy to miss because it is set behind an unobtrusive gray fence, whose only distinguishing feature is the stars that are cut out along the top. The stars provided us with a hint of what to expect beyond the fence, and the small sign on the gate indicated that this was indeed the Merlinn Guesthouse.

Most of the guest houses in Key West are blessed with a central garden and pool set amid lush tropical plantings, but the Merlinn is a step beyond the norm. After passing through the gate, guests enter a lush jungle of trees, ferns, and assorted flowers. Water flows through tiny streams, swirling into small pools containing exotic fish. A series of tiered decks flow away from the inn toward paths that lead over tiny bridges to quiet corners of the property. The massive trunk of a giant Maho tree wends along the ground, through hibiscus and other foliage, before it climbs skyward to provide a dense canopy for a portion of the gardens. There is a distinct Japanese look to the grounds, with a pergola spanning one stream and small statues and carvings tucked under immense leaves or alongside the pool. Small cages contain tropical birds, and deep within the labyrinth of paths leading to the guest rooms is a large aviary filled with finches and mourning doves. This is, of course, Hemingway country, and cats can usually be seen wandering freely about the property.

The opulence of the gardens envelopes the gray-stained buildings and cottages, which are joined by many secret alcoves and walkways. We found Pat in the tiered living room, where a wall of windows provides yet another glimpse of the exterior landscape. Comfortable rattan furnishings are set in small groupings, and it was here that we sat with Pat to talk about the guest house. She bought the guest house in the mid-1980s from two gentlemen who had spent a number of years creating the Merlinn. Theirs had been a successful venture and Pat wanted to maintain their traditions; yet, she wanted to make her own changes, too—to create an even more eclectic and appealing place. The breakfasts are one way in which Pat has sought to balance the past and the future. This has always been an ample meal, which begins with fresh tropical fruits and muffins topped with homemade preserves. It is complemented with a choice of granola or vegetable quiche. The latter has been a mainstay through the years. Morning is generally a peaceful time of day, when the only audible sounds are the chattering of birds against a backdrop of quiet conversation.

While the inn and grounds are not expansive, there are a variety of rooms available to guests. The smallest of these are located in one long wing that resembles an old fashioned motel. It runs along the property's perimeter and easily goes unnoticed, unless guests are looking specifically for it. There is nothing fancy here, just brightly decorated rooms that have a typical Key West charm. Because of their small size, these are not really appropriate for Bowser. Guests will find that the additional space and privacy afforded by the cottages and apartments are ideal for their canine friends.

One of these more roomy accommodations is the Conch House, a small cottage on the far edge of the property. What might have been a dark space has been enlivened by the bright green and blue sponge-painted walls. The cottage's front door opens directly into the bedroom containing a queen-size bed that is covered in a festive, tropical spread. A narrow doorway separates this room from the small living area furnished with a twin bed that doubles as a couch. In here, as in all the other cottages and apartments, is a fully-equipped kitchen. The Islander is another good alternative for guests and their dogs, as it is tucked behind the main building, close to an aviary filled with finches. This cavernous space has exposed rafters that are supported by pillars. Upon closer inspection, the festive, patterned bedspreads reveal cavorting tropical fish. Pat told us that she first found the whimsical spreads, then commissioned a local artist (who also painted Key West's Reef Relief mural) to create a mural for this room. The effect is stunning, with an entire wall dedicated to a lively reef scene.

The Deck House is a terrific choice for two couples or a family. There are two levels, with the first floor containing a 1950s-style, yellow tiled, eat-in kitchen and a small sitting are just off of that. Upstairs are two bedrooms and a shared bathroom. Our favorite is the sun-drenched purple bedroom, with a private sundeck that is brightened by flowers cascading down one trellised wall. Although we were unable to see the Patio House and Pool House, these are also decorated with a tropical and Far Eastern theme. The Patio House has one king-bed and a sleep sofa, while the Pool House is more expansive, with a pair of double beds in the master bedroom and a sleep sofa in the living room. While most of the accommodations are lightened by the sunlight pouring in through modern skylights, their bathrooms and kitchens would not be considered state of the art.

One of the many endearing features about the Merlinn is that people can either mix socially with the other guests or hide away in the very private rooms. The pool is one great place to meet other people and is set on the sunniest part of the property. The formal gardens are lovely to look at and walk through, but are not meant for romps with Bowser. Duval Street is only a block from the Merlinn, but guests would be better served to investigate some of the quieter back streets that run parallel to Duval. Here, they will discover wonderful residential neighborhoods with a mix of tiny conch houses amid more opulent homes. Those who wish to get the lay of the land will find that Old Town can be easily explored by foot. The Merlinn is located closer to the north end of town, where the famous (and heavily touristed) Sunset Festival takes place each evening in the Old Mallory Square. At the end of the day, though, it is just as easy to relax in the private enclave that is the Merlinn.

Whispers
at the Gideon Lowe House

409 William Street
Key West, Florida   33040
(800) 856-SHHH, (305) 294-5969

Hosts: Bonnie and John Marburg
Rooms: 6 doubles, 1 cottage
Rates: Doubles and Cottage $69-150 (B&B)
Payment: AE, MC, and VISA
Children: Not appropriate for children
Dogs: Welcome
Open: All year

The name Whispers is certain to conjure up plenty of images for most guests; however, for John and Bonnie Marburg, and all the owners who have preceded them, it represents a bit of Nirvana tucked within an island paradise. The Marburgs bought the inn over two years ago from another couple who had owned it for several years, who had bought it from someone else, who had bought it from someone else...and so on. As John tells it, he was offered some stock options a few years ago, took them, sold them, and bought the inn. His once diversified assets are now just one big asset: Whispers. We instantly liked both Bonnie and John, as much for their openness as for their energy, humor, and wit. These are essential qualities to have when running an inn and catering to a wide array of personalities.

We arrived in the middle of the day, having ridden our bikes up from Duval Street. The antique house is located on a side street in Old Town's residential district. Most of the guest houses in Key West are architecturally appealing, but this one is even more so. Built in 1845, with an addition in 1866, Victorian and Bahamian elements combine to create a distinctive look. A picket fence lines the tiny front gardens, with a walk leading up to the first veranda. The facade has two levels of verandas, fronted by gingerbread railings and backed by fully shuttered windows. The front of the house is a bit like an ornately decorated cake, except this one is topped by narrow eaves framing a single double-hung window.

When we arrived, it was that hectic time between check-in and check-out, when rooms were being cleaned, breakfast dishes were being put away, and an inventory was being taken of what was needed for incoming guests. Bonnie was in the middle of her busy routine, but happily took a break to give us the grand tour of their inn. Along the way, she laughingly told us that neither she nor John likes to cook or clean, but since they had to choose, he opted for the cooking and she for the cleaning. All the bedrooms, with one exception, are located in the main house. These are individually decorated with period antiques and contain perhaps a king-size, four-poster bed draped in lace, or an antique mahogany bed fitted with a half canopy. We liked the Periwinkle Room, with its bright blue walls and doors opening onto the upper veranda. In the attic, accessible by way of a steep flight of stairs, guests sleep under peaked ceilings. This top floor contains two rooms, better known as Grandma's Attic and Captain's Hideaway. These are the most casual spaces here, and they share a bathroom. Guests visiting with a dog are welcome out in the Garden House. Dog or no dog, this was our favorite room at Whispers. It seems more like a dollhouse than a cottage, and is set amid the lush tropical gardens found toward the rear of the inn. Guests who stay here enjoy the utmost in privacy. The mahogany antiques in the Garden House surround a four-poster bed set into an alcove. A small-print wallpaper, in mauve, lightens what might otherwise be a rather dark space. Within the nooks and crannies, is an intimate loft containing a double bed. An interesting array of collectibles displayed throughout this charming chamber add still more charm and interest to it.

Most of the guest houses in Key West serve a Continental breakfast; however, the Marburgs outdo themselves with their gourmet creations.

Small tables, set with a different tablecloth each day, are arranged across the outdoor brick patio. Lush plantings and potted flowers seemingly envelop guests, while finches and parrots chirp merrily in the nearby aviary, creating a truly memorable experience for the guests. Either John or his assistant prepares this repast, which is as beautifully presented as it is delicious. The menus vary, depending upon the whims of the cooks. One day, a croissant is dipped in a cinnamon egg batter and lightly fried, accompanied by an asparagus and dill omelette sautéed in garlic butter. On another morning, the croissant is dipped in nutmeg and egg, quickly fried, and then covered with fresh strawberries and a touch of rum. Other creations include the Eggs Florentine topped with cheddar cheese or the French toast à l'orange. Fresh fruit, juice, and coffee complete the meal.

If there is one drawback to Whispers, it is that it is without a pool; however, guests are free to use the swimming pool, private sandy beach, and health spa at The Reach Hotel. Bowser is not allowed on this expedition; however, there are still plenty of walks around the neighborhood and down to Duval Street, which should prove most intriguing. A self-guided walking tour, called the Pelican Path, leads visitors through Old Town. Guests may want to grab a map at the Chamber of Commerce and spend a relaxing morning with Bowser following the pelican signs to explore the many sights and attractions in the area. Although Mallory Square is usually filled with tourists who come to participate in the nightly sunset festival, it is fun to bring Bowser and check out the local street performers. When we were there, a man and a woman were doing all sorts of great tricks, accompanied by their cute (and highly talented) mutt and pot-belly pig.

The William House

1317 Duval Street
Key West, Florida 33040
(800) 848-1317, Fax (305) 294-9044

Innkeeper: William Wakeley
Rooms: 5 doubles, 3 suites, 1 apartment, 1 cottage
Rates: $83-170 (B&B)
Payment: AE, DC, DSC, MC, and VISA
Children: Welcome, but not especially appropriate for young children
Dogs: Welcome
Open: All year

Duval Street is a curiosity for many reasons. It has been called the longest street in the world, because it links the Atlantic Ocean with the Gulf of Mexico. Yet it is no more than a mile long. The street's personae seems to shift as visitors travel it's long but short span. The northern end has the famous open-air bars, t-shirt shops, and carnival atmosphere. It was here that we encountered one of Key West's local characters, his possessions strapped to the back of a bike and his endearing mutt lying comfortably up front in the basket. Of course, this was not an ordinary dog, it was a Key West critter who seemed to enjoy surveying the passing scene though his pair of green-tinted sunglasses. The southern end of Duval Street appears to widen, and the overall caliber of shops increases and the commotion from the throngs of tourists almost disappears. Nearing the "southernmost point", there are no stores at all, just a few guest houses and a large hotel. This is where we found The William House.

The building has been here since the 1920s, when it was called the Oceanview Hotel. Unfortunately, for much of its life it was better known as the Casa Blanca Boarding House where it housed transients and more recently, served as a crack house for drug addicts. Not a pretty picture, but an important piece of history, particularly given its most recent metamorphosis. Three years ago, William Wakeley came to Key West in search of a building he could turn into an inn. After looking at existing inns that were for sale, he settled on the old Casa Blanca Boarding House, which was virtually abandoned. He told us that it was easy for him to see past the beat up metal furniture, the hospital green paint, broken windows, sloping floors, and general filth, to the inherent potential of the building. When guests look through his "before and after" book for a clearer picture of the building, they will discover its checkered past has been physically erased and the original integrity of the building restored with a wonderful modern decorative twist.

The exterior of William House is in many ways right out of a New England landscape. A white picket fence frames the two story white shingled house. It's veranda and upper deck, dotted by tables set with red umbrellas, give it a distinctly Key Westian twist. Stepping inside, guests enter an enormous living room that runs the entire width of the house. This room, like many of the others, is decorated in an Art Deco style with triangular wall sconces, unusual standing lamps, a black leather sectional sofa, and a few decorative vases and bowls overflowing with flowers. The white walls are necessary, because throughout the inn there are bold accents of lacquered cherry red. The lustrous hardwood floor is covered with an Oriental rug. The other side of the room is taken up by an elegant baby grand piano backed by a mirrored wall that reflects the light from the crystal chandeliers. (William told us that he was so excited about these chandeliers that he hung them before the floors had even been finished.) On weekends, a pianist plays here in the afternoon, while guests sip their wine and sample the hors d'oeuvres. There is always an interesting knickknack or collectible displayed in the most unexpected places. The piece generating the most comment is an interior wall fountain that gurgles endlessly and has proven to be quite a curiosity.

The front and side doors are generally left open at the William House, allowing people to enjoy the refreshing sea breezes as they flow through the building. Each of the several first floor bedrooms is decorated in a distinctive manner, but all with a contemporary touch that we did not see duplicated anywhere else in Key West. The bright red bedroom doors open to reveal a very different color scheme which utilizes combinations of chocolate brown, deep green, and taupe that have been incorporated into intricate fabrics that cover the beds, sofas, and chairs. Gray carpeting provides a neutral backdrop for this rich use of color, as well as for the enormous, sleek, gray lacquered armoires that conceal the cable televisions. Tropical netting is draped from the ceilings and around the beds, forming a canopy that is purely esthetic. The ceilings soar 15 feet overhead and are broken up by the paddle fans that provide a gentle breeze on still nights. There is a variety of room configurations to choose from, with the two-room suites providing the most space. These contain a pair of queen-size beds and a sleep sofa. The cottage is set apart from the inn, and has a little more privacy than the rooms in the main building. Guests will find it by following a deck along the side of the house to the hot tub. A red French door marks the entrance to this exceptionally secluded space. Regular travelers will discover that standard amenities found in most first class hotels are also present at The William House, including voice mail telephones, faxes, cable televisions, clock radios, and refrigerators.

Each morning guests are invited to enjoy a Continental breakfast on the side deck or at one of the umbrella tables on the second floor deck overlooking the street. Anyone who wants to watch the parade of early morning beach goers or to just enjoy the sun, should opt for the porch. The William House is literally only a block from "the" beach, and although Bowser is not welcome on this postage-stamp size beach, it is still possible to walk along the sea wall with him. There are also plenty of side streets that are worth exploring on this end of town which lead visitors into the quieter, less traveled residential sections. We liked the feeling of actually being able to smell the ocean and feel the sea breeze, something that the guest houses located a few blocks away are unable to deliver.

We also liked William. His enthusiasm, coupled with a straight forward and hospitable manner, make him a very affable and delightful host. He took a great deal of time to offer suggestions for quiet local hangouts, serving authentic Cuban and Caribbean dishes and plenty of atmosphere. It isn't often that visitors stumble upon a family-owned restaurant where the chickens are running through the yard, music is playing, and you are the only out-of-towner eating there that night. That is a wonderful part of Key West that is easily missed unless you are willing to travel a bit off the beaten path. Anyone who truly wants to sample an unusual Key West spot, should definitely visit the cemetary. The caskets are in above-ground tombs, because it is too difficult to cut through the rock and coral for a more traditional below-ground burial. Read the epitahs, some of which reveal the true "character," or shall we say "characters," of old Key West.

Homewood Suites

3100 Parkway Boulevard
Kissimmee, Florida 34746
(800) 255-4543, (407) 396-2229, Fax (407) 396-4833

General Manager: Douglas Roos
Rooms: 156 suites
Rates: $94-189 (B&B)
Payment: AE, CB, DC, DSC, MC, and VISA
Children: Welcome (cribs, cots, and high chairs are available)
Dogs: Welcome with a $275 pet deposit, $75 of which is non-refundable
Open: All year

Disney World is always a wonderful destination, whether it is visitors' first trip or fifth, or somewhere in between. While there are seemingly countless ways to enjoy Disney's many expansive theme parks, the costs associated with these visits can be staggering. Though visitors cannot really hope for deep discounts on admission prices, they can cut down on "miscellaneous" expenses, such as food, accommodations, and transportation. One of the largest price variables is the accommodation option. Since we are a family of five, and two dogs make us seven, the ideal situation is usually a combination of rooms, or perhaps a suite, where we can easily cook, nap, sleep, play games, and just enjoy being close—but not too close. Just outside the gates of Disney World lies the Homewood Suites, which is fast becoming the accommodation of choice for families who want to travel economically, yet in style.

The Homewood Suites in Kissimmee is only one mile from Disney World's main gate. The hotel entrance is marked by shade trees, grass, and vibrant flower gardens. The villas are grouped in very attractive, two- and three-story, peach stucco buildings with interesting roofs. Expanses of grass, palm trees, and bedding plants surround these villas, along with a pond or two that provide a sense of visual coolness. Our first impressions are usually quite telling, and we were impressed with the lobby, which is more reminiscent of a country inn than a suite hotel. Boxed-beam ceilings make the space seem all the more intimate, as does the elaborate woodworking. A soft, taupe color has been used to paint the paneled walls and boxed columns that define these charming common areas. Low, contemporary flared armchairs are placed around a fireplace, while the brass coffee tables, harvest tables, and assorted accent pieces are more reminiscent of English country antiques.

When reserving a villa, keep in mind that there are four different styles from which to choose, ranging in size from 585 square feet to 900 square feet. Couples or families with only two children would be very comfortable in the standard Homewood Suite. The one thing that impressed us most was the emphasis on quality throughout these spaces. The decor in most of these is quite similar, with dove gray carpeting setting a neutral basis for the coral and slate blue, coordinated color schemes. Furnishings are very attractive contemporary pieces, combined with more traditional Florida-style glass and rattan. All suites have two televisions, with one containing a video cassette recorder. Walking into the expansive living room, guests will find a small dining room table placed at the far end, separating this chamber from the tiled kitchen. The kitchens have new Euro-style cabinets and are fully equipped with all the conveniences, including refrigerators with ice makers, microwave ovens, coffee makers, and dishwashers. A pair of doors open into the large bedroom, which contains either a pair of double beds or one king-size bed set opposite a second cable television. Pairs of windows generally look out to attractive views of the grounds or courtyards. Bathrooms have an adjoining dressing area where a counter contains the sink. Guests may also request the two-bedroom Homewood Suite, which is essentially the same configuration as we just described, but with a second, smaller bedroom.

The next grade of accommodations is the one-bedroom Master Suite, which is 700 square feet. There are fewer of these on the property, but the decor and number of amenities have both been increased. The living rooms are substantially larger and are equipped with fireplaces. We liked the big kitchens, as they are completely separate from the main living area. For the ultimate in space and privacy, guests may reserve a two-bedroom Master Suite. Both of these bedrooms are oversized and contain separate bathrooms and dressing areas. Guests should keep in mind that even the most expensive and luxurious two-bedroom Master Suite is far less expensive than anything comparable on the Disney property.

By staying outside the park, guests may give up easy access to Epcot, Magic Kingdom, and MGM Studios, but the Homewood Suites does offer free transportation to each of these attractions. We recommend starting the day early, very early. The management has made this proposition quiet painless by providing deluxe Continental breakfasts for their guests. Baskets of freshly baked muffins, breads, and pastries are laid out in the lobby each morning, along with cereals and fresh fruits. Top this off with coffee and juice and most people are ready to get started with their day's adventure. Whether guests plan to return mid-day or as the parks are closing, they will appreciate the opportunity to take a swim in the pool. Children have their own kiddie pool and fenced-in play area. Adults may also wish to rejuvenate in the whirlpool, or head over to the sports' court and fitness center to exercise a bit more. Social hour takes place in the early evening, which is a nice time to get acquainted with the other guests and enjoy a complimentary glass of wine, beer, soda, or bag of popcorn. We especially liked the idea of being able to cook our own meals, whether in the kitchens or out on the grill. We know this should be a vacation for everyone; therefore, it makes sense to take advantage of the complimentary grocery shopping service, which leaves guests' cupboards and refrigerator fully stocked and ready to be consumed.

Bowser nicely fits into this picture, too. If guests are planning to be out and about for just a few hours, then they may wish to leave their canine companions at home in air conditioned comfort. Guests should keep in mind, though, that the maids will not clean the suites if there is a dog inside. Those who are gone a full day can bring the dog along and board him at any of the three kennels located outside the gates to MGM Studios, Epcot, and the Magic Kingdom. (See Disney World, kennels for detailed information.) Trips to Universal Studios and Sea World can also be taken with a dog, as there are air conditioned kennels on these properties as well. There are plenty of places to walk dogs around the Homewood Suites, although once off the property the roads can get very busy. We found though, that all in all, for those who want to "do" Disney World and Orlando with their dogs, this is one of the better accommodation options in terms of convenience, quality, and value.

Wynfield Inn
Main Gate

5335 Irlo Bronson Highway
Kissimmee, Florida 34746
(800) 468-8374, (407) 396-2121, Fax (407) 396-1142

General Manager: Richard Kalas
Rooms: 216 doubles
Rates: $49-79 (EP)
Payment: AE, CB, DC, DSC, MC, and VISA
Children: Welcome; under 17 years of age are free of charge when sharing a room with parents (cribs, cots, and high chairs are available)
Dogs: Welcome in select pet rooms, with a $10 nightly fee
Open: All year

The majority of Orlando's hotels and motels that welcome dogs may be found in the appendix; however, we have selected a few of the best to review individually. The accommodations located on the Disney World property are decidedly the most fun and convenient, but they can be expensive. The Homewood Suites is a high-end property that is more affordable than most of the Disney choices, and is situated just a mile from the main gate. Those searching for more of a bargain hotel will discover that the Wynfield Inn is both affordable and fairly convenient.

There are actually two Wynfield Inns, one just four miles outside Disney World's main gate, and another that is ten miles away, with an Orlando address. We preferred the Kissimmee location, but if it is full, Wynfield Inn's Orlando hotel is a good backup. The Wynfield Inns are presented as offering "affordability with style," and we would agree with that assessment. The two- and three-story buildings are clapboarded and their rooflines are gabled, in places. The architecture is somewhat reminiscent of a Cape Cod style, with a Florida twist. The inn in Kissimmee is fairly intimate, making it terrific for families who want to avoid the larger hotels, where it is easy to get lost in the fray. The guest rooms are centered around a heated swimming pool and children's pool, which are surrounded by beautifully landscaped grounds consisting of large grassy areas, flower gardens, and palm trees. The swimming pool is one of the nicest in the area. When guests are not visiting the theme parks, most tend to be found rejuvenating near one of the pools.

Some of the accommodations overlook the pool, while others face the parking lot. Guests traveling with a dog are asked to stay in the rooms designated for pets. These generally have parking lot views, and are all located on the first floor, providing canines easy access to the outdoors. While we would have preferred pool-side vistas, we found that all of the guest rooms shared the same amenities. These accommodations have identical interiors, and are large enough to easily accommodate two to four people, as well as their dogs. Furnishings are standard, hotel variety, and made of good quality, lightly stained woods. Festive floral spreads cover the two double beds, brass lamps provide ample reading light, and bureaus and closets contain enough storage space to hold a family's belongings for several days. Aside from the usual standard features like cable televisions, private telephones, and central air conditioning, guests may also request rooms with refrigerators and safes.

The Wynfield Inn may be more budget-oriented than others, but they include some extras not commonly associated with inexpensive motels. Complimentary coffee and tea are served 24 hours a day in the comfortable lobby. For a slight additional charge, guests may also enjoy a substantial Continental breakfast, served pool-side each morning. The small hut where this repast is presented, known as Windjammers, also offers old-fashioned hot dogs, assorted snacks, and a variety of soft drinks and frozen concoctions throughout the day. Guests at the Wynfield Inn are given coupons that entitle them to 10% off their food at neighboring restaurants. Since most people stay for more than a day, the convenience of on-site laundry facilities is also helpful; however, the children are more likely to appreciate the game room.

Guests may walk their dogs about the property, and either leave them in the room during the day or board them at Disney's kennels. If visiting Universal Studios or Sea World, there are also staffed and air conditioned kennels that are ideal daytime accommodations for dogs. While there are not a lot of state parks or recreation spots in this area that welcome dogs, there is far more greenery around the inn than we had expected to see.

Chalet Suzanne Country Inn

3800 Chalet Suzanne Drive
Lake Wales, Florida 33853
(813) 676-6011, Fax (813) 676-1814

Innkeepers: *Carl and Vita Hinshaw*
Rooms: *30 doubles*
Rates: *$125-185 (B&B)*
Payment: *AE, CB, DC, DSC, MC, and VISA*
Children: *Welcome (high chairs, cribs, and babysitters are available)*
Dogs: *Welcome with a $20 daily fee, per pet*
Open: *All year*

During our years of research, we have seen literally thousands of inns, and we can safely say that the Chalet Suzanne is one of the most unique. We aren't the only ones who think so, as it has won accolades (along with four stars and diamonds) not only for its cuisine, but also for its accommodations. The countryside around the inn is blanketed by citrus groves—not by stands of palm trees, sand, and ocean. Chalet Suzanne is south of Orlando, but it feels as though it is millions of miles from the hubbub of Disney World and the masses of people lining the coastal beaches. The concept for the inn and restaurant first began back in the 1920s, when Bertha Hinshaw's husband passed away. He left her with two children, a small house, and plenty of land near Lake Wales. She was an industrious soul, filled with a sense of whimsy and style, and an aptitude for cooking. Her personality, perseverance, and talents parlayed themselves into the creation of the now-famous Chalet Suzanne.

Driving along back-country roads, we at last came across a narrow driveway that edged through orange groves, past shade and palm trees, near the kaleidoscopic colors of the flower gardens, and finally emerged at the inn. It was then that our mouths fell open. Mix the Munchkins' village in the Wizard of Oz with an Italian villa, throw in a few turrets and spires from the Spanish Moorish architecture, and the result is, in a nutshell, the Chalet Suzanne. This compilation of styles and motifs is an endearing sight, created over the years by Bertha, who simply added to her home as the need arose. The end result is a collection of cottages, all joined together by different roof lines, angles, eaves, and architectural styles. The exteriors may be stucco or clapboard, and the color schemes range from peach to various hues of yellow and blue. The one constant is the beautiful imported tile she had inlaid on the exterior walls and around the fountains, along the brick walkways, and throughout the interior spaces. These tiles don't necessarily match, but then again, nothing else does either. We liked it and are sure you will too.

As one might imagine, the bedrooms here are unique. They are literally filled with collectibles and antiques that Bertha acquired during her 18 trips around the world. Beds might be fashioned with ornately carved, mahogany headboards, brass accents, or hand-painted headboards with a pair of lavender finials. Pretty floral spreads set a feminine overtone to some spaces, while others exude a more tropical feeling. Bedside lamps reflect Victorian, Art Deco, and Georgian styles. Armchairs are wingback, high back, or no back at all. The hardwood floors generally run off at funny angles, as do the ceilings, which follow the inn's unusual exterior roof lines. Each piece of furniture is wonderful by itself; however, combined, they form an eclectic combination of furnishings that give each chamber a distinctive and fanciful personality.

The accommodations alone are worth a visit; however, Chalet Suzanne's restaurant is equally appealing, both visually and gastronomically. It is so popular that the Hinshaws have even put in a landing strip to accommodate guests jet-setting in from other parts of the state. We loved the physical space in here, as it is broken up with nooks, crannies, steps, landings, and of course, decorative tile. Along the walls are photographs of famous people who have visited the inn. These are interspersed with decorative ceramic plates and shelves lined with their much-heralded cans of soups. Bertha originally started the business with her soup creations, which are now quite famous and are carried in countless gourmet shops throughout the country. The soups are produced right on the premises, and visitors are welcome to tour the small factory where the Hinshaw family's soups are canned. Bertha may have started making the soup, but it was her son Carl who worked next to her his entire life and grew the soup business into what it is today. After Carl married Vita, they both worked with Bertha for years, until her death in 1973 at the age of 90. They are the life behind this place today.

While a full breakfast is served to guests of the inn each morning, it is the lunches—and especially the dinners—that most guests really look forward to. The different styles of tables overlooking the grounds and small lake are set with unusual mismatched plates, goblets, flatware, and crystal. Lunch is a four-course affair, while dinner boasts six separate courses. Dinner starts with a grapefruit, broiled with cinnamon and sugar and topped by a chicken liver. This is followed with the soup Romain (nicknamed Moon Soup, as it was taken on the Apollo 15 and 16 space flights), which is served in an unusual Norwegian ceramic ashtray. (Don't ask, just enjoy!) Most people find the multi-use ash trays so appealing that they buy a few at the ceramic studio to take home. The soup Romain is the most popular of all the Chalet Suzanne soups. The salad course is omitted at lunch, but is included at dinner. Entrées are delicious and each is noteworthy. A perennial favorite is the lobster Newburg, which is enriched with fresh butter and cream and a dash of sherry. The lump crab meat is served with a delicious herb butter, and the lamb chop grill is accompanied by sautéed chicken liver, country sausage, and bacon. It is, however, the chicken that everyone seems to rave about. This bird is carefully basted during the entire baking process, so that the juices permeate every delicate morsel. The one thing that is difficult to describe are the seasonings, which are distinctive without being overwhelming. We recommend saving a little room for the miniature crèpes Suzanne, the rum cream pie, or possibly the gâteau Christina, where toasted almond meringues are layered with rich, dark chocolate.

Where does Bowser fit into all this? We were pleased to note that every room has a separate outside entrance, making it easy to take dogs for impromptu strolls. The grounds are expansive, and the inn buildings comprise only a small portion of the 70 acres. While Bowser would probably be interested in taking a dip in the heated swimming pool, we recommend that guests take him, instead, over to investigate the lake or Payness Creek, a 367-acre historic preserve just south of Lake Wales. Early in the morning, guests can walk with Bowser to the edge of the property and follow the country road for a while. Of general interest to guests are the nearby Bok Tower Gardens (with a few outdoor kennels) and Cypress Gardens.

Cedars Tennis Club

645 Cedars Court
(5600 Block of the Gulf of Mexico Drive)
Longboat Key, Florida   34228
(800) 433-4621, (813) 383-4621, Fax (813) 383-5534

General Manager: *Perry Landis*
Rooms: *96 condominiums*
Rates: *$800-1,400 per week (EP)*
Payment: *MC and VISA*
Children: *Welcome (cots are available for $31.30 per week)*
Dogs: *Welcome with a $35 fee and a $300 refundable security deposit*
Open: *All year*

Longboat Key is located just outside of Sarasota. Twelve miles in length, it is the longest in a series of islands linked to the mainland by the John Ringling Causeway. (Yes, Sarasota is the home of the famous Ringling Brothers Circus). Longboat Key, along with the neighboring St. Armands Key, also happens to be one of Florida's more affluent areas. Visitors' first impressions certainly do little to discourage the image. Upon leaving the causeway, travelers emerge onto St. Armands Circle, which is a ring of exclusive shops and restaurants set amid perfectly manicured tropical gardens and foliage. This enclave is perhaps three times larger and more elaborate than Palm Beach's prestigious Worth Avenue, lacking for little except, perhaps, a "doggie bar." The shopkeepers are fond of the pedigreed pooches, though, who sometimes accompany their owners out shopping.

From St. Armands Circle, the Gulf of Mexico Drive leads past exclusive country clubs, lavish Gulfside apartments, and private homes until it reaches the Cedars Tennis Club. Situated on Sarasota Bay, well off the busy thoroughfare, the large complex is comprised of three groupings of attractive condominiums standing amidst a 33-acre nature preserve. Cedars was built in stages. The newest section, Evergreen

Place, was completed just four years ago. Although each complex is almost identical to the others, each is also in some way distinctive. Forest Way is the complex closet to the main road, yet it is only a three-minute walk to the private white sand beach that lines the Gulf of Mexico. Guests may walk along a wooden boardwalk or drive along the lane to the second section, called Cedars Court. This segment is built around the tennis complex, the Olympic-size swimming pool, and the café. Finally, there is Evergreen Place, a more intimate collection of condominiums situated just off Sarasota Bay. As we mentioned, each section is linked by wooden boardwalks, which are just right for leisurely walks with Bowser.

Although the tennis courts are usually busy, it is clear that many guests don't feel they have to play tennis to enjoy their vacation at Cedars. For those who are interested, however, there are excellent tennis pros, a great lesson program, and 10 lighted Har-Tru courts. Many of the condominium complexes we visited in Florida did not have an on-site staff; instead, a rental agent handled the bookings. This is not the case, however, at Cedars, where the office seems to be just as busy as the other facilities. We were impressed with the staff's overall friendliness, both with us and with other guests. People wandered in and out of the main building during our visit—many with their dogs in tow—just to chat or to check on the schedule for the day. The swimming pool was also hopping, with children playing water games or adults swimming laps. This is an active place, serving as a natural draw for active people.

We liked the feeling of life around the place, but equally appealing are the gray clapboard condominiums. These are well designed contemporary structures with multiple roof lines, plenty of paned and Palladian windows, and an array of mature plantings surrounding them. The abundant windows in these three-story condominiums reveal distant views of the water and the surrounding vegetation, while also permitting good cross-ventilation from the Gulf's refreshing breezes. The floor plans are well designed and also fairly consistent from one building to the next. Each unit has a private garage with a set of stairs leading up to the enormous living and dining room. We noticed that some of the living rooms had hardwood floors, while the remainder used a combination of tile and wall-to-wall carpeting.

When we were here the management had just completed a massive redecoration project, infusing some $20,000 into each of the units. Here again, the style of furnishings is quite consistent from one condominium to next: soft, taupe-toned leather sofas in the living rooms; sleek, glass-topped dining room tables in the dining areas; and balloon shades or jabots framing the windows. The contemporary kitchens have every conceivable modern convenience, including new dishwashers, microwaves, and coffee makers, as well as full sets of china, silver, and glassware. Sliding glass doors lead to the screened lanais, which add to the already ample living spaces. On the top floor are two bedrooms. The master bedroom has a king-size bed, as well as a separate dressing area and a private bathroom with two sinks. A second bedroom contains a pair of twin beds and has access to a hall bathroom. These are light and open spaces—particularly the master bedroom, where four windows on one wall and a pair on another offer some of the best views of the surrounding area. The bedroom's bureaus and tables are crafted from lightly stained and pickled woods, while white rattan or woven, fan-shaped headboards back beds draped in thick, quilted floral spreads. Decorative accents include botanical prints and the bright colors of the Haitian, pressed tin drum art. As we looked around, it was clear that a decorator's touch had carefully coordinated the color schemes and overall look of these units.

The beach is only a four- to ten-minute walk, depending on which condominium guests are staying in. Leashed dogs are frequently seen on the sand in the early morning and evening hours, although we understand they are not technically permitted on the beaches. As we mentioned earlier, Cedars also has acres of beautiful, preserved land that lends itself to long walks. Others enjoy taking a stroll along the Gulf of Mexico Drive, where there is plenty to look at along the way. Non-doggie diversions might include a visit to the Mote Marine Aquarium on City Island, just south of Longboat Key. Here, the Mote Marine Laboratory has put together displays that illustrate what the local marine and mangrove ecosystems are all about. Another excellent choice is the 15-acre Marie Selby Botanical Gardens in Sarasota, which is rich with thousands of species of plants and orchids.

Lighthouse Bed and Breakfast

13355 Second Street East
Madeira Beach, Florida   33708
(813) 391-0015

Hosts: Joyce Drew and John Michael Dickinson
Rooms: 4 doubles, 2 suites, 1 cottage
Rates: Doubles $60-75 (B&B), Suites $60-75 (B&B),
*   Cottage $90-120 (B&B)*
Payment: MC and VISA
Children: Most appropriate for ages 5 years and up
Dogs: Welcome, with advance notice and prior approval
Open: All year

Madeira Beach lies on one of a series of islands located near the bustling Tampa/St. Petersburg area. The islands are connected to one another by busy Route 699, otherwise known as Gulf Drive. This is Florida at its more crowded. However, a quiet spot can be found near the Gulf of Mexico's sandy beaches, next to the Boca Ciega Bay. This is certainly not the land of Bed and Breakfasts, as most accommodations are found in the high-rise apartments and condominiums that dot the Gulf shores. We were surprised to discover the Lighthouse Bed & Breakfast, on the opposite side of the drive, situated among other private homes in a low-key residential neighborhood.

We knew we were in the right place when we spotted the distinctive lighthouse, which anchors one corner of the property. The small complex is actually a series of wings built off the lighthouse, forming a courtyard reminiscent of a Key West guest house. Joyce and John purchased the B&B in early 1995. We could see that they had already accomplished a number of renovations and were planning more. Initially, though, we were most focused on the Cape-style house, as it contains the most creative and interesting use of space. Inside, a large area—created by the curved interior walls of the lighthouse joining with those of the main house—has been transformed into a charming, white-tiled breakfast room. From the white iron, glass-topped tables, guests may sample one of John's gourmet morning meals. During high season, fresh fruit is accompanied by cereals, or by more elaborate waffles, pancakes, or overstuffed omelettes. In the off season, the meal becomes a Continental affair, with delicious muffins and breads topping the menu. Afterwards, guests may take their coffee outside to the courtyard, where palms and flowering cactus plants add to the tropical environment.

The bedrooms lie in the two wings just off the courtyard, in unobtrusive, one-story buildings that are partially concealed by the lush foliage. When we were visiting, some of the guest rooms had already been redecorated, while others were slated to be redone in the near future. Joyce assured us that all the rooms would be getting a facelift, and that they hoped to be finished by the end of 1995. The newer units had attractive Key West color schemes, interspersed with a mishmash of modern furnishings and collectibles. The effect was appealing and casual. We're sure that once Joyce and John are able to tackle the remaining guest rooms, all of them will be quite wonderful. The kitchenettes are great for storing cold foods and creating light meals. Of course, air conditioning and cable television are thoughtful amenities that most will appreciate. To the rear of the B&B, just outside the courtyard, is a larger two-bedroom cottage with a living room and full kitchen. This is terrific for a family looking for a little more space and privacy.

In the afternoon there are always snacks and cool drinks laid out for the guests. Joyce's two Pekinese usually can be found sleeping in the courtyard, completing the domestic scene. For those who are craving an immediate beachfront fix, there is a small sandy landing facing the narrow bay, just a stone's thrown from the B&B. This is not a place for sunning—just for visiting with a dog and catching a glimpse of the water. Most people, however, prefer to head out in the other direction, where they will find the big beach. From here, a short stroll will lead to the famous Johns Pass Village, which used to be a rustic group of tin-roofed fishing shacks. Today, the shacks are joined by a 1,000 foot boardwalk and contain shops and restaurants, along with all sorts of water sport companies (which supply a wide choice of recreational options for tourists). This might also be an appropriate and appealing walk with Bowser. Some visitors will want to drive south to Cabbage Key and Madelaine Key, where they will find the 900-acre Fort Desoto Park. Fort Desoto is a leftover from the Spanish-American War. Dogs are welcome to explore the park's grassy areas—on a six-foot leash. Human visitors might like to know about the miles of beaches, picnic areas, and a bird sanctuary. A trip to the world famous Busch Gardens is a must for tourists. Unfortunately, Bowser must remain in one of the park's kennels, but these are free of charge. Visitors need only bring a bowl for water and some food. The dogs are checked by personnel every hour, but they are not walked; therefore people who are boarding their dogs for the day, should return to walk them. When entering the Busch Gardens parking area, visitors need to drive through the toll booths to find the kennels. If the day is busy, attendants may try to direct visitors to alternate parking across the street. But head for the toll booths anyway—the staff will understand as soon as they see the dog.

Rainbow Bend Resort

Route 1, Box 159
Grassy Key, Mile Marker 58
Marathon, Florida   33050
(800) 929-1505, (305) 289-1505

Manager: Jeanne Ruster
Rooms: 11 doubles, 11 suites
Rates: Doubles $110-165 (B&B), Suites $140-210 (B&B)
Payment: AE, DSC, MC, and VISA
Children: Welcome, infants are free of charge and children are $10 (high
chairs are available)
Dogs: Welcome with a $10 fee, provided they are leashed on the property
Open: All year

Driving through the Florida Keys is always an experience, whether it's the first time or the hundredth. For those unfamiliar with the area, there is one road, known as the Overseas Highway, leading on and off the Keys. Depending upon the time of day and year, the road can be relatively quiet or lined with bumper to bumper traffic. We recommend that first-time visitors come armed with a "don't worry, be happy" attitude and they will be better equipped to understand the subtleties of the Keys. As we were traveling along the highway through Grassy Key, destination uncertain, we stumbled upon the Rainbow Bend Fishing Resort. It is located at Mile Marker 58 (there are few addresses along this highway, everything is referenced by Mile Markers) and is situated behind low walls and lush foliage, thereby reducing the sound of road noise.

We knew that Rainbow Bend was a fishing resort and, for some reason, we could only envision a glorified bait and tackle shop surrounded by innocuous bungalows. We were therefore pleasantly surprised to come across this Caribbean-style resort, where clutches of bright pink stucco cottages line the beach amid gently swaying palm trees. As we walked out onto the hard sand beach, lined with thatched huts, we found a man reading quietly in the shade of a palm tree, while children sorted through some of the beach toys that are stored in an old wooden dory. A line of 15-foot Boston Whalers bobbed alongside the dock, and a couple of Sunfish were tacking back and forth just offshore. Strangely enough, even though there were people around and plenty of activity, it was very quiet and serene.

After a while, we pulled ourselves away from the beach and went off in search of the office, which, it turns out, is also a tiny general store offering everything from casual resort wear to soft drinks. As we were talking with Jeanne, a distressed woman walked in with her family and asked if there was a room available. It seems the family had made reservations at another large hotel in the area, sight unseen, and were disappointed with the rooms and impersonal feeling of the place. Jeanne gave her a quick tour of a few available units. The woman returned a few minutes later, looking very relieved, and asked to reserve one. We were just as curious to see some of the rooms as she was, and were pleasantly surprised as well.

The accommodations are located in six different buildings, and range from an intimate Jacuzzi Room to a large Oceanfront Suite in the Octagon House. Guests in search of a romantic hideaway should consider the Jacuzzi Suite. It does not have direct ocean views, but it is very private. We stepped across the lanai and through sliding glass doors onto the cool white tile floors. The natural wood walls and skylights, coupled with the informal rattan furnishings, lend a casual feeling to this space. As in the rest of the resort, the colors in here reflect the tropics. In this case, the room is lightened by a green cotton spread covering the bed. The bathroom has no door, just a wide arch that reveals the corner Jacuzzi and a pair of sinks. As we walked from the Jacuzzi Room to another oceanfront unit, we noted that some areas could use a little landscaping and some of the old stucco walls were in need of a fresh coat of paint. Generally, the resort is in excellent shape; there are just a few out of the way spots that could use some tending to.

A unit entitled "Lower D" faces the water and has sliding glass doors that open to reveal a small sitting room and fully-appointed kitchen. The natural wood walls in here, and throughout the rest of the unit, are painted out white. This area is tiled, but the two small bedrooms in the back have coral-colored carpeting. The beds are twins, but can be pushed together to form a king, depending on guests' preference. There is little else in the rooms, except for armoires crafted from rough-hewn wood. Contemporary furnishings are comfortable and easy on the eye. In the morning, guests can make a pot of coffee, grab one of the bright pink or green mugs from the cabinet, and enjoy a leisurely hour or so on the lanai. Just beyond this unit is a large thatched hut with a barbecue and picnic table, which guests tend to use at night for cooking dinner.

Our favorite spot is the two-story Octagon Building, set on the edge of the resort and separated from the rest of the accommodations by a large, grassy area. There are just two units inside, one on each level. Because the building has eight sides, the interior walls have all sorts of interesting angles that allow for maximum breezes and, even more importantly, incredible water views. The living room in the first-floor unit has matching rattan furnishings accented by pale blue and coral, tropical-patterned pillows. These sofas also convert into beds. A dining area and kitchen adjoin the living room, along with two bedrooms and one and a half baths. Regardless of room choice, guests may expect contemporary furnishings constructed from light woods or rattan, and color schemes designed to enhance the lightness of these good-sized chambers. Some of the bathrooms are a bit dated, but without exception, the interior spaces are immaculate. Our advice, when deciding where to stay, would be to opt for the Octagon Building, Upper or Lower A-D, or Rooms 6-8, as each of these have unobstructed water views. When inquiring about accommodations, guests may ask the receptionist to send a map of the resort, which clearly indicates where the units are located in relationship to the beach and the highway.

The rates may seem a bit steep, considering the simplicity of the accommodations; however, this is a waterfront resort and there are many hidden extras. While guests are staying at Rainbow Bend they have unlimited use of the Boston Whalers, Sunfish, and canoes (guests pay only for the motor boats' gasoline). VCRs can be rented by the day, and guests may borrow any of the videos at no extra charge. Swimming off the beach is a little tricky, as it is mostly coral and rock; however, guests may borrow a boat and take it offshore about a mile to the sandbars. This is a surprising little swimming beach, which also happens to have some of the best snorkeling in the area. Bowser will certainly enjoy accompanying his human companion on this outing, and he'll love the chance to swim offshore. We recommend that guests bring their own mask, snorkel, and fins to explore the coral reefs around here. The brochure suggests, and the staff confirms, that some of the best snorkeling in the Keys lies at Mile Marker 45, where a living coral reef contains an amazing abundance of sea life. After a busy day, it is always nice to return for a rejuvenating dip in the swimming pool or the adjacent spa.

Most like to begin their day with a full complimentary breakfast at Mike's Hideaway Café. "Hideaway" is an appropriate name for this place, as it is tucked into the top floor of the main building and guests have to search for the unobtrusive stairway leading up to it. The gourmet restaurant is owned and operated independently of Rainbow Bend, but is integrated right into the resort. Inside, most people are drawn to the floor-to-ceiling windows, and beyond to the screened-in deck, where turquoise waters extend as far as the eye can see. Simple formica tables and rattan chairs are set on terra-cotta tiled floors and framed by pale green walls, dotted with coral accents. There is very little about the physical space that indicates what type of meal will follow.

The appetizer list is long and includes three types of escargôt. One is baked en croute; another is served "à la Mike," where the escargôt is baked with mushrooms, garlic, spinach, and proscuitto. The final escargôt selection is sautéed with fresh vegetables, garlic, black pepper, cognac, and heavy cream. The two-page menu changes frequently, but there is always a wide array of offerings. During our visit, grouper was prepared three different ways. It was baked in parchment paper with shrimp, scallops, mushrooms and a lobster sauce; it was covered with peppercorns and cognac; and it was sautéed in a light egg batter with lemon and white wine. The finest cuts of beef are well-aged—by Mike of course. Guests might try the filet mignon with a bernaise sauce, the medallions of beef sautéed with black butter and garlic, then flamed with cognac and served with shrimp, or the chateaubriand with a bouquetière of vegetables. After a dinner such as this, those staying here are fortunate; they can just head back to their room, open their windows, and smell the salt air as it wafts in off the ocean.

Bowser is a most welcome guest at the Rainbow Bend, and is free to explore the beachfront at the resort and further along the coast. Walking along the highway is not recommended during the heat of the day, but early in the morning it is usually still quiet, and an invigorating stroll can be quite pleasant. Rainbow Bend has been here for over 20 years and has retained its old Keys atmosphere. We hope it can hold onto its casual and relaxed feeling for another 20 years.

Faro Blanco Marine Resort

1996 Overseas Highway
Marathon, Florida 33050
(800) 759-3276, (305) 743-9018, Fax (305) 743-2918

General Manager: Melanie Tank
Rooms: 27 cottages, 71 houseboats, 2 lighthouse apartments, 30 condominiums
Rates: Cottages $55-145 (EP), Houseboats $79-185 (EP), Lighthouse
    Apartments $135-175 (EP), Condominiums $205-232 (EP)
Payment: AE, MC, VISA
Children: Welcome (cribs and babysitters are available)
Dogs: Welcome in the cottages and houseboats for an $18 one-time fee
Open: All year

Marathon is not necessarily the first town people think of when planning a trip to the Keys. For those traveling by yacht, though, the lighthouse at the Faro Blanco Marine Resort has been a navigational landmark and favorite overnight anchorage for many years. The resort actually lies on both sides of the Overseas Highway, which is a well-traveled road connecting Florida's mainland with the Keys. The Faro Blanco offers cottages, houseboats, and docking facilities, all of which are accessible from the water. Unlike most seafaring souls who frequent these parts, we approached the resort by land, found the office, and checked in. Although this resort was new to us, we quickly learned that many of the guests have been coming here for decades. The cottages are the first-choice of accommodations for many visitors, who like the small stucco and clapboard buildings painted in cheery tropical yellows, greens, and peaches. The best of these small buildings are located closest to the Gulf. Although guests cannot see the turquoise water, they can certainly feel the breezes emanating from it. Each cottage is different from the others inside, but all are minimally furnished. In some, natural board walls are painted white and the rooms are filled with bamboo furniture. Others contain a spacious main room with a king-size bed and small sitting area consisting of a sofa and armchair. Although there are few knickknacks, all the basics—such as good reading lamps, refrigerators, cable television, and telephones—have been thoughtfully provided. Some cottages contain extremely clean kitchenettes, although these are strictly out of the 1940s, with vintage linoleum and fixtures. The bathrooms are also somewhat dated, but again, they are immaculate and well equipped with soaps, shampoos, and towels. Each of the cottages is individually air conditioned and they also have paddle fans. Best of all, there is a strong sense of "Keys casual" felt throughout the resort.

Surrounding the cottages are shade trees, grassy areas, and scattered flower gardens, although we felt the grounds were looking a bit scraggly during the height of the season. In the center of the cottage complex, nestled in the shade, is a picnic area, with a small playground for the children. Closer to the waterfront there is an enormous freshwater pool, which seems to be the biggest draw for most of the guests. Anyone unfamiliar with the Keys will soon realize that while it may be surrounded by water, there are few sandy beaches to swim from, making a swimming pool almost mandatory. Most visitors access the saltwater by chartering a boat and spending the day exploring the underwater beauty of the surrounding coral reefs. Drive a short distance to the beautiful Bahia Honda State Park for the most beautiful beaches in the Keys—unfortunately, Bowser has to stay home for this one.

Adjacent to the pool stands a cozy two-story building. On its second floor is the rustic Angler's Lounge. Lunch is served here daily, although its busiest time is from four o'clock in the afternoon until one in the morning. The Goombay Smash—containing coconut, rum, banana liqueur, pineapple and orange juices, and topped with 151 rum—seems to be the drink of preference with the spring break crowd. From their perch at the old time wooden bar, patrons need only turn around to watch the boats bobbing in the marina and see beyond to the sparkling waters of the Gulf of Mexico. On the first floor of the building is the casually elegant and intimate Kelsey's, which is open for dinner. We liked the two small dining rooms, both of which are paneled with dark wood and have low ceilings. Paddles emblazoned with different boat names hang from the walls and are tacked to the pillars, adding to the nautical motif. The glassed-in porch offers patrons the best view of the marina, while they enjoy their gourmet fare. Oysters dominate the appetizer menu, with oysters Rockefeller topping the list of patron favorites, and oysters Moscow (served with horseradish and sour cream) coming in a close second. Entrées include quail with a mustard glaze, Long Island duck, rack of lamb, Chateaubriand, and a variety of fish. The seafood selection is perhaps the best option, with a fresh lobster tail served with sautéed mushrooms, artichokes, and almonds; stone crab claws (in season); and jumbo shrimp served barbecued, sautéed, or stuffed with crabmeat. As a special service, guests are always encouraged to bring in their own catch, which the chef will fry, blacken, or grill for them. Guests should be sure to save room for the macadamia pie, peanut butter pie, Key lime cheesecake, or the raspberry cheesecake. It is an easy walk back to the cottages; however, houseboat guests might prefer driving to and from this excellent dinner spot.

While the cottages are nice, we preferred the houseboats. Even though they are not located in the main complex and they lack grassy areas for a dog, they are unique and worth investigating. New arrivals should ignore the rather seedy looking trailers that line the main highway and a section of the lane leading to the Faro Blanco property; once guests arrive at the marina they will quickly forget their existence. At the Faro Blanco Resort, attractive two-story houseboats line a series of low-lying cement piers, which end at the marina's office. Each boat is configured slightly differently, with some containing four individual staterooms and private patios, and others providing a full floor suite. Houseboat guests enjoy the best of both worlds, land and sea. They are often surrounded at night by visiting yachts, and they can feel the sea breeze, without getting seasick. Although the houseboats are permanently anchored to the dock, guests may experience a subtle sense of feeling slightly off-kilter when on board. We feel it merely enhances the overall experience. French doors open from a patio into a good-sized room containing an immaculate galley kitchen, with stools alongside the counter. The fir floors gleam under a heavy coat of varnish. In each houseboat a queen-size bed is set off by itself, usually covered with an attractive pink and blue floral comforter, with matching curtains framing the small windows. On most boats, the heads (or bathrooms) are strictly utilitarian and are hardly large enough to turn around in; however, that is certainly not the case here. The heads here have new white tiles and ample space for the shower, sink and toilet. The only thing guests need to keep in mind is that the boats are hooked into marine plumbing, which can be sensitive. Guests can open the windows at night and hear the faint and comforting sound of the stays clinking against the masts. When reserving a houseboat, people should consider choosing those in the Boat Basin first, as they have the best views of the mangrove hammocks and open water. Those in the Inner Basin are more densely docked. For greater privacy, it is important to request an outward-facing room, rather than one overlooking the dock. During our visit, there were a few visiting boat dogs who were obviously enjoying the company of the other land-based canines.

Anyone traveling with a dog will find many enjoyable ways to exercise them at the Faro Blanco. Those staying on the houseboats can walk along the property over to the area near Crocodiles, another one of the resort's restaurants. Further afield, there is a bike path leading to the seven-mile bridge where visitors can walk or jog with their dogs. The main thoroughfare that runs through Marathon is clearly not the most scenic place for walks (the road is quite busy and lined with strip malls and government buildings); however, within the confines of the resort, on the Gulf side, there is a lot of greenery and a fairly nice dog walk down by the marina. The lighthouse contains two apartments and a well stocked marine store. From it, visitors may rent a small motor boat for the day and explore some of the Keys by water, with Bowser manning the stern. It might be advisable to request a boat with a small bimini, so that visitors and their canine companions don't get too much sun during their travels.

The Lafayette Hotel

944 *Collins Avenue*
Miami Beach, Florida   33139
(305) 673-2262, Fax (305) 534-5399

Owners: *The Castrossi Family*
Rooms: *41 doubles*
Rates: *$135-150 (B&B)*
Payment: *AE, DC, MC, and VISA*
Children: *Welcome*
Dogs: *Special ground floor rooms are available for those traveling with a dog*
Open: *All year*

Driving into Miami Beach's Art Deco district is like stepping back in time. While many of the 1920s and '30s buildings have been restored, others are still waiting for new owners and extensive face lifts. But this is definitely an area that has begun the long road back from decay; and, we must say, it has succeeded with flair. Within a relatively small region there are trendy shops, art galleries, and international cafés serving everything from Italian to Thai foods. The beach is only a block or two from most hotels. There, white sand and people-watching predominate.

The Lafayette Hotel is so European that we could just as easily have been staying in a Mediterranean villa on the coast of Italy as in Miami Beach. Tucked amid small private apartment buildings and residential hotels, the Lafayette's yellow walls and white trim are a standout. A raised terra-cotta terrace dotted with umbrella tables fronts the attractive, semi-circular building. We entered one of the series of paired French doors topped by Palladian windows to find an intimate interior lined with terra-cotta floors and enhanced by potted palms. We were immediately greeted by a staff member, whose heavy French accent merely added to the international flavor of the place. She graciously gave us the lay of the land, describing the hotel and the next morning's breakfast. She explained in detail everything about the area, telling us where it was safe to walk at night (just about anywhere), where to go for dinner, and some of the more popular diversions available in the nearby area.

A small elevator is available to take guests to the upper floors, but we decided to walk up the curved staircase. The hallways are simple, void of decoration, with the exception of a large, antique table at the top of each landing. The naturally-stained wood doors are also surprisingly plain, but they open to reveal very attractive bedrooms. The decor is similar in all the rooms, with pale peach-colored walls and wall-to-wall sage green carpeting. The furnishings are of pickled oak, and one of the standouts is the enormous armoire containing a cable television. Contemporary oak headboards back bedsteads covered with cotton, floral-print comforters that come in a variety of sage greens, gray blues, and pale peaches. A pair of glass lamps sits on the bedside tables, and a large oak writing desk gives business travelers room to work. The walls have little adornment, other than a pair of framed architectural prints placed behind the beds, and a gilt-framed mirror situated over the bureaus. Much of the hotel's original architectural details have been removed over the years; however, the pedestal sink and tiles in the bathrooms do lend an Art Deco feeling to this chamber.

Larger guest rooms contain a small sitting area and separate table. Rooms along the front side of the building allow guests to watch the action along the busy street below. Not surprisingly, these rooms can also be noisy. Those who prefer a quieter stay may wish to reserve a room toward the rear of the hotel. It happens that the suite of rooms available to people traveling with a dog is located on the first floor, to the back of the building. These rooms have just been completed and, in our view, are ideal. Four rooms, two bedrooms, and two living rooms can all be combined in a variety of ways to suit guests' needs. A couple traveling with their dog might want to reserve the queen-bedded room and the adjoining living room, or just the bedroom alone. Families might prefer to reserve both bedrooms and the two living rooms. These spaces have hardwood floors, not carpet; but they are decorated with the same sage green, gray blue, and pale peach color scheme found on the upper levels. Like the rooms upstairs, they are furnished with pine armoires and desks.

Each morning, a Continental breakfast is served on the very private back patio. As we walked to breakfast, we wandered through two common rooms that were rather sparsely furnished. When we talked with the manager, she informed us that the family who owns the

Lafayette has put so much money into rebuilding and redecorating the guest rooms that they haven't been able to focus on the sitting areas quite yet. In one of these spaces, which will soon be transformed into a library, there is a beautiful stained glass window. Beyond this is a room where the Continental breakfast is presented each morning. This is a simple meal of fresh fruit, a variety of muffins and breads, juice, and coffee or tea. We ate on the terra-cotta terrace, which is furnished with wrought iron furniture and royal blue umbrellas. The terrace's charming fountain contains no water, but is lined with plants and seashells. There are also plans for adding a small swimming pool, along with a roof terrace. At this juncture, the Lafayette Hotel is truly a work in progress, but one which guests will find thoroughly charming.

This is a very intimate hotel, with an emphasis on service. We were given excellent advice on where to dine in the evening and we found a variety of restaurants within a three-block radius of the hotel. Cellular telephones are made available to guests, should they be expecting an important call. Those who want to get the lay of the land will find many boutiques and restaurants on Washington Avenue. Bowser, however, would probably prefer to head down one of the side streets to Ocean Drive and the white sand beaches along the Atlantic. Here, the people-watching is excellent and the oceanfront walks seem endless. The many cafés lining one side of the street are the perfect place for a mid-morning respite with Bowser. A 15-minute stroll will bring walkers to South Pointe Park and Tower, where the greenery and open spaces are especially appealing. There is beach access here, as well, and usually a few surfers who put on a good show. At the end of the day, returning to the Lafayette feels like coming home again. It was exactly what we needed to feel comfortable in a city as large and exotic as Miami Beach.

Marlin

1200 Collins Avenue
Miami Beach, Florida   33139
(800) OUTPOST, (305) 673-8770, Fax (305) 531-5543

Manager: Gary Farmer
Rooms: 12 suites
Rates: $200-325 (EP)
Payment: AE, CB, DC, DSC, MC, and VISA
Children: Welcome
Dogs: Welcome
Open: All year

Miami Beach's Art Deco district is so architecturally varied and so alive with action that it is tough for anything to stand out amid the mélange of color and sound. Tough, unless you happen to be the Marlin, whose lilac exterior (lit at night by neon) and pulsating Jamaican music catch the attention of most who pass by the hotel. The Marlin is the brainchild of Chris Blackwell, the former owner of Island Records. He opened it in 1992, after a complete renovation of the building, to much fanfare and press. The hoopla has settled somewhat, but the intimate hotel retains its sense of Hollywood panache amid the backdrop of musicians and entertainers who use the recording studio in the basement.

We walked in during the middle of the day, and immediately started tapping our feet to the fabulous Jamaican tunes. This place was unlike most anything we had ever experienced in a hotel. Though its corner location offers prime street-side viewing, most people are more intrigued with the action going on inside the walls. The building was decorated by Barbara Hulanicki, who obviously knew what kind of mood she wanted to create. The Marlin's main floor is actually on four levels. On the first is a sitting area set along the front of the building; then there is a two-level bar that reaches into the deepest corner of the hotel; and finally, an upstairs platform, with tables well-placed to observe the activity below. The deep blues and purples are flecked with gold and bronze tones, causing the room to almost shimmer. The unusual effect is coupled with artsy furnishings to create a truly upbeat and festive atmosphere.

Amoeba-shaped couches and chairs are grouped into sitting areas on the first level. Shell-motif wall sconces maintain the subdued lighting, and a wave pattern is created from the undulating multiple rails separating the sitting area from the bar. Patrons can easily check out their reflection in the free-form mirror (also amoeba-shaped), which covers an entire side wall. In the far reaches of this space is the famous Shabeen's cookshack and bar. Except for its deep purple walls, this area looks as though it has been transplanted directly from a sandy Caribbean beach. This isn't a hotel, it is a Hollywood creation.

The front desk staff are just as hip as their surroundings, and are unusually protective of their patrons. Only hotel guests are allowed on the upper floors, which are even more distinct, unique, and colorful than the main common areas. A strong Jamaican/Haitian theme is ever present, with the use of bright colors and funky furnishings to create a casual island ambiance. The simple rooms have been creatively furnished with Balinese carved wood chairs, bentwood rattan couches set with multicolored cushions, and wicker or iron tables topped with glass. In stark contrast to electric yellow, turquoise blue, or deep vibrant purple walls, guests may come upon an all-white bedroom with traditional balloon shades framing the windows. For the most part, though, whimsical caricatures of crabs, sea horses, or mermaids are hand painted on the walls, and occasionally there will be a face or jungle scene handpainted on a table. It is impossible to escape the abundant use of striking color schemes, the exception being the subdued terra-cotta brick floors. Haitian paintings and oil drum sculptures, painted and enameled in electrifying colors, line the walls. Tropical plants, both real and fake, add a subtle touch of hominess to the place. Hanging from hooks on bathroom doors are batik, patterned robes for guests to wrap up in after a shower. There are also hair dryers and a full array of island toiletries.

The additional amenities are equally well thought out, with music, of course, being the first consideration. A combination CD-radio-cassette player is set up in each suite, along with a library of CDs that are worth investigating. After a few nights here, most visitors elect to add several kinds of Jamaican music to their personal collections. The television has a VCR, along with another library of tapes, and the mini-bar is well stocked with an array of libations. The full kitchens are fine for anyone who feels like cooking; however, most people prefer ordering the spicy and exotic foods that are prepared at Shabeens. While waiting for the meal to arrive, we recommend ordering a Shabeen Punch, a concoction of rums and fruit juices that is guaranteed to extinguish, or at least smooth out, any memories of a stressful life.

Anyone staying at the Marlin can easily find places to explore with Bowser. During the day, the cafés along Ocean Drive are filled with people enjoying the sun and something light to drink. Unfortunately, the white sand beach across the way is off limits, but it's just as easy to walk along the sidewalk near the beach front. The shopping is interesting in South Beach, and it might be fun to take a stroll with Bowser over to Lincoln Road, a pedestrian mall lined with an eclectic array of art galleries and outdoor eateries. On the way back, many enjoy taking a shortcut through Española Way, a narrow street with a strong Spanish heritage, and still more unusual boutiques. Finally, those with pint-sized dogs may enjoy renting a bicycle, putting Bowser in the basket and covering the entire beach area in the course of a day. Larger dogs may opt to trot alongside the bicycle.

World Tennis Center
Resort and Club

4800 Airport-Pulling Road
Naples, Florida 33942
(800) 292-6663, (813) 263-1900, Fax (813) 649-7855

Manager: Laura Legue
Rooms: 148 2-bedroom condominiums
Rates: $80-160 (EP)
Payment: AE, DSC, MC, and VISA
Children: Welcome
Dogs: Welcome in selected units. Pets may not be left on balconies or tied
  up outside the units. Must be leashed when walking the grounds.
Open: All year

Naples has always been an appealing spot to those who "discover" it. There is Old Naples, where the affluent still reside in their million dollar homes that line the beach. They shop in the exclusive little boutiques on Third Street South, and still buy their groceries in neighborhood markets on Fifth Avenue South. There is a social season here, and a symphony, and all the trappings of wealth and sophistication. However, even with all this, Naples is not the west coast version of Palm Beach, nor does it try to be.

We appreciated the fact that visitors can still park along the quiet back streets and walk out to the beautiful, white sand beaches. The tropical climate, unspoiled beaches, and the warm Gulf waters have lured people here for years. Those who were responsible for the original development of Old Naples set up tight restrictions regarding height requirements, view easements, setbacks, etc. For the most part, this has kept high-rise buildings off the beachfront and it has set the tone for this lovely community. Unfortunately, few places remain "undiscovered" for long, and over the past ten years the outskirts of this once sleepy town have exploded with malls, commercial buildings, houses, and condominiums. In general, the developments are unobtrusive and tasteful, if not luxurious. Those who have lived here for years, though, are likely to tell visitors that the once rural landscape is being gobbled up by the seemingly insatiable developers. While real estate near the beach remains very expensive, some of the attractive condominium complexes east of the Tamiami Trail, or Route 41, offer both terrific values, lovely accommodations, and beautifully landscaped surroundings.

One of these, the World Tennis Center, is a relatively new complex set on 82 acres of tropical gardens and lakes, as well as a cypress preserve. Built in a Mediterranean style, it is reminiscent of the white stucco houses we have seen dotting the hills of the Greek Isles. This place is not just for the tennis set, but a penchant for the game certainly helps. With 16 tennis courts (11 clay and 5 hard courts) along with a 2,500-seat stadium, those who don't know how to play are undoubtedly tempted to give it a try. There is, of course, a USPTA tennis pro and various assistants who will teach the sport to newcomers or enhance the technique of even the most veteran players. They will also set up matches between players, hold clinics, and organize informal tournaments. When not playing tennis, guests tend to congregate around the huge swimming pool, or they may rejuvenate in the whirlpool spa or saunas. The tennis courts, pro shop, swimming pool, and small café are all housed in a central area, with the condominiums set in clusters around the rest of the property.

The condominiums are attractive, and the most desirable overlook the cypress groves and lakes. The layout from one unit to the next is fairly standard. Guests walk in past the kitchen and dining area to the good-sized living room, which is lined with sliding glass doors that open onto a balcony or cement patio. The landscaping around the patios and surrounding the complexes is still fairly immature, but it already provides just enough greenery to soften the starkness of the white exteriors. Just off the living room is a master bedroom, where another set of sliding glass doors opens to reveal another portion of the balcony or patio. The expansive private bathroom off the master suite is tiled. A second bedroom, containing twin beds, generally overlooks the parking area. The kitchens are completely modern and all white, with good quality General Electric appliances that include microwaves, ovens, toasters, and oversized refrigerators. Long-term guests are certain to appreciate the washer/dryer combination provided in each unit. The dove gray carpeting and neutral wall color schemes make these spaces seem a little utilitarian; however, the contemporary sofas and armchairs, along with a scattering of framed prints, potted plants, and knickknacks provide some character.

We preferred the first floor units, as it is easy to take Bowser out for impromptu walks around the grounds. There are vast expanses of grass, plenty of shade trees, and even a few flower gardens here and there. Canine friends will certainly enjoy investigating the seven acres of man-made lakes on the property. The lakes may be the creation of man, but the alligators who inhabit them are very natural. While they are "non-aggressive," we would still recommend keeping Bowser on a leash. Another option is a run along the main road leading toward the ocean. We suggest doing this early in the morning, as the traffic becomes heavy during the commuting hours. Others may prefer jumping in the car and taking a drive over to Old Naples to investigate the Naples Pier and the many people who can usually be found fishing from this landmark. Afterwards, peaceful walks through the surrounding neighborhoods or along Gulf Shore Boulevard give visitors a good feeling for the quieter sections of Naples. Loudermilk Park, just north of Old Naples, is situated next to the beach and generally has plenty of intriguing action —for both Bowser and his friends.

As a final aside, accommodations that accept dogs are extremely limited in Naples. The World Tennis Center, surprisingly enough, is one of the few places that welcomes canine travelers.

Walt Disney World
Kennel Accommodations

Walt Disney World Central Reservations
P.O. Box 10100
Lake Buena Vista, Florida 32830-0100
(407) 824-4321

Kennel Club: (407) 824-6568
Fort Wilderness Kennel: (407) 824-2735
Epcot Kennel: (407) 560-6229
Disney/MGM Studios Kennel: (407) 560-4282
Kennel Fees: Resort guests pay $6 per day or $9 for an overnight stay . Non-
resort guest dogs are $11 per 24-hour period.

Walt Disney World is a vast subject to write about, so please keep in mind that our purpose is not to supply you with all the nitty gritty details, entire books are dedicated to that, but instead to specifically describe the kennel situation. We will provide you with an overview of the doggie domains within this magic kingdom—a kingdom, we might add, that is primarily geared for people, not their dogs. Before visiting Disney World it is very important to do plenty of research. We read through a few books, knew where to stay and in what order we would visit the parks, but were not clear on how our dogs would fit into this Disney wonderland. It was only after we arrived and spent hours investigating the different facilities, conferring with the kennel staff, and speaking with assorted dog owners, that we more easily understood how to best visit with our canine companions.

While there are plenty of hotels and motels around the perimeter of Disney World that will accept dogs, it is not really feasible to keep them there all day, while the rest of the family is out touring the various attractions. The folks at Disney realized this and have set up kennels at the entrances to all the major parks. The basic rules for the four kennels are as follows:

• These are indoor/outdoor kennels of varying sizes designed to provide the bare essentials for daytime and overnight animal guests. It used to be that only Disney World Resort guests could board their dogs in the kennels. This is no longer the case, but resort guests are entitled to a discount for overnight boarding.

• The indoor kennels are air conditioned. The outdoor kennels are not. Because we have big dogs, the outdoor kennels were more appealing, as they appeared to be larger than those inside (although the staff told us the biggest kennels were all the same size). The outdoor kennels are shaded; however, it is critical during the often oppressive heat of the summer that dogs stay inside.

• Dogs should arrive at the facility with their own bowl, toy or chew bone, and any special food or medication. The corporation that owns Friskees oversees the operation of the kennels, and their food is fed to the dogs.

• Reservations are not accepted, but the kennels do open an hour before, and stay open an hour after, the parks' opening and closing times. These times vary with the day and the time of year, so it is advisable to check in advance. (As an aside, it is highly recommended that even those traveling without a dog, plan on being in the parks at least an hour before the official opening as this is the best way to beat the crowds.)

• Technically, owners are required to walk their dogs three times a day. Unofficially, we talked with a number of people who said the staff sometimes made exceptions and would help out with the walking if absolutely necessary. However, don't expect them to break with the rules, just occasionally bend them slightly.

Our first stop was the **Kennel Club**, which is located just outside the Magic Kingdom's ticket and transportation center, near the monorail. When we arrived it was quite early, but people were already at the kennels dropping off or picking up their dogs. We saw a pair of Golden Retrievers, a Scottish terrier, and a curly haired mutt all heading out for their morning constitutional. This is a pretty area to walk one's dog, particularly for those who find the secluded spot back under the monorail, near the Wilderness Resort. This is an old grassed over airstrip, that is rarely used, and provides people with acres of open space to play on with their dog. Head off in the other direction over toward the Palm Golf Course and the Disney Inn, and although Bowser is not allowed on the course, the walk is a nice one. The **Kennel Club** makes sense for those visiting the Magic Kingdom for the day. It is the perfect location for anyone staying at the Polynesian Resort Hotel, the Grand Floridian, the Contemporary Resort Hotel, or the Disney Inn.

All of these resorts are considered to be Disney's luxury level and ease of access to the **Kennel Club** or the Magic Kingdom is unmatched. The Grand Floridian is the grand dame of them all, a sprawling white

Victorian-style hotel with red roofed turrets, gables, and eaves. Balconies and pillars are edged with gingerbread molding, and inside is the unforgettable five-story atrium topped by stained glass skylights. Furnishings are classic Victorian, but they are upholstered in light color schemes. Bedroom decor is equally sophisticated, with pale peach and green accenting the lovely formal pine furnishings. Our second choice would be the Polynesian Resort, as much for the tropical atmosphere and beautifully decorated rooms, as for its proximity to the **Kennel Club**. The resort is literally steps from the kennel, allowing guests of the Polynesian easy access to their dogs. This hotel was remodeled a few years ago, and the contemporary rattan furnishings and beds utilize dark, tropical fabrics that reflect the theme for the rest of the resort. Once again, the lobby is the primary focal point for the Polynesian Resort with its cascading waterfalls and lush foliage, giving us the illusion of that we were sitting in a rain forest. The Contemporary Resort is the final monorail stop, with the monorail running right through the center of the building. The futuristic look and sleek design made it feel slightly eerie, if that is possible at Disney World. Rooms are streamlined creations decorated with neutral colors. We thought it lacked a little of the personality found in the other resorts.

Our next tour was of the **Fort Wilderness Kennel**. In terms of overall surroundings, and a feeling of open space, this kennel seemed to have it all. We felt as though we were entering a National Park when we drove through the gates, as Disney has made it a point to keep as much of the surrounding forest as intact as possible. The physical kennel was somewhat smaller than the one over at the Magic Kingdom, but the actual cages were similar. The outdoor kennels are also near the horse stables, supplying some interesting smells for Bowser's sensitive nose, as well as plenty of grassy areas around the corrals. This is the perfect choice for people staying in the Fort Wilderness Resort and Campground, whether they choose the Wilderness Homes or the tent and RV campsites. The campsites are arranged in loops, and the kennel staff informed us that the 1600-1900 loop was going to soon be accessible to tent campers who want to stay here with their dogs. If this policy has not already been implemented, it soon will be. Another excellent choice, and more affordable than the three grouped around the Magic Kingdom, is Disney's newest addition, the Wilderness Lodge. Set on the edge of the Fort Wilderness Resort, the striking lodge was designed to replicate the massive lodges built in the Pacific Northwest around the turn of the century. Rough hewn logs and stone create the enormous timbers, slate floors, and elaborate vaulted roof lines. The main lodge and its wings protect the hotel's centerpiece, a system of geysers and waterfalls that spill from interior spaces to the outside, creating rock faced swimming pools. Guests staying here can opt to keep their dog at either the **Fort Wilderness Kennel** or the **Kennel Club**.

Two additional kennels are located at **Epcot** and the **Disney-MGM Studios Theme Park**. The **Epcot Kennel** is to the left of the park's main entrance. There are grassy areas near the kennel, along with stands of trees, which Bowser will certainly find desirable for walks. Visitors who have chosen the luxurious Yacht and Beach Club Resorts or the Walt Disney World Swan and Dolphin Resorts, will want to utilize the **Epcot Kennel** since the kennel near the Magic Kingdom is just too far away to make regular visits to your canine companion. The last kennel of choice is the **Disney-MGM Studios Kennel,** primarily because it is rather small and there is limited open space to walk your dog. This is incorporated into a building to the left of the entrance plaza.

One final note about kennels and Walt Disney World. After personally talking with the staff and visiting each of the facilities, we feel comfortable recommending the kennels for day trips and short term visits to Walt Disney World. The staff obviously enjoys taking care of these animals, and are exceptionally kind to them. But there are limits, both for the dogs and for you. The kennels, while clean and pleasant, are not luxurious and not, perhaps, the best place to leave a dog all day for several days on end. These kennels make perfect sense for those who feel they can approach Walt Disney World in a leisurely fashion, perhaps spending the morning touring, taking a break at lunch, and then swimming or casually exploring the outlying areas in the afternoon. Bowser also can join you in those expeditions that do not involve the theme parks. We met plenty of people who were in town for the week with their dogs, but most were planning on spending practically as much time with their dogs as they were visiting the assorted parks. We learned from them, and from personal experience, that guests and their canine companions can thoroughly enjoy Disney World, as long as Bowser's needs are factored in when setting up the vacation schedule.

Animals are never allowed in the hotel rooms, or on the hotel properties. We learned of one instance where a guest smuggled in a cat, left it in the room, and the maid inadvertently let it out. The cat was eventually caught, but no one would claim her because they were so embarrassed. We know that plenty of people try to sneak their animals into hotels; however, this is definitely not the place to attempt such an escapade. All in all, with Disney's usual attention to the smallest details of vacationer's needs and desires, guests and their dogs can have a great resort-style vacation here with the understanding that dogs can be happily accommodated by, if not totally integrated into, the wonderful world of Disney.

The Ocean Grand

2800 South Ocean Blvd.
Palm Beach, Florida 33480
(800) 332-3442, (407) 586-2690, Fax (407) 547-1557

General Manager: *William Mackay*
Rooms: *198 doubles, 12 suites*
Rates: *Doubles $245-525 (EP), Suites $600-1,800 (EP)*
Payment: *AE, DC, DSC, Eurocard, JCB, MC, and VISA*
Children: *Welcome, children under 17 are free of charge when staying with*
parents; extensive children's programs are available (cribs, cots,
and high chairs are available)
Dogs: *Welcome*
Open: *All year*

Palm Beach has long been thought of as the exclusive winter retreat for the ultra-rich and famous. We wanted to judge the city for ourselves, and what we found both confirmed and dispelled a few myths. Driving along Palm Beach's Royal Palm Way, we felt like Dorothy entering the land of Oz, telling Toto, "We aren't in Kansas anymore." The buildings are architecturally distinct and the streets are wide and immaculate. American cars are an endangered species here, with sleek European automobiles quietly purring along the byways. We were in search of The Ocean Grand, but would not find it near the exclusive shops along Worth Avenue. Instead, we followed the famed Ocean Boulevard to the hotel and, along the way, caught our first glimpses of the renowned Palm Beach estates. It can be difficult to see the mansions, as they are fronted by lush, flowering hedges and gates; however, just catching a glimpse of these spectacular homes is enough.

Nearing The Ocean Grand, the narrow seaside road widens and the overall neighborhood becomes slightly less residential. Private homes give way to high-rise condominiums, which begin to dot the landscape. As with the many nearby estates, the hotel is mostly obscured by large green hedges, and visitors must look carefully for the entrance. Upon our arrival, the attentive staff instantly appeared, offering to park the car and attend to our needs. As we stepped inside, the light marble floors and taupe colored walls created a sense of coolness. The public rooms are furnished on a grand scale, with huge vases of fresh orchids and spring flowers set on marble-topped tables, and potted palms lining the two main corridors that lead to the restaurants and sitting areas. We especially liked the Living Room, with its long wall of floor-to-ceiling French doors. One end of this room is comprised of an elegant bar, which is set unobtrusively behind large pillars supporting the recessed ceiling. Deep, soft couches pulled up around the fireplace, have a way of enveloping guests. In the evening, there is always live music played by a pianist or jazz band. Just off the Living Room is an intimate library that is one of our favorite spaces. The chintz covered sofa, backed by a Chinese silk screen, and Chippendale-style armchairs are arranged well for private conversations. Keep in mind, though, that this is Palm Beach, and the sparkling ocean and tropical landscape usually draw guests to the out of doors.

Viewing the hotel from outside, guests will see that the hotel building forms a semi-circular backdrop to the enormous heated pool and Jacuzzi. These are surrounded by expansive terraces extending to the white sandy beach beyond. The staff, who are never intrusive, move quietly amid the lush surroundings, always available to take drink orders, supply a towel, or secure a beach cabaña. Casual lunches can be ordered from the beach and poolside grill, or guests may retreat to the inviting Ocean Bistro for more lavish fare. Set on a covered slate patio and framed by palms and impatiens, guests may dine on stone crab claws, Indian River She crab soup, and a variety of salads made with organic lettuces and vegetables. The five-spice duck salad is served with wontons, Oriental greens, and a guava essence. Diners may also choose a grilled chicken yogurt and red grape salad, or the Caesar salad adorned with rock shrimp or grilled chicken. The jumbo lump crab cakes, smoked salmon, caper, lemon cream and vegetable pasta, and the focaccia pizzas topped with shrimp or fresh vegetables are not to be passed up.

Another gourmet dining experience awaits in The Restaurant. It has won awards from all corners of the culinary world, as a result of Chef Hubert Des Marais' inspired menus. Taking advantage of fresh local ingredients, he imbues these foods with a style reminiscent of the Caribbean, Native America, South and Central America—and a touch of his grandmother's American south. Guests may take tours of Chef Hubert's kitchen early in the morning, or they may wait until evening to enjoy the entire culinary experience. The decor is as exquisite as the food, where ivory-colored walls, Chinese silk screens, and lush flower arrangements set the tone. Walls of floor-to-ceiling glass doors reveal glimpses of the ocean through the thick plantings. Although the menu changes nightly, some appetizer favorites include the Indian River blue crab, served with plantain crisps; the Caspian and Amur River caviars; and the grilled South Carolina squab with a pan-fried grit cake and wild forest mushrooms. During our visit, the entrée selection was exotic. The lemon Macadamia nut-crusted lamb served with spinach, yucca, and garlic-smothered onions; the black and blue tuna loin steak with a fiery papaya slaw, cilantro, and ruby grapefruit; or the charred salmon with stir-fried Oriental greens, cilantro, and Keffer lime-scented red pepper essence were just three options on the extensive menu.

Guests will find that walking the beach after dinner is almost a prerequisite before returning to their rooms. In the three years that the Four Seasons has managed the property, the guest rooms have received just as much attention as the public areas. The corner suites are the most spectacular, where marble floors are set with Persian rugs, velvet-covered sofas, Chippendale ball and claw chairs, and baby grand pianos. Suites aside, the standard guest rooms are truly on the luxury level. Taupe walls are a neutral backdrop to the chintz bedspreads and coordinated draperies. In each room, there is usually a small sitting area set with formal French furnishings, complemented by lamps created from Oriental vases and framed botanical prints. We were also impressed with the marble bathrooms, where a single orchid in a vase sets the tone for the other thoughtful amenities. Here, guests will find oversized cotton towels, thick terry bathrobes, a hairdryer, and a full array of European toiletries, along with a telephone and a small television. The immense armoire contains the refrigerator, honor bar, and television, as well as a safe. Just in case it rains, there are extra umbrellas available. Most, but not all, of the bedrooms have unobstructed views of the ocean. We highly recommend requesting an ocean view room when making a reservation.

Bowser will certainly feel welcome at The Ocean Grand. The Four Seasons has a knack for making its canine guests feel particularly comfortable. The hotel supplies dog bowls, Evian water, and homemade dog biscuits to its canine guests. Unfortunately, Palm Beach has an ordinance prohibiting dogs on its beaches; however, a 20-minute drive north will bring visitors to Singer Island, where dogs are allowed full access to the beach. For evening walks with Bowser, guests usually venture out along Ocean Boulevard where there are wide sidewalks and plenty of grass. A drive back into the heart of Palm Beach will provide walkers with quieter residential streets. Human guests have access to three local golf courses and three tennis courts. Others might choose to work out at The Spa, where they may receive the advice of personal trainers or just work out on their own in the 6,000 square-foot facility. Afterwards, a massage or beauty treatment is one of the many therapeutic ways to unwind after another day enjoying the balmy breezes and recreational diversions of Palm Beach.

Hibiscus House Bed and Breakfast

501 30th Street
West Palm Beach, Florida   33407
Telephone/Fax (407) 863-5633

Host: *Raleigh Hill*
Rooms: *5 doubles, 1 suite, 1 cottage*
Rates: *Doubles $55-85 (B&B), Suites $80-110 (B&B),*
Cottage $120-150 (B&B)
Payment: *AE, DC, MC, and VISA*
Children: *Not appropriate for small children*
Dogs: *Welcome in the cottage*
Open: *All year*

Raleigh Hill has spent his life changing and enhancing other people's lives. As an interior decorator for over 30 years, he has designed and decorated hundreds of homes and even a hotel or two. In moving from city to city, he invariably indulged in two of his passions, buying and renovating properties and collecting antiques. His keen interest in antiques has led to an extensive collection of unusual pieces gathered from all over the world, many of which are displayed in the Hibiscus House. For all of his traveling, he is still a native Floridian, and he has returned to West Palm Beach and opened the Hibiscus House.

The Colonial-style home, with a tropical twist, is the centerpiece to Old Northwood. Old Northwood is a ten-block by two-block neighborhood that has recently been listed on the National Register of Historic Places. In 1922, when the [then] Mayor of Palm Beach built the home, it must have been considered opulent. This was not the case, however, in the mid-1980s when Raleigh Hill and his partner Colin Rayner found it. The building was informally known as the "crack house" and lay in the heart of a neighborhood that was less than marginal. Hill and Rayner were able to look at the historic value of the area and see the potential for this house and others around it. Overlooking the general filth and garbage they found around the house—preferring instead to see the intrinsic character of the building—they chose to make an investment in time, money, and energy to turn it all around. The attractive exterior lines are now accentuated by a fresh coat of paint, new porches and decking, and lush tropical foliage. Due in large part to these men's efforts, the neighborhood is now a pleasant place to live, with new people moving in and restoring many of the older cottages. Those who have lived here for years are also beginning to refurbish their houses, further shaping the area into a lovely historic district. One never knows what surprises lie behind the doors of these charming homes, but a peek into the Hibiscus House might reveal some interesting clues.

The front door opens into a foyer, where French doors then beckon guests into the formal living room. Here, Oriental and Egyptian antiques intermix with European pieces. The chairs and sofas are from the Louis XV and XVI periods and are upholstered in handsome fabrics. Porcelain vases and pots contain fresh flowers or palms. Knickknacks and family photographs are displayed throughout this room and in other parts of the house, lending a personalized atmosphere to these common areas. We found it incredible that some of the intrinsic features of the house actually survived the years of abuse and neglect. A brick fireplace is enhanced by a marble hearth and hand-worked moldings. Adjacent to this is the ornate dining room. It is difficult to pick one outstanding piece of furniture in here, as each is noteworthy in its own right. The oak dining room table and sideboard are from the 1800s and exhibit a rich patina. The caned chairs are Brentwood, and wide enough to provide very comfortable seating for the extended breakfasts that are regularly presented in this chamber. Depending on the viewing angle, the Victorian mirror reflects the light from a graceful brass candelabra or from the sunlight spilling through the French doors. Most guests, at some point, will comment on the wall-mounted columns in here, and will learn that they were recovered from one of New York City's pre-war apartments before it was destroyed. The breakfast is as elaborate as the surroundings, with fine crystal and china as the backdrop for an elegant meal. Depending upon the day, there might be a garden quiche or Eggs Benedict, along with French pastries, fruit, and gourmet coffee. On warm sunny mornings, of which there are many in south Florida, some guests prefer to take their meal out by the swimming pool or in the gazebo.

In redesigning the house, it was important to Raleigh that all his guests feel a sense of privacy. Therefore, the bedrooms have private bathrooms, as well as private terraces that are usually accessed through a pair of French doors. Although most of the guests who travel with their dogs prefer to stay in the cottage, we cannot ignore the rooms in the main house. Each is individually furnished with lovely antiques from Raleigh's private collection. We should note that some pieces resemble authentic antiques; however, they are cleverly disguised knock-offs, though few would be able to recognize as such. The beds usually dominate the guest rooms. Some contain canopy or four-poster rice beds; others have unusual headboards that Raleigh has created from odd pieces of wood. From the Green Room, guests may walk onto their private balcony and pick oranges right from the tree. Guests staying in the Library Room will have to reach a bit, but will still be able to gather their own oranges. One of the most sought-after chambers is the Burgundy Suite, which is accessed by way of a private staircase. The four- poster cherry-wood bed is the highlight of the space, along with the Chinese screen that hangs behind it. Hardwood floors in here and throughout the house are covered with varying types of Oriental rugs from Persia or China.

The cottage is actually composed of two guest rooms, the Poolside Studio and Garden Room. These may be rented separately (an ideal arrangement for a couple) or they may be combined to form an expansive suite. The Garden Room is accessed by way of the rose garden. Guests enter off their private deck, and once inside will find a good-sized chamber with a queen-size, four-poster bed. The Studio is more complete, with a fully-equipped kitchen, along with a living and dining nook. There is no separate bedroom, but there is a sleeping area that can be adjusted to hold a pair of twins or a queen-size bed. Privacy and shade are ensured by the awning that extends over the flagstone patio and fountain. Through the foliage, guests may catch glimpses of the swimming pool. Whichever accommodation guests select, they will discover that each has a color television and air conditioning, although the paddle fan is more than sufficient on most nights.

Once guests have settled in a bit, they will want to explore the other nooks and crannies throughout the house. One favorite is the tiled porch, which is also the site of afternoon tea, where a variety of libations are offered. Some prefer to head outside through the French doors and enjoy their drink by the side of the swimming pool. When Raleigh bought the house there was no swimming pool. Guests would not know that today, though, because the pool looks as though it has always been part of the property. The decking leads from the house and across several terraces to the pool. The entire back of the house is surrounded by an array of tropical shrubs, as well as an abundance of palm and orange trees, and (of course) hibiscus. During the day, most are content to relax by the pool. But if Bowser is getting a little impatient just hanging around, there are also plenty of places where he may stretch his legs. Because the house is in a neighborhood, leisurely walks are pleasant and allow guests to visit with the residents. Some may prefer to hop in the car for a short drive over to Palm Beach. There, once again, Bowser will have fun meeting all the other dogs. Although dogs are not permitted on the beach, the walk along the water is just as pretty and offers ocean vistas, along with views of all the people. The Hibiscus House might be a bit off the beaten track, by Palm Beach standards, but it provides guests with more intimacy and charm than just about anything offered on the other side of the causeway.

Plaza Inn

215 Brazilian Avenue
Palm Beach, Florida   33480
(800) 233-2632, (407) 832-8666, Fax (407) 835-8776

Owner: Ajit Asrani
Rooms: 50 doubles and suites
Rates: Doubles $125-195 (B&B), Suites $225 (B&B)
Payment: AE, MC, and VISA
Children: Welcome, free of charge when staying in room with parents
Dogs: Welcome
Open: All year

The streets of Palm Beach have a distinct European look and feel to them, as do the people who live and play here. For years, visitors to Palm Beach had very few reasonably priced accommodation choices. Expensive options were plentiful, with The Breakers topping the list, along with one or two exclusive small hotels frequented by the country's wealthy and famous families. However, it was many years before the European concept of a pensioné or bed and breakfast filtered to these shores. Luckily for all of us travelers, in 1990 Ajit Asrani and his fiancé changed the status quo by buying and revamping an old Mediterranean-style hotel housing seasonal residents and turning it into a B&B.

Asrani's background is in commercial real estate, but nothing could have prepared him for the work that was needed on the old Hotel Ardma. He easily spent half a million dollars fumigating the interior and renovating the building. Plaster was repaired, windows were replaced, and a mix of European and American antiques selected for the interior. What emerged was an intimate Art Deco-style hotel that looks as though it would fit right into south Miami's Art Deco neighborhoods. Instead, this three-story building is nestled onto a quiet side street, within a few blocks of the exclusive boutiques and restaurants on Worth Avenue.

A short circular driveway provides easy access to the front door leading into the foyer and reception area. This intimate area is just spacious enough to accommodate a baby grand piano and a pair of sitting areas. The pale green walls serve as a backdrop for the elaborate moldings framing the upper walls and encircling the crystal chandeliers that hang from the vaulted ceilings. The room is comfortable, and looks lived in; partly because of the nicely worn mahogany antique furnishings that are combined with draped tables set with pretty collectibles. Hardwood floors are covered with rugs from India and the Orient. When we arrived, all of the outside doors were open, to allow the sea breezes to circulate through the inn. French doors lead out to the garden, pool, and Jacuzzi, which are surrounded by lush tropical plantings and trees. In the evening, the sparkle of lights and the sounds of the small waterfall create just the right effect. If an after-dinner dip in the pool does not sound enticing, then perhaps a visit to the intimate English pub, set just off the lobby, does.

The bedrooms are located on three floors, situated off long straight hallways with sparkling stucco ceilings illuminated by small chandeliers. Interestingly, even though the building has been immaculately restored, it has not lost its understated old Floridian feeling. For instance, the guest room doors still have the original *fleur di lis* ornamentation on them. The doors open to reveal individually and tastefully decorated chambers. The elaborate cornices and moldings adorning the public areas are noticeably absent in the guest rooms, where pastel colors and subtle papers cover the walls instead. These guest rooms contain a mix of furnishings, ranging from white wicker and hand-painted pine to lightly stained cherry. The larger rooms contain king-size four poster beds, draped with canopies or tropical netting. Ours was fitted with Scandinavian furnishings, which were nicely complemented by the coordinated floral fabrics covering the bed and framing the windows. Depending upon the decorative theme of the room, guests may find botanical prints on the walls or reproductions of famous paintings. Some rooms are furnished with a tiger maple dresser, while others are equipped with an armoire concealing both a television and a small refrigerator. Air conditioning is supplemented in some bedrooms by paddle fans. We think the guest rooms facing east receive the best ocean breezes. The exceptionally clean bathrooms — whose decor, tiles, and fixtures are decidedly retro-1940s—are stocked with thick towels, oatmeal soaps, and jojoba shampoos.

Breakfast is a leisurely affair, where guests may arrive as early as 7:30 or as late as 10:30. The intimate breakfast space, which is tucked toward the rear of the inn, consists of two sunny rooms that contain a dozen lace-covered tables. In contrast to the lace, the wallpaper and oil paintings reflect something of a hunting theme. We were able to get our own coffee and tea from the buffet and then casually peruse the menu. Fresh fruit started the meal, and was followed by a variety of egg dishes, sourdough French toast, or pancakes.

Afterwards, it was time for a walk. Anyone thinking of leaving Bowser behind during a stroll along Worth Avenue would be missing a special opportunity. In all of our travels, we have never seen a street more suited for the canine set. The staff in the exclusive boutiques are just as pleasant to the dogs as they are to their human patrons. Because it was still fairly early, many of the shops were in the process of opening, but the window shopping was almost as fun as the real thing. As we walked, we stopped to look in the window of a fine linen shop, with exquisite items that were being carefully watched over by the resident golden retriever and little white Scottish terrier. While the retriever tried to sleep, the terrier would run madly around the store, attempting to convince his friend to play. He had found a roll of paper towels and was systematically destroying it. He then took a tiny Easter basket over to the retriever and flipped it in the air, hoping to catch his companion's attention. The retriever wasn't interested, but we were —as were the other passersby. As we continued back up the other side of Worth Avenue, we came across the "doggie bar." This small trough lined with Italian tiles can be filled with water from a spigot. We thought L.L. Bean, the giant Maine retailer, was being particularly sensitive to dogs when it provided a spigot and metal bowl for its visiting canines; however, this "bar" on Worth Avenue is clearly in a league unto itself. When visitors are not shopping, there are a number of lovely residential side streets around the Plaza Inn that are ideal for long walks. Palm Beach has a "season," which begins in early December and ends abruptly in April. During this time, the weather is perfect, with long sunny days and not too much heat or humidity. It's a beautiful time to visit; however, those who want deeply discounted room rates should consider visiting during the shoulder season or in the quieter summer months.

Marriott at Sawgrass Resort

1000 TPC Blvd.
Ponte Vedra Beach, Florida   32082
(800) 457-GOLF, (904) 285-7777, Fax (904) 285-0906

General Manager: *Mark Vinciguerra*
Rooms: *404 doubles, 105 suites, 16 1-3 bedroom golf villas*
Rates: *Doubles $150-299 (EP), Suites 200-500 (EP), Villas $225-550*
      (EP), Extensive golf, tennis, and sports programs are available
Payment: *AE, CB, DC, DSC, MC, and VISA*
Children: *Welcome; an extensive children's program is offered (cribs, cots,*
      babysitters, and high chairs are available)
Dogs: *Welcome in the Island Green Villas*
Open: *All year*

The Marriott at Sawgrass has won just about every conceivable award and accolade, including being ranked among the top 50 all around and family-oriented resorts in the country. The resort have also earned the Gold Key, Gold Tee, and Gold Medal awards from various national travel industry publications. Its 99 holes of golf stand are virtually unmatched in the United States, both for course quality and difficulty. Sawgrass Resort is best known in golfing circles for being the home of the prestigious Tournament Player's Club (TPC) and for hosting The Players Championship each March. Of course, all of this is incidental to Bowser, who is probably more interested in exploring the 4,800 acres of lush gardens, nature trails—and grass, grass, and more grass.

The centerpiece for this lavish resort is the enormous seven-story hotel with its 70-foot high indoor atrium. The atrium is backed by a three-story wall of emerald green glass that overlooks a lake and a picturesque waterfall. Sounds of rushing water fill the interior as well, as it cascades into a waterfall and jumps from fountains. A small stream wends past palm trees and flowers, then seemingly disappears, only to reappear again elsewhere in the atrium. Bowser is not allowed to stay in the main hotel, nor would he be very comfortable here. However, just a short walk over footbridges and boardwalks are the Island Green Villas. Here, guests are certain to feel completely at ease amid the lovely accommodations and surroundings.

We were very impressed with the villa suites. The decor is sophisticated, with teal green, bright blue, and an array of tropical colors blending together to exude a tranquil Caribbean ambiance. The bedrooms are enormous, with brightly colored spreads fitted on beds backed by huge, carved, pickled-wood headboards. The doors on the naturally-stained armoires and bureaus are accented by wood trim resembling strands of rope. Good-sized bathrooms are outfitted with double sinks, thick towels, and an extensive array of toiletries. The galley kitchen is equipped for most cooking needs and opens to a formica island that is backed by four stools. Some may want to pull up a stool and chat with the chef, while others will find it even more relaxing to rest in a wing chair with their feet on an ottoman. The deep sofas are well-placed for napping, or perhaps for watching a little golf on television. Sliding glass doors open to patios overlooking stands of giant oak, palm, and magnolia trees, which overhang ponds surrounded by lush foliage and walls of azaleas. Guests traveling with a dog should probably request a first-floor unit with a pond view, as these provide easy access to the grounds, as well as the best views. The end units are usually private and have interesting room configurations.

When it comes to activities, there are plenty of things to do, both with or without a dog. Immediately adjacent to the main hotel are 15 acres of lagoons. In addition, there are 350 acres of freshwater lakes and lagoons on the property. Dogs who enjoy swimming might sneak in for a dip every now and then, just to cool off a bit. There are also miles of jogging and bicycling paths that wend through many lush and scenic settings. Bowser is not permitted on the golf course, but there are so many other options for walks that this is not really a hardship. After a little exercise, Bowser might enjoy a brief rest, while his human caretakers take a shuttle bus down to Sawgrass' beach. Here, an assortment of amenities are available, including Hobie cats, boogie boards, and beach bicycles. There are 2 1/2 miles of shoreline to explore on foot or by bicycle. The property also boasts 19 tennis courts with four different types of surfaces. Three swimming pools are located at Sawgrass, along with two kiddie pools. Families will want to know about the extensive children's program available through the resort. The younger set, ages 3-12, can join the Grasshopper Gang. Staff trained in youth education offer such activities as shell jewelry design and sandcastle sculpting classes, along with nature hikes and shark's teeth hunts. Teenagers, ages 13-15, can spend their time at Camp Sawgrass. Here, they might participate in horseback riding or pool-side games, as well as organized dances and movie nights.

In the evening, while the children and Bowser sleep, many make a point to have dinner in the Augustine Room — Sawgrass' five-star restaurant that reflects the history of its historic neighbor, St. Augustine. Amid fresh flowers, Belgian linen, and candlelight, diners can peruse the extensive gourmet menu. Guests might select an appetizer such as the boneless marinated quail glazed with apricots or the salmon and sweet pepper cannelloni with a tomato concasse. An ever popular entrée is the bouillabaisse made with Mayport shrimp, lobster, and

New Zealand mussels. The grilled veal chops are served with roasted shallots in a port wine demi glace. By all means, guests should save room for the Passionate Sunset, a blend of six tropical sauces swirled artfully around a passion fruit, orange, and Bavarian cream bombé. Chocolate fans should not miss sampling the Clincy, an almond sponge cake covered with dark chocolate, mocha cream, and Kahlua. Other more informal Sawgrass restaurants include the Café on the Green, The 100th Hole, Champs, and Cascades, which is a lounge set next to the indoor waterfall.

The villas at the Marriott at Sawgrass impressed us with their sense of privacy and roomy dimensions, as well as with their lush open space and beautifully landscaped grounds. Few resorts on the east coast of Florida can offer the acreage, amenities, and activities found at the Marriott at Sawgrass.

The Castaways

6460 Sanibel-Captiva Road
Sanibel, Florida   33957
(813) 472-1252 or 472-1112, Fax (813) 472-1020

Manager: Tammy Thompson
Rooms: 37 cottages
Rates: Efficiencies $75-160 (EP), 1-Bedroom $85-190 (EP),
*   2-Bedroom $135-230 (EP), 3-Bedroom $265-280 (EP)*
Payment: DSC, MC, and VISA
Children: Welcome; under 12 years of age are free of charge
Dogs: Welcome in 11 units, $10 per pet per day
Open: All year

Blind Pass is the last point on Sanibel before the short bridge crosses over onto Captiva. It is quite a hot spot for fishermen, but is also just as appealing to sunbathers and swimmers because of its wide, half-moon shaped, white sand beach. Sanibel is so narrow here that people can walk from one side of the island to the other in just five minutes. The Castaways at Blind Pass also happens to be the last resort on the northern tip of Sanibel. It lies on both sides of the road and is surrounded by huge pine, banyan, and palm trees that provide plenty of shade for the surrounding grassy areas (which are more wild than the lush lawns found in other parts of the state). Grass is somewhat of a rarity on Sanibel, as water is a precious commodity and using it to create lawns is seen as a waste of a natural resource. More often, native vegetation is used to create the attractive landscapes. The Castaways has a combination of both, with lanes wending through the attractive ground cover, leading guests to the various clutches of cottages and motel units. Throughout this book we have mentioned the Old Florida architectural style. The Castaways is one more resort that seems to reflect a little bit of it all. Most of these cottages are painted a pretty Wedgewood blue, but each seems to utilize different materials, including block, tin, and wood.

At The Castaways, the management prefers that those traveling with a dog stay in one of the freestanding cottages on the property—in other words, one not sharing walls with another unit. The most requested and desirable cottages are those located on the beach. These have blue vertical board siding, double hung windows, and tin roofs, and they range in size from 1-3 bedrooms. Families often prefer these cottages because they don't have to cross the busy road to get to the beach. Six of the eleven beachfront cottages are available to people traveling with a dog. We liked the appearance of the cottages situated across the street near the marina, where four of the buildings permit guests and their canine cohorts. The blue clapboard siding and crisp white trim, inset with paned double hung windows, give the impression that these buildings would be more appropriate in a New England seaside setting. White lattice adds a decorative touch, while small porches provide a little extra outdoor space. The interiors are contemporary and bright. The beachfront and marina cottages sometimes have to contend with a little roadway noise. Therefore, anyone looking for a very quiet setting and a little more privacy should consider reserving the two-bedroom waterfront cottage that is set toward the rear of the property. The views from here are peaceful, as they look across the mangroves and back toward the marina.

In all the units, the furnishings are a mishmash of rattan and light woods that look as though they have been collected over a period of years. Some walls are painted in neutral colors, others are papered in small contemporary prints. This casual Florida decor, with its Caribbean accents, is in evidence throughout the units. These places have personality and we like them. Aside from not providing private telephones, the cottages are otherwise well equipped with assorted modern amenities. As these are housekeeping units, maids clean only once a week and guests are left to fend for themselves for the remainder of their stay. The staff does supply all of the linens and towels, replacing the towels daily—which is a necessity in this tropical climate. Cable television and air conditioning are also standard features. Guests who wish to do a little laundry will find facilities right on the premises. The kitchens are well equipped for creating just about any meal, but most people feel they are on vacation and try to eat out whenever possible.

The Mad Hatter, a four-star gourmet restaurant located right on the beach, is within walking distance of The Castaways. Another popular choice is the neighboring raw bar and a casual eatery, just down the road.

The cottages may have a distinct Old Florida appeal, but what usually inspires most people to reserve a room months in advance is the white sandy beach. Leashed dogs will also enjoy spending some time out here, and will probably find the bird life quite intriguing. The calm waters and soft sand beaches usually found on Sanibel change at Blind Pass, where the waters contain more rips and the beach has more texture. We were informed that this beach can change dramatically when storms hit the area, causing the overall width of the beach to diminish as the sands swirl out into the Gulf. The tiny marina is always hopping with activity, and it is here that guests may inquire about renting a boat, hiring a captain to take them fishing, or buying some bait to fish off the beach. Some may want to walk with Bowser around the grounds or over the bridge that leads to Captiva. The road can be busy, but just south of The Castaways a bike path emerges. The path is a terrific, safe avenue for cycling, Rollerblading, or walking. At the end of the day, the beach offers some of the most spectacular ocean sunsets around.

Signal Inn

1811 Olde Middle Gulf Drive
Sanibel, Florida   33957
(800) 472-4690, (813) 472-4690, Fax (813) 472-3988

Property Manager: *Greta G. Swain*
Rooms: *12 1-2 bedroom cottages, 4 townhouses*
Rates: *1-Bedroom Cottages $605-1,100 per week (EP), 2-Bedroom Cottages*
$750-1,290 per week (EP), Townhouses $920-2,050 per week (EP)
Payment: *MC and VISA*
Children: *Welcome (high chairs are available)*
Dogs: *Welcome in all 2-bedroom cottages, in 2 of the 1-bedroom cottages,*
and in a few of the townhouses. There is a fee of $50 per week and a
credit card imprint is required for a damage deposit.
Open: *All year*

Sometimes we find a vacation destination that is so beautiful and unspoiled that it makes a lasting impression. Sanibel and Captiva are two such places. As first-time visitors, we were overwhelmed by the immense natural beauty that has been preserved on these islands. Long-time residents might yearn for the old days before the causeway, when ferries shuttled visitors between the islands and the mainland. The causeway seems to have changed little about the landscape, however, primarily because there was little left to develop by the time it was built. Sanibel was fortunate, because early in its history there were those who recognized the ecological value of these barrier islands. One of the more celebrated conservationists, Jay Norwood Darling, bought land that otherwise would have been sold to developers. This land, and much more—ultimately totaling some 5,000 acres—was privately held until it was finally designated a National Wildlife Refuge. Another 1,100 acres are currently under the jurisdiction of local conservation groups, which form a strong coalition for the preservation of, and education about, the ecosystem around the islands.

To appreciate Sanibel's beauty, visitors don't necessarily need to be well versed in the island's long history of conservation. Anyone's initial impressions are of dense stands of trees dripping with moss amid lush foliage. Fortunately, there is very little sign of commercialism along the roadways. This is due, in part, to the blanket of greenery fronting the small complexes of exclusive shops. The other part of this equation is that all signboards have been kept to a minimum. Gas stations, eateries, and small chain stores exhibit low, unobtrusive placards. Perhaps this is also why we had some trouble locating the Signal Inn. Once we did spy the small red sign discreetly marking the driveway, we proceeded down a road, through what seemed a jungle, and finally emerged in a clearing. Here, we found a dozen raised, Tahitian-style cottages dotting the landscape. The dark wood exterior walls and pyramid-shaped roofs lacked only the thatching commonly found in the South Pacific. This a peaceful place, but not without life, as there are usually children swimming in the pool, guests heading out for walks along the beach, and still others enjoying some quiet time on their private screened-in porches. These are often very cool places, as each has three exterior walls that allow for terrific cross-ventilation.

The floor plans of the cottages may be similar to one another, but each cottage is individually decorated and furnished. Any of the two-bedroom units are appropriate for people traveling with a dog. Guests enter through a great room containing the living and dining areas, as well as a kitchen. Just off this are two small bedrooms and one shared bath. Also available are two one-bedroom units, which are ideal for singles or couples and a dog. These have one bedroom, combined with a smaller living room/dining room/kitchen combination. Families with several children will probably opt for the spacious townhouses. Here, the living/dining room areas are quite spacious, and the kitchen is larger and more separate from the living space. Toward the rear of these units, there is a large master bedroom with a dressing room and private bathroom. The upstairs is comprised of an even larger bedroom and another bath, along with a spiral staircase leading to a captain's walk. Some of the ceilings are cathedral with skylights, allowing for a greater sense of spaciousness.

As we mentioned, the decor is a little different in each of the cottages, with some reflecting neutral earth-tones and others containing more festive and tropical color schemes. Furnishings include glass-topped dining room tables, rattan sofas and armchairs, and soft peach and white floral patterned sofas. We also found that the management takes excellent care of the property. The moment we walked into one unit, Greta, the resident manager, instantly noticed a strange mark on the carpet. She was clearly bothered by it, and we knew she would attend to it immediately after leaving us. Besides being meticulously maintained, the cottages have numerous modern amenities. The kitchens are well appointed with ice makers, microwaves, self-cleaning ovens, and garbage disposals. Paddle fans help circulate the breezes, although air conditioning is also available to cool down rooms during the height of the summer. Guests may also be interested to know that the water at the inn is heated by solar energy panels.

We were impressed with the cottages, but they wouldn't be the same were it not for the well- maintained property. Palms, along with flowering hibiscus and bougainvillaea, line the sandy paths which are dotted by an occasional starfish or shell. The majority of the cottages are set around the swimming pool and spa, which are adjacent to the Jacuzzi and sauna. Next to the pool there are also barbecues, where many guests gather and visit while preparing their meals. An air conditioned racquetball and volleyball court are pleasant alternatives on non-beach days. The beach is accessed by way of a boardwalk that cuts through trees and dense foliage, eventually emerging onto a quiet, pristine beach. Bowser will enjoy early morning or late afternoon jaunts along the water's edge, when things are quiet. At other times of the day, it is almost easier for guests to head back down the lane, until they reach Middle Gulf Drive. Either a left or right turn will bring explorers to bicycle paths that meander along the coastline and inland. There are 20 miles of bicycle paths on Sanibel. They don't necessarily parallel the roads, but they do head off toward quieter and more scenic destinations and preserves.

A final note on making reservations: The Signal Inn is a popular resort. Most visitors make reservations a year in advance. The weekly rentals run from one Saturday to the next. To make a reservation during the high season, the management allows prospective guests to telephone exactly one year in advance of the date they are interested in visiting. During the off-season, there are also three-day reservation blocks, but potential guests would be well-advised to call sooner, rather than later.

Mitchell's Sand Castles

3951 West Gulf Drive
Sanibel, Florida 33957
(813) 472-1282, Fax (813) 472-1477

Manager: *Roxanne Palmer*
Rooms: *18 cottages, 1 beachfront home*
Rates: *Cottages $75-140 (EP), Beachfront home $150-200 (EP)*
Payment: *Travelers checks*
Children: *Welcome (cribs and cots are available)*
Dogs: *Welcome with a $5 daily fee*
Open: *All year*

The term Old Florida may be used to define an architectural style, or it may refer to a disappearing lifestyle. Some developers want to bulldoze away anything reminiscent of the past, while others are constantly trying to recapture and/or preserve it. There are pockets of Old Florida that still exist, and one of these is Mitchell's Sand Castles. The main cottage complex has fourteen 35-year-old cottages dotting a white sandy beach, as well as a separate property with two honeymoon cottages nestled just off the beach at Blind Pass, in a stand of pine trees.

The first grouping of cottages is situated in the heart of Sanibel, on a cul-de-sac in a residential neighborhood. It is a simple place where sandy paths, nicely landscaped grounds, and assorted stands of trees encircle the cottages. There are lovely views out toward the beach that are somewhat reminiscent of the Caribbean, where pure white sand, turquoise blue waters, and even a thatched hut create a lasting impression. This was such a casual place, and the sand looked so soft, that we quickly made some excuse to remove our shoes—so we could begin to feel as if we belonged. We checked in with the office, a tiny edifice filled with a few beach essentials and a complicated chart of reservation bookings. This is another one of those secret, yet not so secret places, where travelers find a good thing and keep coming back.

One of the endearing aspects about this place is the pink seashells that are stenciled on the side of the cottages that reflect their names. Ocean Mist, Sea Spray, and Sea Star are right on the beach, whereas Sea Grape, Coquina, and Driftwood are set one cottage off the water. Each is slightly different, although all are rustic yet immaculately kept. The white- or gray-stained exteriors are fashioned with tiny windows and, with two exceptions, also have screened-in porches. The interiors have exposed wood slat ceilings and linoleum floors. Even the largest cottage is really quite small by most standards. The kitchens and bathrooms appear to be circa 1950, but they are well stocked with the usual cooking accoutrements. Furnishings are also dated, but it doesn't matter, as most people spend the majority of their time relaxing on the beach. This is a very relaxed sort of place, where people don't feel compelled to wash off every drop of sand before entering their cottage, and guests are comfortable putting their feet up and relaxing at the end of the day. Televisions, along with individual air conditioning and heating, provide a few welcome, modern conveniences.

Those who require a little additional space or are looking for oceanfront accommodations should try to reserve Sea Spray, which has an oversized bedroom containing two double beds, and a couch bed in the living room. Sea Star is another good choice, with a similar setup. Small and cozy, Coquina has just one room, but the vista is unequalled. No one should feel left out when it comes to views, though, as each cottage seems to have some sort of peek at the ocean. Another option, for those who are looking for a more private setting, is to consider renting one of the two Honeymoon Gulf Front Cottages. However, be forewarned: what guests may gain in exclusivity, they lose in tranquility, as the cottages back onto a busy road that links Captiva with Sanibel.

Calmer ocean waters can be found in front of the main cottage complex, where children and dogs can swim without concern. There is also a heated swimming pool on the property, which is nice when the Gulf water temperature drops off a bit. Of course, Sanibel is known for its fantastic shelling, and the Sand Castles' beach is no exception. Best of all, dogs are more than welcome to accompany their human friends on these expeditions. Another popular walk is along the quiet road that runs behind the cottages. Many enjoy combining both, as there are numerous public access points along the road, which allow guests to cross over to the beach and return to the tiny resort.

Heron Lagoon Club

8212 Midnight Pass Road
Siesta Key, Florida 34242
(813) 346-0617

Owner: Nick Emery
Rooms: 10 suites
Rates: $65-120 daily (EP), $375-650 weekly (EP)
Payment: MC and VISA
Children: Welcome
Dogs: Welcome and encouraged
Open: All year

Siesta Key was a pleasant surprise for us, particularly after spending a day checking out the more densely populated islands off the coast of St. Petersburg and Tampa Bay. Siesta Key is far smaller and has a more jungle-like quality than most of its northern neighbors. There are also more "hammocks" of wildness found in this region, where dense stands of trees, dripping with moss, and native flora and fauna line many of the narrow roads. This is not to say that it is without its developments, because there are plenty of places to stay along the water. But there are just as many private homes, which are either set well back from view or line the many lagoons and waterways that weave along the key.

Set unobtrusively among mostly private homes is the Heron Lagoon Club. This small complex of single-story, peach colored stucco and brick cottages is virtually indistinguishable from the lush gardens that surround it. We almost missed the entrance, as it is marked by a tiny sign. We were also misled by the word "club," thinking it meant the resort was private, but we soon learned that many of the cottages and apartments around here refer to themselves as clubs. After further inspection, we decided that the Heron Lagoon Club may just as well be private, because most of its patrons tend to book rooms a year in advance and stay for as long as three months at a time. Its steadfast reputation was built by word of mouth, and attracts affluent guests from all over the United States. At the time of our visit, we met people from Bloomfield Hills, Michigan and Chestnut Hill and Chatham, Massachusetts. All were raving about the owner, Nick Emery, who, over the last ten years, has carefully created his little piece of island paradise.

The collection of suites and apartments is intimate. The rooms are contained in small cottages that date back over 30 years. Nick told us that the property is grandfathered, meaning the town has said he cannot change anything about the cottages' facades. This gives the exterior an Old Florida feeling, but as we soon discovered, the interior spaces are a lovely mix of tradition and "new" Florida. Paths leading to these suites wend between small grassy areas and lanais crafted from coquina, a native stone made from crushed shells. At times, the lush plantings partially obscure the way, and most people are surprised at how friendly the resident squirrels and birds seem to be in this natural environment. As we wandered about, we happened upon one couple and their terrier. All three were out basking in the sunshine. This was their first trip to the Heron Lagoon Club and they were already planning a more extended stay for the following season. They appreciated not only the completely private setting, but also the assortment of amenities the club provided. We thought the small swimming pool they were lounging by was especially appealing, as it overlooks the lagoon and mangrove hammocks.

As we mentioned, Old Florida meets new when guests step inside their bungalow or suite. Each is designed and decorated differently, but all have been updated over the last few years. The original terrazzo floors are now covered in soft carpeting. The furniture and decor is primarily done in pastel hues. The furnishings are either high quality wicker or rattan, set with chintz cushions, combined with an occasional Louis XVI or Chippendale reproduction thrown in for good measure. We especially liked Suite 10, where three walls of windows allow refreshing breezes to waft through the room. They also provide unparalleled views of the lagoon. This spacious one-bedroom suite's living room is furnished with coordinated pieces. The chintz sofa, which converts to an inner spring foldout bed, and the matching love seat are complemented by dark wicker tables and chairs. Set off to one side of the room is the Chippendale-style writing desk. Guests may watch television on an oversized 25" console set, or walk out to the porch to read a bit. This particular suite also has a small private yard, accessed through the bathroom. The kitchen in this suite, as in all of the others, is completely modern. The sleek, European style cabinets are complemented by new appliances that include dishwashers, microwave ovens, ice makers, and sinks with Kohler faucets. We were pleased to learn that when entertaining guests, visitors to the club can rest assured that all the china, silverware, and glassware match—no jelly jar glasses or chipped hand-me-downs from a local garage sale are found in these cupboards. Central air conditioning and individually controlled heat make all the accommodations comfortable year round.

Guests should keep in mind that each suite varies dramatically in size. Some are ideal for a couple; others are large enough for extended families. We liked Suite 8, if only for its private lanai. Nick informed us that long-term guests—those who have been staying here for years—have first pick of the suites. All other guests may choose what is left over on a first come, first served basis. Whatever suite guests ultimately select, they will discover that the club supples just about everything to make their stay exceptionally comfortable. Grills are set out for those who want to barbecue; and once a week, there is the traditional Heron Lagoon Club barbecue, which most guests look forward to attending. Nick said there are some who come here to unwind, preferring to keep to themselves, whereas others are very social and outgoing. Nick is an unobtrusive host, but we can tell that he enjoys his guests as much as they enjoy him.

When not gathered around the pool, many enjoy taking a leisurely stroll along the short dock that edges the lagoon, where they will come across a motor boat. This can be used for exploring the mangroves or heading out to the open waters of the Gulf. Another popular walk leads guests out onto the main road and towards Turtle Beach. Unfortunately, dogs are not allowed out on the beach, although we have it on good authority that they have been seen way down the beach near the "nonexistent" nudist beach. The walk is quite pretty, and well worth the effort. Some 15 miles inland on Route 72, visitors will come upon the beautiful Myakka River State Park. Leashed dogs are welcome in the day-use areas and on the hardtop roads in the 28,000-acre preserve. This park follows the path of the Myakka River and has an abundance of bird and animal life, including a few alligators.

Tropical Breeze Inn

140 Columbus Boulevard/Avenida Navarra
Siesta Key, Sarasota, Florida 34242
(813) 349-1125, Fax (813) 349-0057

Managers: Marie-Louise and Jorg Leuenberger
Rooms: 13 suites, 2 cottages, 1 townhouse
Rates: Suites $70-155 (EP), Cottages $109-175 (EP),
*   Townhouse $155-195 (EP)*
Payment: AE, DSC, MC, and VISA
Children: Welcome, under 12 years of age are free (cribs are available)
Dogs: Welcome, fee is 10% of final bill or a $40 minimum
Open: All year

Traveling along the keys that line Florida's west coast, we discovered that each had a distinct personality. Sanibel and Captiva are dense tropical jungles, where nature preserves seem to occupy more space than the resorts and private homes. The small keys north of here are equally lush and possibly even more beautiful, although most are exclusive and hard to reach. As we neared Sarasota, the keys off its coast lost some of their pristine appeal; however, they still exuded a strong tropical feeling and were blessed with pure white sandy beaches.

The Tropical Breeze Inn lies on the northern side of the island, in the heart of Siesta Key Village. While this is decidedly not secluded, hotel guests are privy to the village's beachside setting, and are within walking distance of its many funky cafés, international boutiques, and intimate night spots. When we arrived, it was the height of spring break for many college students, and the village was hopping. We found some of the students enjoying their warm weather respite at the Tropical Breeze Inn, along with families and older couples. There are actually three parts to this intimate resort—a group of garden suites, the pool cottages, and the beach suites, which are just 100 yards from the beach.

We checked in with Marie-Louise at the office, near the garden suites. We had to step around the workmen who were laying a circular brick courtyard over the old lawn. Evidently, the area was getting so much use that there was more dirt than grass, and the Leuenbergers thought a courtyard would be more practical. We would agree, particularly because the courtyard is still surrounded by lush plantings. Each of the ground-level garden suites overlook this landscape, with separate outside entrances that open to a shared and shaded lanai. We like the pristine interiors, where white walls have a smattering of framed posters and lithographs depicting sailboats, groves of palm trees, and other tropical vistas. The honey colored rattan and wicker sofas and chairs are set with either bright floral patterns or muted, tropical colored cushions. We walked into one suite, where florals and electric yellow or pink cushions all combined to create a festive tone. Glass is used with rattan for both the coffee and dining room tables, enhancing the already light feeling of these places. Also scattered about the rooms are director's chairs and ceramic lamps resting on rattan tables set upon the terazzo floors. Kitchens or kitchenettes are exceptionally clean, with new white European-style cabinets, coffee makers, and plenty of pots, pans, china, and flatware. Guests may expect remote controlled televisions, private telephones, and air conditioning in all the accommodations. The bathrooms are Art Deco, which means guests may expect a variety of funky styles. The garden suites are all one bedroom; however, they range from units that are quite small to those that appear more spacious.

The beach suites are the other choice that is the highest on our list of recommendations. These are located two blocks away in a small, white brick, two-story building, which is recognizable by the turquoise green and salmon trim. A white board fence and mature plantings surround the property, allowing for optimum privacy. The upper floor's two-bedroom townhouse is our favorite room configuration, as it has a private deck that offers exceptional views of the Gulf. Walls of jalousied windows are reminiscent of Old Florida, but once again, the furnishings and decor are a blend of both. Rag rugs are scattered about the floors, and the dining room table is placed to take optimum advantage of the view. On the first floor are four, one-bedroom beach suites. These may not offer the same views as the townhouse, but this is compensated for by the private garden setting. Stepping outside the gate and across the street, the water and white sands beckon. Finally, there are the two small, two-bedroom pool cottages that lie back up the road away from the water, closer to the village. These are equally well furnished and designed, and are built around a central swimming pool.

Guests and their dogs will find plenty of things to do in the area. There are walks, upon walks, upon walks, to enjoy. Guests may want to head over to the village for a little early morning cappucino in one of the outdoor cafés, or stroll down near the beach. The dog laws state that dogs are not allowed on the beach; once again, though, we kept seeing them here in the early morning and late evening. Hmmm....we advise guests to use their better judgement. Guests may bring a bicycle and ride for miles along Siesta Key, where highrise buildings are kept to a minimum and the million dollar houses that line the water are certainly worth further inspection. A popular day trip leads visitors south to Gasparilla Island, where they may explore the beaches or hire a boat and head over to Cayo Costa for the rest of the day. Here, humans and dogs alike will find over 2,000 acres of trails and unspoiled beaches, which are great for shelling or for just relaxing.

Turtle Beach Resort

9049 Midnight Pass Road
Siesta Key, Florida 34242
(941) 349-4554, (813) 918-0203

Owners: *Gail and David Rubenfeld*
Rooms: *2 studios, 3 two-bedroom suites*
Rates: *Studios $89-140 per day (EP), Villas $99-165 per night (EP)*
Payment: *Personal checks*
Children: *Welcome, and they can stay free of charge (babysitters are available)*
Dogs: *Welcome with a 10% surcharge added to final bill*
Open: *All year*

Siesta Key, with its soft, white sand beaches and lush tropical setting, is a lovely place to vacation, especially with a dog. This is a quiet, laid back sort of place, which is accessible to the mainland by two causeways—yet it still manages to retain an island ambiance. A single road leads past mostly residential homes concealed by dense foliage to the southernmost point on the key. Finding the Turtle Beach Resort shouldn't be hard—just try not to blink as the road nears its end or you might miss it. The tiny property, which is surrounded by small houses and a few discrete restaurants, is a lovely oasis, where brick-lined walkways weave among grassy areas, palm trees, and flowering hibiscus and jasmine. Of course, the crown jewels are the four cottages overlooking Sarasota Bay and the pristine neighboring island.

The taupe colored stucco and board cottages exude a Key West flavor. However, unlike most guest houses in that town, each of these is privy to water views. Glass is used in lieu of wall space whenever possible, whether it be in the jalousied or full view windows, or in the sliding glass doors. Three cottages, the Key West, the Victorian, and the Country Cottage, contain two bedrooms, a living room, dining area, and kitchen. The Country French Studio and Southwestern Studio are the two most recent additions. Although they are smaller and do not feature separate bedrooms, they are just as unique and lovely as their predecessors. We learned that Gail has a background in interior design, and she has nicely parlayed these talents into creating five lovely accommodations.

The Country Cottage is often guests' first choice, as it is built virtually over the water's edge. Surrounded by lush plantings, guests step inside to find a crisp French blue and white interior, where striped cotton curtains frame the windows, and an overstuffed blue and white couch rests against a wall. The sophisticated country look is enhanced by English-country oak tables and chairs. The fully-equipped kitchen is similar to the rest of the cottages, and includes both a microwave oven and a coffee maker. The Key West cottage is fashioned with white wicker and glass, with slate blue and peach floral fabrics as accents. The white tiled floors throughout this space lend it a cool and distinct Florida feel. The backdrop for the Victorian cottage is also white; however, the color scheme consists of muted mauve and blue gray. Old fashioned floral fabrics are used throughout the cottage, whether as fluffy comforters for the beds or as decorative accents in the living room. We thought the variety of knickknacks and baskets of silk flowers set on coffee tables, dining room tables, and draped tables, tied the entire effect together quite nicely.

Finally, there are the Country French and the Southwestern Studios, which may lack the spaciousness of the other cottages, but they make up for this shortcoming with an abundance of charm. In here, the beds seem to set the theme. We liked the unusual canopied bedstead in the

Country French Studio, built to resemble intricately patterned black wrought iron. It would seemingly overwhelm the room, were it not for the vaulted ceiling. The florals in the French Provincial bedspread are fresh, especially against the darker woods of the corner hutch and hardwood floors. The bed in the Southwestern Studio is exactly like the one in the Country French Studio, but is four-poster. The walls may be white, but it is the reddish hues of the hardwood floors that set the tone for the rich combination of jade, russet, and chocolate brown colors more typically found in the desert Southwest. These may be studios, but guests still benefit from fully-equipped kitchens and dining areas. In fact, all the cottages and studios have certain standard amenities, which include remote controlled cable televisions, private telephones, and individually heated and cooled chambers. A mere step outside and guests will find their own private whirlpool spa.

The Rubenfelds have recently added a good-sized swimming pool to the property, which is as attractive as it is refreshing. Guests can take a swim and then relax in the pool-side hammock. They can also walk out to the dock, to either dip their feet in the water and fish, or bask in the Florida sun. Some may want to borrow the paddle boat and take Bowser for a little tour of the bay. Turtle Beach, the most secluded of the beaches, is literally a three minute walk from the cottages. Here, the soft Gulf sands are conducive to uninterrupted walks, especially further south where very few people tend to congregate. Just up the road is Siesta Beach, which is a busier spot and even has a few concession areas for buying food or renting umbrellas. We preferred the former option, as it is easier there to get away from it all. Technically, Bowser is not allowed on Turtle Beach. (This is not unusual for Florida's beaches.) Once again, what we read on the sign and what we actually observed during the early morning and evening hours, seemed to be a contradiction in terms—a contradiction the locals seemed to grasp quite well. The area around Turtle Bay is quiet, and great for walks with Bowser, as there are mostly private homes and a few restaurants. Guests may want to borrow a bicycle and take Bowser on an early morning ride along Siesta Key, when all is still.

We found the Turtle Beach Resort to be many things to many people. It appealed to those looking for a romantic weekend getaway, a week-long family retreat, or just a relaxing hideaway. Whatever guests' reasons for staying here, if they are traveling with Bowser then they are certain to find the Rubenfelds to be exceptionally dog-friendly hosts. As Gail mentioned to us, "We tend to treat our dog guests as well, if not better, than their human companions."

Barefoot Trace

6240 A1A South
St. Augustine, Florida 32084
(904) 471-9212

Manager: *Five Star Property Management, Inc.*
Rooms: *66 2-bedroom condominium suites*
Rates: *$652-816 per week (EP)*
Payment: *MC and VISA*
Children: *Welcome*
Dogs: *Welcome with a $40 fee*
Open: *All year*

According to historians, it is neither Plymouth nor Jamestown that should be claiming first colony status in America—it is St. Augustine. Juan Ponce de León first saw North America in 1513, claiming it for Spain, although the resident Timucuan Indians would rightfully dismiss the idea of Europeans having discovered anything new in their land. After this initial sighting, the Spanish returned six times in an attempt to establish a colony here. The French finally slipped in around 1564 and built a fort on the St. Johns River. Not to be outdone, Spain sent Pedro Menéndez de Avilés to destroy the French fort and establish a Spanish stronghold. Menéndez came ashore south of the fort, built his settlement, and then sent the French back to Europe. The date was 1565, and it would be a long and difficult struggle for Spain to maintain its presence here. Over the centuries, the area has come under the jurisdiction of many different countries. It has survived fires, hurricanes, war, and millionaires who wanted to exploit its natural beauty. Surprisingly, it remains virtually intact, and most of the historic portions of this colony have been carefully preserved, restored, or recreated.

This is a lovely spot along Florida's east coast, where an historic site or event can be found on virtually every corner, plaza, or building. The Castillo De San Marcos National Monument is one of the more famous attractions. The Spanish began building this fort in 1672 and completed it some years later. To build it, they used the native coquina brought over from Anastasia Island. The fort is a fascinating place that reveals just a portion of the city's intriguing history. Trips further into town bring visitors to the Cathedral of St. Augustine, which was built in the late 1700s and rebuilt in 1887, making it the country's oldest Catholic church. Guests may enjoy bringing Bowser on a walking tour of town where they will find the oldest house, the oldest wooden schoolhouse, and the oldest museum store, each of which is filled with various historic artifacts. This is one of the easier cities to walk through, and probably one of the most fascinating. We looked all around town for inns to stay in, but none of them accepted dogs. There are a few motels, but nothing out of the ordinary. Luckily, just slightly out of town, we found an ideal solution—Barefoot Trace.

To reach Barefoot Trace, visitors drive south from St. Augustine, along scenic A1A, to Crescent Beach, where Barefoot Trace is found. We have visited countless condominiums in Florida, and this is one of the better ones. Its expansive two-bedroom units are housed in three separate four-story, Mediterranean-style buildings set just off the beach. There is a strong residential feeling here, perhaps because during our visit the "snowbirds" were here for their three-month hiatus from the cold. The floor plans and amenities are virtually identical, and with the exception of the first floor units, all are privy to ocean views. The decor does vary, though, as each condominium is individually owned. When the owner is not in residence (which is frequently) the condominiums are placed into a rental pool. Some of these owners allow pets; we even met a few of the canine vacationers while we were visiting.

Barefoot Trace is positioned to take advantage of the ocean. This considerably enhances the guest chambers, as walls of windows overlook the water and sliding glass doors open to private patios. The only room that does not benefit from the sea breeze or vista is the back bedroom. This bedroom and the kitchen are separated by a tiled foyer that marks the condominium's entrance. Walking past these rooms, guests enter a spacious living room and dining area. Just next to this is a master bedroom with its own private bathroom.

The floor plan works well, but the well maintained amenities are what set Barefoot Trace apart from the rest. Unlike some of the shoddier units we have seen, Barefoot Trace's guest rooms were well constructed from the beginning, with thick floor joists, good soundproofing, and quality windows that do not allow the wind to whistle through the cracks. Tile is used in the high traffic areas and in the bathroom, but otherwise guests will find beautiful wall-to-wall carpeting throughout. While there are a variety of good restaurants in St. Augustine, most people often prefer to cook at home, making a well-equipped and designed kitchen an important feature. White General Electric appliances are surrounded by a full complement of light oak cabinets. Coffee makers, microwave ovens, and oversized refrigerators with ice makers are just a few of the conveniences. The kitchen may be separate, but one wall is open so that the cook can either visit with guests in the living room, or look past them to the ocean. An optional wet bar is terrific for those planning to entertain frequently during their stay. The already ample space generally has a wall of mirrors to give the illusion of even more spacious chambers. The furnishings are good-quality and very tasteful contemporary pieces covered in light fabrics, which we consider to be Florida formal. Sofas are generally sectional, and face an entertainment center set up along the wall. The master bedroom usually contains a king-size bed, and the second bedroom, a pair of twins. We liked the two private bathrooms, one off each bedroom. Of course, the master bedroom's is more elaborate, where the toilet and whirlpool spa/tub are separate from the sink and dressing area. The walk-in closet can easily hold a month's supply of clothes. Best of all, for those who are staying for longer intervals, there is a small utility area with a full-size washer and dryer, located toward the rear of the unit.

Guests are attracted not only to the luxury of these units, but also to the shared amenities. A private parking garage keeps cars well protected, trash chutes make disposal easy, and elevators take guests to the upper floors with ease. The Olympic-size swimming pool is terrific, as is the heated spa. Tennis is available on the lighted courts. But it is the beach to which most guests gravitate each day, whether to walk, swim, or just relax in the sun. Well manicured grassy areas lead some to the two boardwalks, which rise above the dunes and drop down to the white sand beach. Here people and their dogs can walk for miles. Guests can drive into St. Augustine with their dog, stop by the visitors' center, and pick up a walking tour map, which will certainly outline some of the more notable excursions for visitors traveling with Bowser. Further south, some may want to visit to the Fort Matanazas National Monument and the many pristine beaches along the way. If travelers drive far enough, they will arrive at Marineland, the country's first oceanographic park.

Indian River Plantation Beach Resort

555 Northeast Ocean Blvd.
Stuart, Florida 34996
(800) 444-3389, (407) 225-3700, Fax (407) 225-0003

General Manager: *Steve Powers*
Rooms: *174 doubles, 10 suites, 70 villas*
Rates: *Doubles $135-175 (EP), Suites $225-415 (EP),*
Villas $150-425 (EP)
Payment: *AE, CB, DC, DSC, MC, and VISA*
Children: *Welcome; extensive children's program is available (cribs, cots,*
babysitters, and high chairs are available)
Dogs: *Welcome with a $75 one-time charge in hotel and a $200 one-time*
charge in suites or villas
Open: *All year*

The Indian River Plantation lies on Hutchinson Island, which parallels southeastern Florida's "Treasure Coast." The Gulf Stream has always played a major role in the history of the area. In the 1600s, Spanish Galleons filled with gold and other riches sunk here, while trying to navigate the tricky coastal sandbars. The same warm waters also created a climate that was conducive to growing pineapples, and the island quickly became known for its pineapple plantations. Today, visitors will not see plantations, only private homes and low-density developments. This is an active community, with sailing, sportfishing, tennis, and golf comprising some of the more popular activities. We know of many people who have settled here, lured by the low-key and relaxed pace of life, which is without the usual signs of commercialism found further south.

Hutchinson Island is also an ideal destination for families. However, the Indian River Plantation Beach Resort takes family vacationing one step further, allowing the family dog to participate in the vacation. The resort claims to combine a bit of Old Florida with first-class accommodations and amenities. After spending some time here, we think this is an apt description. The overnight accommodations are divided between the main hotel and three oceanfront condominiums. Guests register at the hotel, which is tucked discreetly off the main road amid native flora and fauna. Most will appreciate the fact that there is a tram shuttle, which brings guests from one end of the resort to the other. This allows them to park their cars on arrival and leave them for the duration of their stay. As we walked into the lobby, we found a tropical setting reminiscent of Old Florida. This was combined with the lime green, bright yellow, and hot pinks more commonly associated with the eye-catching Lily Pulitzer fabrics. Formal chintz sofas and armchairs are placed around glass-topped tables in a raised sitting area, which is illuminated during the day by passive light from the floor-to-ceiling windows. Rather than walls, the room is framed by panels of white lattice lined with potted palms.

The bedrooms in the main hotel are located in three buildings, which surround an enormous pool and Tiki bar. These are spacious chambers, with private balconies accessed through sliding glass doors. The bedrooms are fully carpeted spaces and are brightened by coordinated floral fabrics that appear both on the quilted bedspreads and in the draperies. White wicker chairs are set next to tables arranged alongside the windows, so that guests may enjoy their breakfast and the surrounding views at the same time. The amenities found in the hotel rooms are similar to those in the condominium villas. The bedrooms contain not only cable televisions, but also a wet bar and refrigerator. The modern bathrooms are fully stocked with toiletries and an array of bathing accoutrements.

The hotel rooms work well for a short-term stay; however, we recommend the Sandpiper Villas for longer visits. These are located along the shoreline, standing four stories above the dunes. Most of these units have terrific ocean views, but not all of them do. Therefore, it is important to request a room that actually faces the water. These villas range from accommodations as small as a studio to space as large as a one-bedroom suite. The basic decor is comprised of pale greens and peaches, combined with Scandinavian furnishings made of bleached wood. The one-bedroom units offer separate, oversized living rooms and dining areas, with televisions hidden in the massive armoires. The kitchens are modern and well stocked, and some are even privy to ocean views—which is more than enough incentive to volunteer for cooking duty. The tiled bathrooms are equally well appointed, containing separate telephone lines and blow dryers, along with the usual complement of toiletries. These are vacation rentals, with just enough pictures on the walls and knickknacks set out to make them seem homey and attractive, but not overdone. We also liked the idea of being able to open the sliding glass doors to the balconies, where we could enjoy the refreshing breezes and listen to the ocean crash against the shore as we drifted off to sleep.

There are many protected areas on Hutchinson Island, which makes this sleepy community all the more appealing. We saw all sorts of vacationing dogs at the Indian River Plantation, ranging from standard poodles to wire-haired terriers. Loggerhead turtles can frequently be found on the beaches here, and are highly protected, making it all the more important to keep Bowser on a leash when visiting these beaches. The turtles lay their eggs in August, offering a prime opportunity for human visitors to learn more about these intriguing creatures. There are 25 miles of beachfront to explore with a canine companion, and much of it is remote and wild. From the Sandpiper Villas, guests usually access the beach by walking along wooden boardwalks that climb over the dunes. Bathtub Beach is another popular spot for many, as there are trails to explore that wend along the river and over the dunes. There are also plenty of nature preserves on the island, both inland and along the water. Bike paths make it easy and safe to take leisurely rides with both Bowser and the children.

Within the resort, there are a myriad of excellent people-oriented diversions. Children may be enrolled in the Pineapple Bunch Children's Camp, which is divided into morning and afternoon sessions for children ages 4-14. This allows parents to play golf on one of the two 18-hole golf courses, or perhaps to take advantage of the resort's 13 courts over at the tennis club. Later in the day, many like to rent a boat at the nearby marina for some water-oriented activities, such as water skiing or snorkeling around the nearby ocean reefs. The resort also has a good supply of wave runners, jet skis, and boogie boards that guests may rent. The waters off Hutchinson Island are famous for their deep sea fishing, particularly for sailfish. Guests may choose from one of the four swimming pools to have a refreshing dip—a nice change of pace from swimming in the ocean.

During the day's and evening's adventures, there are plenty of places to stop for sustenance. The most casual is The Emporium, where there are a variety of choices for breakfast or lunch, as well as the kids' perennial favorite — an ice cream parlor. Our dogs always love the last bite of cone, making it their favorite place to visit, as well. The most elegant and formal restaurant at the Indian River Plantation is called Scalawags. The extensive menu emphasizes local fruit, produce, and fish. Some of the appetizer selections include an avocado stuffed with snow crab meat or the jumbo sea scallops and shrimp sautéed in garlic, Shiitake mushrooms and ginger, topped with a Key Lime butter sauce. The selection of fresh fish truly stands out. The dolphin, swordfish, red snapper or Florida grouper can be broiled, sautéed, poached, grilled, blackened and then covered with a Key Lime or Dijon mustard sauce. Shrimp Creole is also a popular request. Or guests may choose to combine fish and meat dishes in the Florida surf and turf. It is fortunate that there are plenty of athletic options around the resort. This gives guests leeway to indulge in the restaurant's elaborate dessert concoctions. These feature chocolate or apricot mousses, which are spooned into a small chocolate shell and then topped with a raspberry coulis and whipped cream. The dessert cart usually is loaded with wonderful creations, the exact assortment depending on the dessert chef's whims of the day. After a round of golf, players may also choose to eat at the 19th Hole or dine seasonally at The Porch, which is a traditional steak house located next to the tennis complex.

There are a variety of ways to enjoy the Indian River Plantation, as it is a multifaceted place. It is tough to find an lightly developed, low-key, and uncommercial part of southeastern Florida that is so accessible to those traveling with a dog. Hutchinson Island is one of the last refuges for those who thoroughly enjoy this relaxing and uncomplicated type of vacation.

Seahorse Cottages

10356 Gulf Boulevard.
Treasure Island, Florida 33706
(800) 741-2291, (813) 367-2291, Fax (813) 367-8891

Managers: *Larry and Pat Lynch*
Rooms: *6 cottages, 3 apartments*
Rates: *Cottages $40-92 (EP), Apartments $35-72 (EP)*
Payment: *DSC, MC, and VISA*
Children: *Welcome (cribs, cots, high chairs, and babysitters are available)*
Dogs: *Welcome but they must be either under 20 pounds or under 20*
    inches high
Open: *All year*

Let's face it, finding a beachfront bungalow that is affordable, clean, and charming is not an easy task. So we were lucky to come across the Seahorse Cottages, which consist of a small group of cottages and a few apartments situated directly on the enormous, white sandy beach of Treasure Island. We were especially surprised with this discovery, because much of Treasure Island tends toward the commercial, with an assortment of fast food restaurants and stores interspersed among high-rise buildings tightly packed along the beach. This area is not without its charm; visitors just need to look a little harder to find it. And find it we did at the Seahorse Cottages.

The Cottages were built in 1939, making them the first cottages on Treasure Island and probably the best for anyone who loves the beach. The Petits are only the third owners in all these years, and have established a reputation for friendliness and first-rate service during their tenure. Some guests came as children and now bring their grandchildren back for multi-generational family vacations. Although the Petits own the cottages, Larry and Pat Lynch are the managers. Pat told us the occupancy rate averages 92% year round. After talking with her and looking around the complex, we can understand why this

245

might be the case. When we arrived, Pat was busy juggling several different things. On the one hand, she was trying to ready one of the apartments for new arrivals; at the same time, she was visiting with and helping the other guests. As we walked around outside, the resident egrets caught us off guard as they casually strolled up to us in search of a handout. Pat tries to dissuade guests from feeding them, but with little success — as they are so friendly and such fun to see up close.

The egrets are as integral to the complex as are the crisp white bungalows trimmed in turquoise blue. The most desirable cottages are the ones on the beach, because they are furthest from the busy main road and closest to the sounds of the waves and cool Gulf breezes. The interiors of each vary slightly in their room configurations and furnishings, although they are similar to one another in physical appearance. All have darkly-stained, knotty pine paneled walls and ceilings; wall-to-wall carpeting combined with some linoleum; and fully-equipped kitchens. Surprisingly, there are even a few built-in corner cupboards, which add interest to the small, but immaculately maintained cottages. The cottages are made to seem larger through the use of multiple double-hung windows that seem to fill any wall that might offer an interesting view.

Cottage 9 is perhaps the most private, as it is set along the far edge of the beachfront cottages. The separate bedroom has a king-size bed covered with a richly patterned cotton spread. It has plenty of closet space and bureaus for holding a week's worth of clothes. The attractive furnishings are of dark oak or pine and fit in well with the woody surroundings. The living room is equally well-sized and has a sleep sofa. Cottage 2, just next door, is the only two-bedroom unit, which is not to say that it is overly spacious. Two double beds virtually fill one bedroom, and a double bed rests in a second miniscule chamber. Most of the knickknacks or artwork have a strong seaside theme; framed posters of shells or mirrors etched with sea gulls set the predominant tone. There are also plenty of modern amenities, such as cable color televisions, air conditioning, and new coffee makers and microwaves in the kitchens. In addition, guests have the option of using the overhead fans. But when all is said and done, it is the beach that is truly remarkable.

The cottages form a semi-circle around the edge of the sandy beach. In front of the cottages are chaise lounges for sunning, a small inflatable kiddie pool for cooling off, and even a swing set. The Gulf of Mexico can be seen from the cottages, but it actually takes a minute or two to walk from them across the beach to the water's edge. The wide beach is similar to many that line the coast of Southern California, except the sand here is whiter and the water is much warmer. Guests usually spend their days relaxing in the sun, walking along the beach, and swimming. Even as the sun is setting, most people are reluctant to go inside, which is why many choose to grill their dinner and enjoy it at the picnic tables on the beach. This is truly a casual beachfront vacation spot, which everyone, including Bowser, is certain to enjoy.

A park across the street from the cottages is a popular place for walking dogs. Some people enjoy strolling along the road that runs next to the beach, which is lined with all sorts of hotels, motels, and cottages. Technically, dogs are not allowed on the beach. In fact, during the day, if a dog is found on the beach the owner will be fined. The dog laws on Treasure Island are similar to those in other parts of the state, where dogs are not allowed on the beaches at all; but during the early morning hours and evenings there seems to be some leniency, provided the dogs are under control. We do not encourage people to break the law, but we feel guests should be informed about the local customs.

Chain Hotels/Motels-800 Numbers

Best Inns-America: (800)237-8466
Best Western: (800) 528-1234
Budgetel Inns: (800) 4-BUDGET
Comfort Inns: (800) 228-5150
Days Inn: (800) 325-2525
Econo Lodge: (800) 446-6900
Embassy Suites: (800) 362-2779
Fairfield Inn/Marriott: (800) 228-2800
Four Seasons Hotels: (800) 332-3442
Guest Quarters: (800) 424-2900
Hampton Inns: (800) HAMPTON
Hawthorne Suites: (800) 527-1133
Hilton Hotels: (800) HILTON
Holiday Inn: (800) HOLIDAY
Homewood Suites: (800) 225-5466
Howard Johnson: (800) 654-2000
Hyatt Corp: (800) 228-9000
La Quinta: (800) 531-5900
Marriott Hotels: (800) 228-9290
Quality Inns: (800) 228-5151
Radisson Hotels: (800) 333-3333
Ramada Inns: (800) 2-RAMADA
Red Roof Inns: (800) 843-7663
Residence Inn: (800) 331-3131
Ritz-Carlton: (800) 241-3333
Sheraton Hotels: (800) 325-3535

Shoney's Inns: (800) 222-2222
Stouffer Hotels: (800) HOTELS-1
Super Eight: (800) 800-8000
Travelodge: (800) 255-3050
Westin: (800) 228-3000
Wyndham Hotels: (800) 822-4200

Helpful Telephone Numbers

American Animal Hospital Association..(303) 986-2800
American Humane Association.. (800) 227-4645
A.S.P.C.A ....(212) 876-7700
Assistance Dogs International .... (303) 234-9512
Guide Dog Foundation for the Blind ....(800) 548-4337
Humane Society for the U.S. .... (202) 452-1100
National Animal Poison Control Center .... (800) 548-2423
Pet Loss Support Hot line .... (916) 752-4200
Pet Finders...(800) 666-5678
Tattoo-A-Pet International...(800) TAT-TOOS

The Best of the Rest

B&Bs, Inns, Hotels, and Motels

North Carolina

ABERDEEN
   Best Western
      (910) 944-2367
      1500 Sandhills Blvd
ASHEVILLE
   Best Inns of America
      (704) 298-4000
      1445 Tunnel Rd.
   Comfort Suites
      (704) 665-4000
      890 Brevard Rd.
   Days Inn East
      (704) 298-5140
      1500 Tunnel Rd.
   Holiday Inn East
      (704) 298-5611
      1450 Tunnel Rd
ATLANTIC BEACH
   Atlantis Lodge
      (919) 247-2636
      Salter Path Rd.
BOONE
   Grandma Jean's B&B
      (704) 262-3670
      254 MeadowView Rd.
BURLINGTON
   Comfort Inn
      (910) 227-3681
      978 Plantation Dr
   Holiday Inn
      (910) 229-5203
      2444 Maple Ave.
CANTON
   Comfort Inn
      (714) 648-4881
      737 Champion Dr.
CARY
   Courtyard by Marriott
      (919) 481-9666
      102 Edinburgh Dr.
CHARLOTTE
   Adams Mark Hotel
      (704) 372-4100
      555 South McDowell Dr.

Comfort Inn
   (704) 375-8444
   2721 East Independence Dr.
Comfort Inn-UNCC
   (704) 598-0007
   Sugar Creek Rd,
Days Inn - Airport
   (704) 394-3381
   3101 I-85 Service Rd,
Holiday Inn
   (704) 547-0999
   8520 Univ. Executive Pk.
Homewood Suites
   (704) 525-2600
   4920 S. Tryon St.
Hyatt at South Park
   (704) 554-1234
   Tyvola Rd.
La Quinta Inn-South
   (704) 522-7110
   Nations Ford Rd.
Masters Economy Inn
   (704) 377-6581
   2701 E. Independence
Orchard Inn
   (704) 525-2551
   5822West Park Dr.
Radisson Hotel
   (704) 527-8000
   5624 West Park Dr.
Ramada-Airport
   (704) 527-3000
   515 Clanton Rd.
Red Roof Inn-Univ. Place
   (704) 596-8222
   Sugar Creek Rd.
Residence Inn
   (704) 527-8110
   5800 West Park Dr.
Wyndham Garden Hotel
   (704) 357-9100
   2600 Yorkmont Rd.

Hampton Inn
(704) 497-3115
Rte 19 South
CORNELIUS
Best Western
(704) 896-0660
19608 Liverpool Pkwy.
Holiday Inn
(704) 892-9120
19901 Holiday Lane
DUNN
Ramada Inn
(919) 892-8101
Rte 421
DURHAM
Best Western
(919) 383-2508
5400 Hillsborough Rd.
Red Roof Inn
(919) 489-9421
5623 Chapel Hill Blvd.
Sheraton
(919) 383-8575
2800 Middleton Ave.
FAYETTEVILLE
Comfort Inn
(910) 867-1777
1922 Skibo Rd.
Comfort Inn
(910) 323-8333
1957 Cedar Creek Rd.
Holiday Inn
(910) 323-0111
1707 Owen Dr.
Howard Johnson
(910) 323-8282
1965 Cedar Creek Rd.
FLAT ROCK
Lakemont Cottages
(704) 693-5174
100 Lakemont Dr.
FRANKLIN
Country Inntown Motel
(704) 524-4451
277 E. Main St.
Sleepy Hollow Cottages
(704) 524-4311
314 Leatherman Gap Rd.

GASTONIA
Knights Inn
(704) 868-4900
1721 Broadcast St.
GOLD ROCK
Comfort Inn
(919) 972-9426
I-95
Days Inn
(919) 446-0621
Route 48
Masters Economy Inn
(919) 442-8075
I-95
Ramada Inn
(919) 446-2041
I-95
GOLDSBORO
Best Western
(919) 735-7911
801 Rte 70 East
Holiday Inn
(919) 735-7901
William St.
GREENSBORO
Biltmore Greensboro Hotel
(910) 272-3474
111 W. Washington St.
Journey's End Motel
(910) 288-5611
2310 Battleground Ave.
Marriott-Airport
(910) 852-6450
Marriott Dr.
Ramada Inn-Airport
(910) 668-3900
7067 Albert Pick Rd.
Red Roof Inn-Highpoint
(910) 271-2636
615 Regional Rd. South
GREENVILLE
Comfort Inn
(919) 756-2792
301 S.E. Greenville Blvd.
HENDERSONVILLE
Comfort Inn
(704) 693-8800
206 Mitchell Drive

HICKORY
Best Western
(910) 465-2378
1710 Fair Grove Church Rd.
Holiday Inn
(704) 323-1000
1385 Lenoir Rhyne Blvd. SE
Howard Johnson
(704) 322-1600
483 Rte 70
Red Roof Inn
(704) 323-1500
1184 Lenoir Rhyne Blvd.
JACKSONVILLE
Onslow Inn
(910) 347-3151
201 Marine Blvd.
JONESVILLE
Holiday Inn
(910) 835-6000
Rte 67
KENLY
Best Western
(919) 284-3800
Truck Stop Rd.
KILL DEVIL HILLS
Hampton Inn
(919) 441-0411
804 N. Virginia Dare Tr.
LAURINBURG
Hampton Inn
(910) 277-1516
115 Hampton Circle
LUMBERTON
Ramada Inn
(910) 738-8261
3608 Kahn Dr.
MAGGIE VALLEY
Cozy Creek Cottages
(704) 926-1231
60 Moody Farm Rd.
Mountain Joy Cottages
(704) 926-1257
Setzer Cove Rd.
MORGANTON
Holiday Inn
(704) 437-0171
2400 S. Sterling St.

MORRISVILLE
Budgetel Inn
(919) 481-3600
1001 Ariel Center Pkwy.
MURPHY
Comfort Inn
(704) 837-8030
Route 64 West
NAGS HEAD
Quality Inn
(919) 441-7191
7123 S. Virginia Dare Tr.
Ramada Inn
(919) 441-2151
1701 S. Virginia Dare Tr.
PINEOLA
Pineola Inn
(704) 733-4979
Hwy 221
RALEIGH
Comfort Inn
(919) 878-9550
2910 Capital Blvd.
Hampton Inn
(919) 828-1813
1001 Wake Towne Dr.
The Plantation Inn Resort
(919) 876-1411
6401 Capital Blvd.
Residence Inn
(919) 878-6100
1000 Navaho Dr.
Sundown Inn
(919) 790-8480
3801 Capital Blvd.
Velvet Cloak Inn
(919) 828-0333
1505 Hillsborough St.
ROANOKE RAPIDS
Comfort Inn
(919) 537-5252
1911 Weldon Rd.
Holiday Inn
(919) 537-1031
100 Holiday Dr.
Interstate Inn
(919) 536-4111
1606 Roanoke RapidsRd.

Sunset Inn B&B
(919) 446-9524
1210 Sunset Ave.

SALISBURY
Days Inn
(704) 633-4211
1810 Lutheran Synod Dr.
Hampton Inn
(704) 637-8000
1001 Klumac Rd.
Holiday Inn
(704) 637-3100
530 Jake Alexander Blvd.

SHELBY
Governor's Inn
(704) 482-3821
825 W. Dixon Blvd.

SMITHFIELD
Log Cabin Motel
(919) 934-1534
Rte. 70

SOUTHERN PINES
Days Inn
(910) 692-7581
1420 Rte 1 South

SPRUCE PINE
Pine Valley Lodge
(704) 765-6276
905 Rte 226

STATESVILLE
Cedar Hill Farm B&B
(704) 873-4332
778 Elmwood Rd.
Comfort Inn
(704) 873-2044
1214 Greenland Dr.
Hampton Inn
(704) 878-2721
715 Sullivan Rd.
Holiday Inn
(704) 872-4101
740 Sullivan Rd.
Howard Johnsons
(704) 878-9691
1215 Garner Bagnall Blvd.
Super Eight
(704) 878-9888
1125 Greenland Dr.

TAYLORSVILLE
Barkley House B&B
(704) 632-9060
Hwy 16 S.

WADE
Days Inn
(910) 323-1255
Rte 13

WAYNESVILLE
Rivermont
(704) 648-3066
Lake Logan Rd.
Wynne's Creekside Lodge
(704) 926-8300
Rte 2

WILMINGTON
Anderson Guest House
(910) 343-8128
520 Orange St.

WILLIAMSTON
Comfort Inn
(919) 792-8400
Rte. 64
Holiday Inn
(919) 792-3184
Rte. 64

WILSON
Quality Inn
(919) 243-5165
Rte 301

WINSTON-SALEM
Hawthorne Inn
(910) 777-3000
420 High St.
Holiday Inn
(910) 723-2911
3050 University Pkwy
Ramada Inn
(910) 767-8240
531 Akron Dr.
Residence Inn
(910) 759-0777
7835 N. Point Blvd.
Salem Inn
(910) 725-8561
127 S. Cherry St.
Sheraton Inn
(910) 767-9595
5790 University Pkwy.

South Carolina

AIKEN
  Best Western
    (803) 649-3968
    3560 Richland Ave. W.
  Days Inn
    (803) 649-5524
    1204 Richland Ave. W.
  Ramada Inn
    (803) 648-4272
    100 W. Frontage Rd.
  Ramada Ltd.
    (803) 648-6821
    1850 Richland Ave.
ANDERSON
  Holiday Inn
    (803) 226-6051
    3025 N. Main St.
  Royal American Motor Inn
    (803) 226-7236
    4515 Clemson Blvd.
BEAUFORT
  Battery Creek Inn
    (803) 521-1441
    102 Marina Blvd.
  Days Inn
    (803) 524-1551
    1809 S. Ribaut
  Holiday Inn
    (803) 524-2144
    Lovejoy St.
  Howard Johnson
    (803) 524-6920
    3127 Boundry St.
CAMDEN
  Colony Inn
    (803) 432-5508
    2020 W. DeKalb St.
  Holiday Inn
    (803) 438-9441
    Rte 1
CAYCE
  Masters Economy Inn
    (803) 791-5850
    2125 Commerce Dr.

CHARLESTON
  Econo Lodge
    (803) 571-1880
    2237 Savannah Hwy.
  HoJo Inn
    (803) 554-4140
    3640 Dorchester Rd.
  Holiday Inn
    (803) 556-7100
    301 Savannah Hwy.
  Indigo Inn
    (803) 577-5900
    1 Maiden Lane
  La Quinta Inn
    (803) 797-8181
    2499 La Quinta Ln.
  Masters Economy Inn
    (803) 744-3530
    6100 Rivers Ave.
  Quality Inn
    (803) 722-3391
    125 Calhoun St.
  Red Roof Inn
    (803) 572-9100
    7480 Northwoods Blvd.
  Residence Inn
    (803) 572-5757
    7645 Northwoods Blvd.
  Town & Country Inn
    (803) 571-1000
    2008 Savannah Hwy.
CHERAW
  Inn Cheraw
    (803) 537-2011
    321 Second St.
CLEMSON
  Holiday Inn
    (803) 654-4450
    894 Tiger Blvd.
COLUMBIA
  Adams Mark
    (803) 771-7000
    1200 Hampton St.
  Super Eight
    (803) 796-4833
    2516 Augusta Rd.

Holiday Inn
(803) 774-5111
Rte 9

EASLEY
Days Inn
(803) 859-9902
121 Days Inn Dr.

ESTILL
Palmetto Inn
(803) 625-4322
64 Wyman Blvd.

FLORENCE
Comfort Inn
(803) 665-4558
Rte 52
Days Inn
(803) 665-8550
Rte 76
Econo Lodge
(803) 665-8558
2251 West Lucas St.
Hampton Inn
(803) 662-7000
826 West Lucas St.
Park Inn International
(803) 662-9421
831 S. Irby St.
Quality Inn
(803) 669-1715
3024 TV Rd.
Ramada Inn
(803) 669-4241
2038 W. Lucas St.
Red Roof Inn
(803) 678-9000
2690 David McLeod Blvd.
Super Eight
(803) 661-7267
1832 W. Lucas St.
Thunderbird Motor Inn
(803) 669-1611
Rte 52
Young's Plantation
(803) 669-4171
Rte 76

FORT MILL
Days Inn
(803) 548-8000
3482 Carowinds Blvd.

GAFFNEY
Comfort Inn
(803) 487-4200
143 Corona Dr.
Days Inn
(803) 489-7172
136 Peachoid Rd.

GREENVILLE
Colonial Inn
(803) 233-5393
755 Wade Hampton Blvd.

Comfort Inn
(803) 277-6730
412 Mauldin Rd.
Hampton Inn
(803) 288-1200
246 Congaree Rd.
Holiday Inn
(803) 277-8921
4295 Augusta Rd.
Howard Johnson
(803) 288-6900
2756 Laurens Rd.
La Quinta Inn
(803) 297-3500
51 Woodruff Rd.
The Phoenix Inn
(803) 233-4651
246 N. Pleasantburg Dr.
Quality Inn
(803) 297-9000
50 Orchard Park Dr.
Ramada Hotel
(803) 232-7666
1001 S. Church St.
Red Roof Inn
(803) 297-4458
2801 Laurens Rd.
Residence Inn
(803) 297-0099
48 McPrice Ct.

GREENWOOD
Econo Lodge
(803) 229-5329
Rte 25

HARDEEVILLE
Days Inn
(803) 784-2281
Rte 17

Howard Johnsons
(803) 784-2271
Rte 17
HILTON HEAD
Comfort Inn
(803) 842-6662
2 Tanglewood Dr.
Red Roof Inn
(803) 686-6808
5 Regency Pkwy.
MANNING
Manning Economy Inn
(803) 473-4021
Rte 261
MT. PLEASANT
Comfort Inn
(803) 884-5853
Rte 17
Days Inn
(803) 881-1800
Rte 17
Holiday Inn
(803) 884-6000
Rte 17
Masters Economy Inn
(803) 884-2814
300 Wingo Way
MYRTLE BEACH
Best Western
(803) 448-9441
1501 S. Ocean Blvd.
Catoe Villa
(803) 448-5706
506 N. Ocean Blvd.
Days Inn
(803) 236-1950
3650 Rte 501
Knights Inn
(803) 236-7400
3622 Rte 501N.
Mariner
(800) 685-8775
7003 N. Ocean Blvd.
Summer Wind Resort
(803) 626-7464
1903 S. Ocean Blvd
Super Eight
(803) 293-6100
3450 Rte 17.

NORTH CHARLESTON
Comfort Inn-Airport
(803) 554-6485
5055 N. Arco Ln.
Fairfield Inn
(803) 572-6677
7415 Northside Dr.
Holiday Inn
(803) 554-1600
2070 McMillian Dr.
Marriott Hotel
(803) 747-1900
4770 Marriott Dr.
Orchard Inn
(803) 747-3672
4725 Saul White Blvd.
Ramada Inn
(803) 744-8281
2934 W. Montague Ave.
ORANGEBURG
Best Western
(803) 534-7630
475 John Calhoun Dr.
Holiday Inn
(803) 531-4600
415 John Calhoun Dr.
POINT SOUTH
Days Inn
(803) 726-8156
Rte 17
Quality Inn
(803) 726-8101
Rte 17
RICHBURG
Super Eight
(803) 789-7888
Rte 9
RIDGE SPRING
Southwood Manor
(803) 685-5100
100 E. Main St.
ROCK HILL
Best Western
(803) 329-1330
Rte 21
Holiday Inn
(803) 329-1122
2640 N. Cherry Rd.

ST. GEORGE
  Best Western
    (803) 563-2277
    Rte 78
  Comfort Inn
    (803) 563-4180
    Rte 78
  Cotton Planters Inn
    (803) 563-5551
    Rte 78
  Econo Lodge
    (803) 563-4027
    128 Interstate Dr.
  Holiday Inn
    (803) 563-4581
    6014 W. JimBitton Blvd.
  Southern Inn
    (803) 563-3775
    114 Winningham Rd.
SANTEE
  Clarks Inn
    (803) 854-2141
    114 Bradford Blvd.
  Days Inn
    (803) 854-2175
    Rte 6
  Ramada Inn
    (803) 854-2192
    123 Mall Dr.
  Super Eight
    (803) 854-3456
    Rte 6
SIMPSONVILLE
  Comfort Inn
    (803) 963-277
    600 Fairview Rd.
SPARTANBURG
  Days Inn
    (803) 585-4311
    578 North Church St.
  Days Inn
    (803) 585-2413
    1355 Boiling Springs Rd.
  Quality Hotel
    (803) 578-5530
    7136 Asheville Hwy
  Residence Inn
    (803) 576-3333
    9011 Fairforest Rd.

Spartan Inn
  (803) 578-5400
  700 Sunbeam Rd.
Wilson World Hotel
  (803) 574-2111
  9027 Fairforest Rd.
SUMMERVILLE
  Econo Lodge
    (803) 875-3022
    110 Holiday Inn Dr.
  Holiday Inn
    (803) 875-3300
    120 Holiday Inn Dr.
SUMTER
  Days Inn
    (803) 469-9210
    Broad St.
  Ramada Inn
    (803) 775-2323
    226 N. Washington St.
TURBEVILLE
  Exit Inn 135
    (803) 659-8060
    Rte 378
WALTERBORO
  Best Western
    (803) 538-3600
    1140 Snider's Hwy
  Comfort Inn
    (803) 538-5403
    1109 Snider's Hwy
  Rice Planter's Inn
    (803) 538-8964
    Rte 63
  Southern Inn
    (803) 538-2280
    1306 Bells Hwy
  Super Eight
    (803) 538-5383
    Rte 64
  Thunderbird Inn
    (803) 538-2503
    Rte 63
WEST COLUMBIA
  Hampton Inn
    (803)791-8940
    1094 Chris Dr.

Georgia

ACWORTH
  Best Western
    (404) 974-0116
    Rte 92
  Days Inn
    (404) 974-1700
    5035 Cowan Rd.
  Quality Inn
    (404) 974-1922
    4980 Cowan Rd.
ALBANY
  Holiday Inn
    (912) 883-8100
    2701 Dawson Rd.
ASBURN
  Comfort Inn
    (912) 567-0080
    803 Shoneys Dr.
ATHENS
  Best Western
    (706) 546-7311
    170 North Milledge Ave.
ATLANTA
  Atlanta Marriott
    (404) 952-7900
    200 Interstate North
  Budgetel Inn
    (404) 321-0999
    2535 Chantilly Dr. NE
  Courtyard by Marriott
    (404) 728-0708
    1236 Executive Park Dr.
  Westin Peachtree Plaza
    (404) 659-1400
    210 Peachtree St.
  Summerfield Suites-Buckhead
    (404) 262-7880
    505 Pharr Rd.
AUGUSTA
  Holiday Inn
    (706) 737-2300
    601 Bobby Jones Hwy.
  La Quinta Inn
    (706) 733-2660
    3020 Washington Rd.

  Radisson Riverfront Hotel
    (706) 722-8900
    Two 10th St.
AUSTELL
  Days Inn Six Flags
    (404) 941-1400
    95 S. Service Rd.
  Knights Inn-Six Flags
    (404) 944-0824
    1595 Blair Bridge Rd.
  La Quinta-Six Flags
    (404) 944-2100
    737 Six Flags Dr.
BAXLEY
  Budget Host Inn
    (912) 367-2200
    714 E. Parker St.
BLUE RIDGE
  Blue Ridge Mountain Cabins
    (706) 632-8999
    Rte 5
  Days Inn
    (706) 632-1200
    4970 Appalachian Hwy.
BREMEN
  Best Western
    (404) 537-4646
    35 Price Creek Rd.
  Days Inn
    (404) 537-3833
    1077 Albama Ave.
BRUNSWICK
  Best Western
    (912) 264-0144
    Routes 341 & 25
  Budgetel
    (912) 265-7725
    105 Tourist Dr.
  Comfort Inn
    (912) 264-6540
    5308 New Jessup Hwy.
  Holiday Inn
    (912) 264-4033
    5252 New Jessup Hwy.

Ramada Inn
(912) 264-3621
Rte 341
Sleep Inn
(912) 261-0670
5272 New Jessup Hwy.
BYRON
Econo Lodge
(912) 956-5600
106 Old Macon Rd.
Super 8 Motel
(912) 956-3311
305 Hwy 49 North
CALHOUN
Best Western
(706) 629-4521
2261 Hwy 41 NE
Budget Host Shepherd Motel
(706) 629-8644
3900 Fairmont Hwy SE
Holiday Inn
(706) 629-9191
1220 Red Bud Rd.
Jameson Inn
(706) 629-8133
189 Jameson St.
Quality Inn
(706) 629-9501
916 Hwy 53 East
CARROLLTON
Days Inn
(404) 830-1000
180 Centennial Rd.
Ramada Inn
(404) 834-7700
1202 S. Park St.
CARTERSVILLE
Budget Host Inn
(404) 386-0350
851 Cass-White Rd.
Comfort Inn
(404) 387-180
29 Hwy 294 SE
Days Inn
(404) 382-1824
5618 Hwy 20 SE
Econo Lodge
(404) 386-0700
25 Carson Loop

Holiday Inn
(404) 386-0830
Hwy 75
Howard Johnson
(404) 386-1449
Hwy 75
Quality Inn
(404) 386-0510
235 Dixie Ave.
Ramada Inn
(404) 382-1515
45 Hwy 294 SE
Red Carpet Inn
(404) 382-8000
35 Carson Loop NW
CHATSWORTH
Key West Inn
(706) 517-1155
501 GI Maddox Pkwy.
COLLEGE PARK
Atlanta Rennaissance Hotel
(404) 762-7676
4736 Best Rd.
Budgetel Inn-Airport
(404) 766-0000
2480 Old National Hwy.
La Quinta Inn (Airport)
(404) 768-1241
Old National Hwy.
Marriott (Airport)
(404) 766-7900
4711 Best Rd.
Ramada Hotel (Airport)
(404) 768-7800
1419 Virginia Ave.
Red Roof Inn
(404) 761-9701
2471 Old National Pkwy.
COLUMBUS
Budgetel Inn
(706) 323-4344
2919 Warm Springs Rd.
Comfort Inn
(706) 568-3300
3443 Macon Rd.
La Quinta Inn
(706) 568-1740
3201 Macon Rd.

CONYERS
　Comfort Inn
　　(404) 760-0300
　　1363 Klondike Rd.
CORDELE
　Colonial Inn
　　(912) 273-5420
　　2016 16th Ave.
　Days Inn
　　(912) 273-1123
　　215 South 7th St.
　Econo Lodge
　　(912) 273-2456
　　1618 East 16th Ave.
　Holiday Inn
　　(912) 273-4117
　　Route 280
　Ramada Inn
　　(912) 273-5000
　　2016 16th Ave. East
COVINGTON
　Best Western
　　(404) 786-5800
　　10130 Alcovy Rd.
DALTON
　Best Inns of America
　　(706) 226-1100
　　1529 West Walnut Ave.
　Best Western
　　(706) 226-5022
　　2106 Chattanooga Rd.
　Holiday Inn
　　(706) 278-0500
　　515 Holiday Drive
DARIEN
　Super Eight
　　(912) 437-6660
　　I-95
DECATUR
　Days Inn
　　(404) 288-7410
　　4200 Wesley Club Drive
　Glenwood Inn
　　(404) 288-5504
　　4460 Glenwood Rd.
　Holiday Inn
　　(404) 981-5670
　　4300 Snapfinger Woods Dr.

DILLARD
　Best Western
　　(706) 746-5321
　　Route 23
DULUTH
　Amerisuites of Gwinnett
　　(404) 623-6800
　　3390 Venture Pkwy.
　Marriott
　　(404) 923-1775
　　1775 Pleasant Hill Rd.
　Days Inn
　　(404) 476-1211
　　1948 Day Drive
ELLIOJAY
　Budget Host Inn
　　(706) 635-5311
　　10 Jeff Dr.
FOLKSTON
　Daystop Tahiti
　　(912) 496-2514
　　1201 S. Second St.
FORSYTH
　Best Western
　　(912) 994-9260
　　Route 42
　Hampton Inn
　　(912) 994-9697
　　520 Holiday Circle
GARDEN CITY
　Masters Economy Inn
　　(912) 964-4344
　　Augusta Rd.
HAPEVILLE
　Residence Inn by Marriott
　　(404) 761-0511
　　3401 International Blvd.
JEKYLL ISLAND
　Best Western
　　(912) 635-2531
　　975 N. Beachview Dr.
　Clarion Resort
　　(912) 635-2261
　　85 S. Beachview Dr.
　Comfort Inn-Island Suites
　　(912) 635-2211
　　711 N. Beachview Dr.

KENNESAW
Comfort Inn
(404) 424-7666
3375 George Busbee Pkwy.
Red Roof Inn
(404) 429-0323
520 Roberts Court N.W.
KINGSLAND
Best Western
(912) 729-7666
1353 Hwy 40 East
Days Inn
(912) 729-5454
1050 East King Ave.
Hampton Inn
(912) 729-1900
1363 Hwy 40 East
LAKE PARK
Days Inn
(912) 559-0229
4913 Timber Dr.
Shoney's Inn
(912) 559-5660
1075 Lakes Blvd.
LAWRENCEVILLE
Days Inn
(404) 995-7782
731 W. Pike St.
LITHONIA
La Quinta Inn
(404) 981-2094
2859 Panola Rd.
LOCUST GROVE
Super Eight
(404) 957-2936
4605 Hampton Rd.
LOUISVILLE
Louisvile Motor Inn
(912) 625-7168
Route 1
MACON
Comfort Inn
(912) 746-8855
2690 Riverside Dr.
Days Inn
(912) 784-1000
6000 Harrison Rd.
Days Inn North
(912) 745-8521
Pierce Ave.

Econo Lodge
(912) 474-1661
4951 Romeiser Rd.
Holiday Inn
(912) 743-1482
2720 Riverside Dr.
Masters Economy Inn
(912) 788-8910
4295 Pionono Ave.
Quality Inn
(912) 781-7000
4630 Chambers Rd.
Rodeway Inn
(912) 781-4343
4999 Eisenhower Pkwy.
MADISON
Days Inn
(706) 342-1839
2001 Eatonton Hwy.
MARIETTA
Best Inns of America
(404) 955-0004
1255 Franklin Rd.
Holiday Inn
(404) 952-7581
2255 Delk Rd.
La Quinta Inn
(404) 951-0026
2170 Delk Rd.
MCDONOUGH
The Brittany Motor Inn
(404) 957-5821
1171 Hwy. 20
Holiday Inn
(404) 957-5291
930 Rte 155 South
MORROW
Red Roof Inn
(404) 968-1483
1348 S. Lake Plaza Dr.
NEWNAN
Comfort Inn
(404) 254-0089
1455 Rte 29 S.
Days Inn
(404) 253-8550
Rte 29
Ramada Inn
(404) 253-1499
1310 South Hwy 29

NORCROSS
Amberley Suite Hotel
(404) 263-0515
5885 Oak Brook Pkwy
Budgetel Inn
(404) 446-2882
5395 Peachtree Ind. Blvd.
Homewood Suites
(404) 448-4663
450 Technology Pkwy.
La Quinta Inn- Jimmy Carter
(404) 448-8686
6187 Dawson Blvd
La Quinta Peachtree
(404) 449-5144
5375 Peachtree Ind. Blvd.
Red Roof Inn
(404) 448-8944
5171 Brook Hollow Pkwy
Shoney's Inn
(404) 564-0492
2050 Willow Trail Pkwy
Travelodge Atlanta
(404) 449-7322
6045 Oakbrook Pkwy

PERRY
Comfort Inn
(912) 987-7710
1602 Sam Nunn Blvd.
Days Inn
(912) 987-2142
800 Valley Dr.
Econo Lodge
(912) 987-2585
624 Valley Dr.
Holiday Inn
(912) 987-3313
700 Valley Dr.

RINGGOLD
Days Inn
(706) 965-5730
Hwy 151
Super Eight
(706) 965-7080
401 S. Hwy 151

ROME
Holiday Inn
(706) 295-110020
Rte 411 East

ROSWELL
Budgetel Inn
(404) 552-0200
575 Holcomb Bridge Rd.
Hampton Inn
(404) 587-5161
9995 Old Dogwood Rd.
Holiday Inn
(404) 992-9600
1075 Holcomb Bridge Rd.

SAVANNAH
Best Western-Central
(912) 355-1000
45 Eisenhower Dr.
Best Western-Savannah
(912) 95-2420
1 Gateway Blvd.
Budgetel Inn
(912) 927-7660
8484 Abercorn St.
Days Inn
(912) 927-7720
11750 Abercorn St.
Econolodge
(912) 925-2280
7 Gateway Blvd. West
La Quinta Inn
(912) 355-3004
6805 Abercorn

SMYRNA
Holiday Inn
(404) 333-9910
1200 Winchester Pkwy
Howard Johnsons
(404) 435-4990
2700 CurtisDr.

STATESBORO
Holiday Inn
(912) 764-6121
230 South Main St.

STOCKBRIDGE
Best Western
(404) 476-8771
3509 Hwy 138
Super Eight
(404) 474-5758
1451 Hudson Bridge Rd.

SUWANEE
Best Western
(404) 945-6751
Suwanee Rd.
Comfort Inn
(404) 945-1608
2945 Hwy 317
Holiday Inn
(404) 945-4921
2955 Hwy 317
THOMASVILLE
Holiday Inn
(912) 226-7111
211 Hwy 19 South
THOMSON
Best Western
(706) 595-8000
1890 Washington Rd.
Ramada Inn
(706) 595-8700
1847 Washington Rd.
TIFTON
Comfort Inn
(912) 382-4410
1104 King Rd.
Days Inn
(912) 382-7210
1008 W. 8th St.
Hampton Inn
(912) 382-8800
720 Hwy 319 South
Holiday Inn
(912) 382-6687
Rtes 82 and 319
Masters Economy Inn
(912) 382-8100
Rtes 82 and 319
Quality Inn
(912) 386-2100
1103 King Rd.
TUCKER
La Quinta
(404) 496-1317
1819 Mtn. Ind.Blvd.
Ramada
(404) 939-8120
2180 N. Lake Pkwy.
Red Roof Inn
(404) 496-1311
2819 Lawrenceville Hwy

VALDOSTA
Best Western
(912) 244-7600
1403 N. St. Augustine Rd.
Comfort Inn
(912) 242-1212
Rte 84
Holiday Inn
(912) 242-3881
Rte 94
Howard Johnsons
(912) 244-4460
Rte 75
Quality Inn
(912) 244-8510
Rte 94
VIDALIA
Days Inn
(912) 537-9251
Rte 280
VILLA RICA
Comfort Inn
(404) 459-8000
Rte 61
WAYCROSS
Holiday Inn
(912) 238-4490
Rte 82

Florida

ALTAMONTE
Embassy Suites
(407) 834-2400
225 E. Altamonte Dr.
La Quinta Inn
(407) 788-1411
150 S. Westmonte Dr.
Residence Inn
(407) 788-7991
270 Douglas Ave.
AMELIA ISLAND
Amelia Island Lodging Sys.
(800) 872-8531
584 South Fletcher Ave.
APOLLO BEACH
Ramada Inn
(813) 645-3271
6414 Surfside
APOPKA
Crosby's Motor Inn
(407) 886-3220
1440 W. Orange Blossom
AVON PARK
Econo Lodge
(813) 453-2000
Rte 27
BARTOW
L. Jon Motel
(813) 533-8191
1460 E. Main
BOCA RATON
Crown Sterling Suites
(407) 997-9500
Yamato Rd.
Radisson
(407) 483-3600
7920 Glades Rd.
Ramada Hotel
(407) 395-6850
Glades Rd.
Residence Inn
(407) 994-3222
525 N.W. 77th St.
BONIFAY
Best Western
(904) 547-4251
2004 S. Waukesha St.

BONITA SPRINGS
Econo Lodge
(813) 947-3366
28090 Quails Nest Ln.
BRADENTON
Econo Lodge
(813) 758-7199
6727 14th St. West
Park Inn
(813) 795-4633
4450 47th St. West
BROOKSVILLE
Holiday Inn
(904) 796-9481
30307 Cortez Blvd.
BUSHNELL
Best Western
(904) 793-5010
Rte 48
CARRAVELLE
The Moorings at Caravelle
(904) 697-2800
Rte 98
CEDAR KEY
Park Place Motel
(904) 543-5737
2nd St.
CLEARWATER
Holiday Inn
(813) 536-7275
Rte. 19
La Quinta
(813) 572-7222
Rte 688
Residence Inn
(813) 573-4444
Rte 688
COCOA
Best Western
(407) 632-1065
4225 W. King St.
Days Inn
(407) 636-6500
5600 Rte 524
Econo Lodge
(407) 632-4561
3220 N. Cocoa Blvd.

COCOA BEACH
Days Inn
(407) 783-7621
5600 N. Atlantic Ave.
Econo Lodge
(407) 784-2550
5500 N. Atlantic Ave.
Surf Studio Resort
(407) 783-7100
Francis St.
CRESTVIEW
Days Inn
(904) 682-8842
Rte 85
Holiday Inn
(904) 682-6111
Rte 85
CRYSTAL RIVER
Best Western
(904) 795-3171
614 N.W. Rte 19
Comfort Inn
(904) 563-1500
4486 N. Suncoast Blvd
DANIA
Hilton
(305) 920-3300
1870 Griffin Rd.
DAVENPORT
Days Inn
(813) 424-2596
2425 Frontage Rd.
DAYTONA BEACH
Aruba Inn
(904) 253-5643
1254 N. Atlantic Ave.
Holiday Inn
(904) 255-2422
1798 W. Intl Speedway
La Quinta Inn
(904) 255-7412
2725 Int. Speedway
Sand Castle Motel
(904) 767-3182
Rte 475
Sea Oat Beach Motel
(904) 767-5684
2539 S. Atlantic Ave.

DEERFIELD BEACH
La Quinta Inn
(305) 421-1004
351 W. Hillsboro Blvd.
DE FUNIAK SPRINGS
Best Western
(904) 892-5111
Rte 331
Econo Lodge
(904) 892-6115
Rte 331
DE LAND
Holiday Inn
(904) 738-5200
Rte 92
Quality Inn
(904) 736-3440
2801 E. New York Ave.
DESTIN
Days Inn
(904) 837-2599
1029 Rte 98
ELKTON
Comfort Inn
(904)829-3435
Rte 207
ELLENTON
Best Western
(813) 729-8505
5218 17th St East
FLORIDA CITY
Coral Roc Motel
(305) 247-4010
1100 N. Krome Ave
Hampton Inn
(305) 247-8833
124 East Palm Dr.
FT. LAUDERDALE
Days Inn
(305) 484-9290
1595 W. Oakland Park Dr.
Ft. Lauderdale Inn
(305) 491-2500
5727 N. Federal Hwy
Guest Quarters Suites
(305) 565-3800
2670 E. Surise Blvd.

FT. MYERS
  Budgetel Inn
    (813) 275-3500
    2717 Colonial Blvd.
  Comfort Suites
    (813) 768-0005
    13651 Indian Paint La.
  La Quinta Inn
    (813) 275-3300
    4850 Cleveland Ave
  Radisson Inn
    (813) 466-1200
    20091 Summerlin Rd SW
  Sleep Inn
    (813) 561-1117
    13651 Indian Paint La.
  Wellesley Inn
    (813) 278-3949
    4400 Ford St
FT. MYERS BEACH
  Best Western
    (813) 463-6000
    684 Estero Blvd.
  Days Inn
    (813) 765-4422
    8701 Estero Blvd.
FT. PIERCE
  Days Inn
    (407) 466-4066
    6651 Darter Court
  Hampton Inn
    (407) 460-9855
    2831 Reynolds Dr.
  Holiday Inn Express
    (407) 464-5000
    7151 Okeechobee Dr.
GAINESVILLE
  Fairfield Inn
    (904) 332-8292
    6901 NW 4th Blvd.
  La Quinta
    (904) 332-6466
    920 NW 69th Tr.
  Residence Inn
    (904) 371-2101
    4001 SW 13th St.
HAINES CITY
  Best Western
    (813) 421-6929
    605 B. Moore Rd

Econo Lodge
    (813) 422-8621
    Rte 27
HOLLYWOOD
  Comfort Inn
    (305) 922-1600
    2520 Sterling Rd.
  Days Inn
    (305) 923-7300
    2601 N. 29th Ave.
  HoJo Inn
    (305) 923-1516
    2900 Polk St.
  Inn at Montreal
    (305) 925-4443
    324 Balboa St.
  Ocean Grand Beach
    (305) 923-2459
    3300 N. Surf Blvd.
HOMESTEAD
  Days Inn
    (305) 245-1260
    51 S. Homestead Blvd.
  Howard Johnson
    (305) 248-2121
    1020 N. Homestead
INDIALANTIC
  Holiday Inn
    (407) 777-4100
    2605 N. A1A
  Melbourne Oceanfront Suites
    (407) 723-4222
    A1A
INDIAN SHORES
  Last Resort
    (813) 595-3336
    19534 Gulf Blvd.
  Sea Club Condominiums
    (813) 596-2046
    19725 Gulf Blvd.
JACKSONVILLE
  Best Inns of America
    (904) 739--3323
    8220 Dix Ellis Tr
  Budgetel Inn
    (904) 268-9999
    3199 Hartley Rd
  Comfort Suites Hotel
    (904) 739-1155
    8333 Dix Ellis Tr.

Courtyard by Marriott
(904) 223-1700
4600 San Pablo Rd
Economy Inn
(904) 281-0198
4300 Salisbury Rd
Hampton Inn
(904) 741-4980
1170 Airport Entrance Rd.
Holiday Inn
(904) 737-1700
9150 Baymeadows Rd.
Homewood Suites
(904) 733-9299
8737 Baymeadows Rd.
La Quinta Inn
(904) 731-9940
8255 Dix Ellis Tr.
Ramada Inn
(904) 737-8000
5624 Cagle Rd.
Residence Inn
(904) 733-8088
8365 Dix Ellis Rd.
JACKSONVILLE BEACH
Days Inn
(904) 249-7231
1031 S. 1st St.
JENNINGS
Holiday Inn
(904) 938-3501
Rte 143
Jennings House Inn
(904) 938-3305
Rte 143
JUPITER
Wellesley Inn
(407) 575-7201
34 Fisherman's Wharf
KEY LARGO
Howard Johnson
(305) 451-1400
Mile Marker 102
KEY WEST
Alexander Palms Court
(800) 858-1943
715 South St.
Hampton Inn
(305) 294-2917
Rte 1

Nassau House
(305) 296-8513
1016 Fleming
Ramada Inn
(305) 294-5541
Rte 1
KISSIMMEE
Best Western - East Gate
(407) 396-0707
5565 W. Irlo Bronson Hwy.
Best Western - Main Gate
(407) 396-0100
8600 W. Irlo Bronson Hwy.
Comfort Inn - Main Gate
(407) 396-7500
7571 W. Irlo Bronon Hwy.
Fantasy World Club Villas
(407) 396-1808
2935 Hart Ave.
Holiday Inn - Main Gate East
(407) 396-4488
5678 W. Irlo Bronson Hwy.
Inns of America
(407) 396-7743
2945 Entry Point Blvd.
Larson's Lodge- Main Gate
(407) 396-6100
6075 W. Irlo Bronson Hwy.
Quality Inn Lake Cecile
(407) 396-4455
4944 W. Irlo Bronson Hwy.
LAKE BUENA VISTA
Comfort Inn
(407) 239-7300
8442 Palm Pkwy.
Days Inn
(407) 239-4646
12490 Apopka-Vineland
Radison Inn
(407) 239-8400
8686 Palm Pkwy.
LAKE CITY
Cypress Inn
(904) 752-9369
Rte 90
Econo Lodge
(904) 755-9311
Rte 441

Wellesley Inn
(813) 859-3399
3420 N. Rte 98
LANTANA
Super Eight
(407) 585-3970
1255 Hypoluxo Rd.
LIVE OAK
Econo Lodge
(904) 362-7459
Rte 129
LONGBOAT KEY
Holiday Inn-Longboat Key
(813) 383-3771
4949 Gulf of Mexico Dr.
Riviera Beach Motel
(813) 383-2552
5451 Gulf of Mexico Dr.
MARATHON
Howard Johnson Resort
(305) 743-8550
13351 Overseas Hwy.
MARIANNA
Best Western Marianna Inn
(904) 526-5666
Rte 71
Comfort Inn
(904) 526-5600
Rte 71
MELBOURNE
Melbourne Hilton
(407) 768-0200
200 Rialto Pl.
MIAMI
Hampton Inn
(305) 854-2070
2500 Brickell Ave.
Holiday Inn-Airport
(305) 266-0000
836 Dolphin Expwy.
Hotel Sofitel
(305) 264-4888
5800 Blue Lagoon Dr.
Radisson
(305) 261-3800
Milam Dairy Rd.
MIAMI BEACH
Fountainbleu Hilton
(305) 538-2000
4441 Collins Ave.

Newport Pier Beachside
(305) 949-1300
16701 Collins Ave.
MIAMI SPRINGS
Crown Sterling Suites
(305) 634-5000
3974 NW South River Dr.
NAPLES
Howard Johnson
(813) 262-6181
221 9th St. South
Spinnaker Inn of Naples
(813) 434-0444
6600 Dudley Dr.
Wellesley Inns
(813) 793-4646
1555 5th Ave. South
NAVARRE
Comfort Inn
(904) 939-1761
8680 Navarre Pkwy
NEW PORT RICHEY
Holiday Inn-Bayside
(813) 849-8551
5015 Rte. 19
Sheraton Inn
(813) 847-9005
Rte. 19
NOKOMIS
Casa Cay Beach Apts.
(813) 768-5591
309 Casey Key Rd.
OCALA
Holiday Inn
(904) 629-0381
3621 West Silver Springs
Howard Johnson Park Sq.
(904) 237-8000
Rte 200
ORLANDO
Best Western
(407) 841-8600
2041 W. Colonial Dr.
Budgetel Inn
(407) 240-0500
2051 Consulate Dr.
Comfort Inn
(407) 855-6060
8421 S. Orange Blossom Tr.

Delta Orlando Resort
(407) 351-3340
5715 Major Blvd.
La Quinta-Airport
(407) 857-9215
7934 Daetwyler Dr.
ORMOND BEACH
Best Western Plantation Inn
(904) 437-3737
2251 S. Old Dixie Hwy.
Comfort Inn on the Beach
(904) 677-8550
507 S. Atlantic Ave.
PALM BEACH
Heart of Palm Beach Hotel
(407) 655-5600
160 Royal Palm Way
Howard Johnson
(407) 582-2581
2870 S. Ocean Blvd.
PALM BEACH GARDENS
Radisson Suites-PGA
(407) 622-1000
4350 PGA Blvd.
PALM BEACH SHORES
Best Western Seaspray Inn
(407) 844-0233
123 S. Ocean Ave.
PANAMA CITY
Best Western Bayside
(904) 763-4622
711 W. Beach Dr.
Days Inn
(904) 784-1777
4111W. Hwy 98
PANAMA CITY BEACH
Best Western Casaloma
(904) 234-1100
13615 Front Beach Rd.
PENSACOLA
Comfort Inn
(904) 478-4499
6919 Pensacola Blvd.
Hampton Inn
(904) 477-3333
7330 Plantation Rd.
La Quinta Inn
(904) 474-0411
7750 N. Davis Hwy.

Pensacola Grand Hotel
(904) 433-3336
200 E. Gregory St.
PORT CHARLOTTE
Days Inn
(813) 627-8900
1941 Tamiami Tr.
Quality Inn
(813) 625-4181
3400 Tamiami Tr.
PORT SALERNO
Pirate's Cove Resort
(407) 287-2500
4307 SE Bayview St.
PUNTA GORDA
Days Inn-Punta Gorda
(813) 637-7200
26560 N. Jones Loop Rd.
ST. AUGUSTINE
Best Western Historical Inn
(904) 829-9088
2015 N. Ponce de Leon
Days Inn-Historic
(904) 829-581
2800 Ponce de Leon
Monson Bayfront Resort
(904) 829-2277
Bayfront Rd.
ST. AUGUSTINE BEACH
Best Western Ocean Inn
(904) 471-8010
3955 AIA South
Holiday Inn
(904) 471-2555
860 A1A South
ST. PETERSBURG
Howard Johnson
(813) 867-6070
3600 34th St. South
Le Mark Charles Motel
(813) 527-7334
6200 34th St. North
SANIBEL
Caribe Beach Resort
(813) 472-1166
2669 West Gulf Dr.
SARASOTA
Comfort Inn
(813) 355-7091
4800 N. Tamiami Tr.

Coquina on the Beach
(813) 388-2141
1008 Ben Franklin Dr.
Days Inn-Siesta Key
(813) 924-4900
6600 S. Tamiami Tr.
Holiday Inn-Lido Beach
(813) 388-3941
233 Ben Franklin Dr.
Hyatt Sarasota
(813) 366-9000
1000 Blvd. of the Arts
SUGARLOAF KEY
Sugar Loaf Lodge
(305) 745-3211
Mile Marker 17, Rte 1
TALLAHASSEE
La Quinta
(904) 878-5099
2850 Apalachee Pkwy
Sheraton
(904) 224-5000
101 S. Adams St.
TAMPA
Budgetel
(813) 626-0885
4811 Rte 301 North
Courtyard
(813) 874-0555
3805 W. Cypress
Days Inn, Busch Gardens E.
(813) 247-3300
2520 N. 50th St.
Embassy Suites
(813) 875-1555
555 North Westshore Blvd.
Holiday Inn, Crowne Plaza
(813) 623-6363
10221 Princess Palm Ave.
La Quinta-Airport
(813) 287-0440
4730 Spruce St.
Residence Inn
(813) 281-5677
3075 N. Rocky Point Dr.
Tahitian Inn
(813) 877-6721
601 S. Dale Mabry

TITUSVILLE
Best Western Space Shuttle
(407) 269-9100
3455 Cheney Hwy.
Day Inn-Kennedy Space Cntr.
(407) 269-4480
3755 Cheney Hwy.
Howard Johnson
(407) 267-7900
1829 Riverside Dr.
VENICE
Best Western Venice Resort
(813) 485-5411
Rte 41
Days Inn
(813) 493-4558
1710 S. Tamiami Tr.
Inn at the Beach
(813) 484-4871
101 The Esplanade
VERO BEACH
Days Inn
(407) 562-9991
8800 20th St.
Hojo
(407) 778-1985
1985 90th Ave.
Holiday Inn-Countryside W.
(407) 576-8321
8797 20th St.
WEEKI WACHEE
Comfort Inn
(904) 596-9000
9373 Cortez Blvd.
Holiday Inn
(904) 596-2007
6172 Commercial Way
WEST PALM BEACH
Comfort Inn
(407) 689-6100
1901 Palm Beach Lakes Rd.
Radisson Suites
(407) 689-61808
1808 Australian Ave. South
Wellesley Inn
(407) 689-8540
1910 Palm Beach Lakes

Regulations for State and National Parks, Forests, and Recreation Areas

North Carolina

Dogs are permitted in the Great Smoky Mountains National Park and in all but three of the state's national forests. They are also allowed in all of North Carolina's state parks and recreation areas, provided they are on a 6-foot leash. They are not permitted in the any of the cabins or bath houses that are located within the state parks.

Dogs are NOT allowed in the following national forests:
Cedar Point, Croatan National Forest
Neuse River, Croatan National Forest
Badin Lake, Uwharrie National Forest

Dogs are NOT allowed in the following national seashore area:
Cape Lookout National Seashore

For more information, please telephone (919) 733-7275 or 733-4181.

South Carolina

Dogs are permitted in the Francis Marios and Sumter National Forests. They are welcome in all of the state parks and recreation areas, provided they are kept on a six-foot leash. They are welcome in the camping areas, but are not allowed in the recreational cabins. The regulations for dogs on beaches varies from one county to the next.

For more information, please telephone: (803) 734-0127 / (803) 756-5222.

Georgia

Dogs are permitted in all of the Chattahoochee and Oconee National Forests. With two exceptions, they are also allowed in all of the state parks and recreation areas, provided they are kept on a six-foot leash. They are not permitted in any cottages or lodges within the parks, nor are they allowed on the state beaches.

Dogs are NOT allowed in the following national seashore area:
Cumberland Island National Seashore

Dogs are <u>NOT</u> allowed in the following state parks:
  Franklin D. Roosevelt Park
  Lake Winfield Scott

For more information, please call (404) 656-3530.

Florida

Florida is unusual, in that they technically allow dogs in the national parks, national forests, along with all state parks and recreation areas, provided they are kept on a six-foot, hand-held leash and are well behaved at all times. The unusual part comes into play because their access to trails, beaches, and the wilderness is severely limited, if not completely restricted. (For instance, dogs can technically enter the Everglades National Park, but cannot walk on the trails, have access to the water, etc.) Pets are <u>not</u> permitted in camping areas, on bathing beaches, or in concession facilities. They may also be restricted to certain areas within most parks.

Dogs <u>ARE</u> permitted in the following state parks and recreation areas (with very few limitations):
  Bulow Plantation Ruins
  Cayo Costa
  Don Pedro Island
  Fort Pierce Inlet
  Gasparilla Island
  Hugh Taylor Birch
  Ichetucknee Springs
  John D. MacArthur Beach
  John U. Lloyd
  Lake Manatee
  Lake Talquin
  Little Manatee River

Dog Law to be aware of for Florida:
  It is illegal in the state of Florida to leave a dog unattended in a car.

For more information, please telephone: (904) 488-9872/(904) 942-9300

Index

On the Road Again
With Man's Best Friend

Reader Input

We research extensively to bring you the best places to stay with a dog. We also appreciate any assistance our readers can give us. Therefore, if you find an interesting B&B, inn, hotel, or resort that welcomes guests traveling with a dog, please let us know. We enjoy hearing from our readers, and are always impressed with their perceptive comments on where to go and what to do with a dog.

If, after researching your suggestion, we include that entry in our next edition of *On The Road Again With Man's Best Friend*, we will send you a complimentary copy of that book.

Please send your information to:

Allison Elliott
Dawbert Press, Inc.
P.O. Box 2758,
Duxbury, Massachusetts 02331

or you may call us at
(800) 93-DAWBERT, Fax (617) 934-2945